INTRODUCING UMBRIA

P9-DGU-138

DISCOVERING UMBRIA

Nestling against the south-eastern flanks of Italy's Apennine range, the region of Umbria is little-visited compared to its neighbour Tuscany. However, the self-dubbed "green heart of Italy" offers a marvellous range of memorable experiences. The wooded hills are alive with wild boar and red deer; the perfectly preserved

Sunflowers growing in the Umbrian Valley

towns perched on hilltops are crammed with medieval and Renaissance art treasures and the local hearty cuisine, which makes use of flavoursome products such as aromatic olive oils, wild mushrooms and truffles, is a treat for any gourmet. The following pages will help visitors plan their holiday to include all of the top sights.

The 13th-century Basilica di San Francesco in Assisi

NORTHERN UMBRIA

- Inspiring Assisi and St Francis
- Magnificent Perugia
- Glorious Lake Trasimeno
- Fascinating medieval Gubbio

The history of the beautiful hilltop town of **Assisi** *(see pp68–80)* is inextricably linked with that of Saint Francis *(see pp24–5)*, founder of the Franciscan order of friars. Dedicated to the memory of this holy man, the 13th-century **basilica** *(see pp72–7)* is decorated with a stunning series of brilliant frescoes by masters such as Giotto and Cimabue. All were restored with expert care in the wake of the devastating 1997 earthquakes that rocked the region.

The captial of Umbria, and its largest city, **Perugia** *(see pp84–91)* demands an extended visit because of the

fascinating architectural heritage it boasts, including massive gateways and city walls, extensive underground walkways and splendid Renaissance palaces. In the magnificent main square, Piazza IV Novembre, stands the well-preserved **Fontana Maggiore** *(see p87)*, dating from the Middle Ages. The **Galleria Nazionale dell'Umbria** *(see pp88–9)* has a collection of works by leading artists from the region, notably the 15th-century painter Perugino

(see p28). Last but not least, engineering enthusiasts will appreciate the marvel of the **Etruscan Well** *(see p90)* in the city centre.

To get away from the bustle of Perugia, take a relaxing ferry trip across **Lake Trasimeno** *(see pp92–5)* and enjoy the placid waters and scattering of pleasant islands. One of these, Isola Maggiore, has a colony of ponies: they double as environmentally sound mowers to keep the grass down. It was on the hilly shores of Lake Trasimeno that Carthaginian general Hannibal brought the Roman army to its knees in 217 BC, a landmark victory *(see p37)*.

Gubbio *(see pp58–61)*, in the northern reaches of the region, is a well-preserved medieval town that climbs in layers up the flank of Monte Ingino. The key attraction is the **Palazzo dei Consoli** *(see p60)*, a castellated palace and museum. However, a good way to get to know Gubbio is by wandering along its cobbled streets and popping into its attractive

Isola Maggiore, a fishermen's haven in Lake Trasimeno

UMBRIA

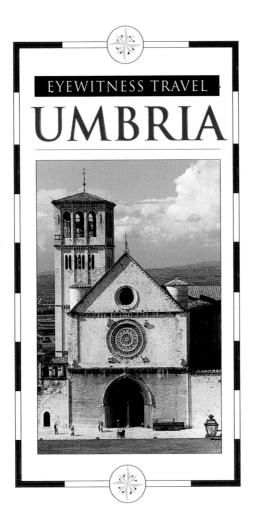

EYEWITNESS TRAVEL
UMBRIA

DK

DK

LONDON, NEW YORK,
MELBOURNE, MUNICH AND DELHI
www.dk.com

PRODUCED BY Fabio Ratti Editoria Srl, Milan, Italy
PROJECT EDITORS Mattia Goffetti, Silvia Riboldi
EDITOR Marina Beretta
DESIGNERS Modi Artistici, Tiziano Perotto
CONTRIBUTORS
Giovanni Francesio, Marina Dragoni, Patrizia Masnini
PHOTOGRAPHER
Ghigo Roli
ILLUSTRATOR
Elisabetta Mancini
CARTOGRAPHY
Laura Belletti

Dorling Kindersley Limited
PUBLISHING MANAGERS Fay Franklin, Kate Poole
SENIOR ART EDITOR Marisa Renzullo
TRANSLATOR Fiona Wild
EDITOR Emily Hatchwell
CONSULTANT Jeffrey Kennedy
FACTCHECKER Leonie Loudon
PRODUCTION Sarah Dodd

Reproduced in Singapore by Colourscan
Printed and bound by in China by Leo Paper Products Ltd

First American Edition, 2004
11 12 13 14 10 9 8 7 6 5 4 3 2
Published in the United States by DK Publishing,
375 Hudson Street, New York, New York 10014.
Reprinted with revisions 2006, 2008, 2011

A CATALOG RECORD FOR THIS BOOK IS AVAILABLE FROM THE LIBRARY OF CONGRESS.

ISSN 1479-344X
ISBN 978-0-75667-007-8

FLOORS ARE REFERRED TO THROUGHOUT IN ACCORDANCE WITH EUROPEAN USAGE;
IE THE "FIRST FLOOR" IS THE FLOOR ABOVE GROUND LEVEL

*Front cover main image: the Scarzuola Garden,
Montegabbione*

MIX
Paper from
responsible sources
FSC
www.fsc.org FSC™ C018179

**The information in this
DK Eyewitness Travel Guide is checked regularly.**

Every effort has been made to ensure that this book is as up-to-date
as possible at the time of going to press. Some details, however,
such as telephone numbers, opening hours, prices, gallery hanging
arrangements and travel information are liable to change. The
publishers cannot accept responsibility for any consequences arising
from the use of this book, nor for any material on third party
websites, and cannot guarantee that any website address in this
book will be a suitable source of travel information. We value the
views and suggestions of our readers very highly. Please write to:
Publisher, DK Eyewitness Travel Guides, Dorling Kindersley, 80 Strand,
London WC2R 0RL, Great Britain, or email: travelguides@dk.com

◁ **Looking over the city of Spoleto, with the cathedral in the foreground**

CONTENTS

HOW TO USE THIS GUIDE 6

Dispute in the Temple, detail,
Cappella Baglioni, Spello

INTRODUCING UMBRIA

DISCOVERING UMBRIA 10

PUTTING UMBRIA ON THE MAP 12

A PORTRAIT OF UMBRIA 14

UMBRIA THROUGH THE YEAR 32

THE HISTORY OF UMBRIA 36

**Opening of the traditional Corsa
all'Anello in Narni**

The medieval Piazza della Repubblica in Foligno

Typical ceramic plate from Deruta

The spectacular Cascata delle Marmore, near Terni

Basilica di San Francesco, Assisi

HOW TO USE THIS GUIDE

This guide helps you to get the most out of your visit to Umbria by giving detailed descriptions of sights, practical information and expert advice. *Introducing Umbria* sets the region in its geographical, cultural as well as historical context.

Umbria Area by Area describes the main sightseeing areas, with maps, detailed illustrations and photographs. Hotels, restaurants and shops are covered in *Travellers' Needs*, while the *Survival Guide* contains invaluable practical advice.

UMBRIA AREA BY AREA

Umbria has been divided into two sightseeing areas, each with its own colour-coded thumb tab: a key to the colours used is on the inside front cover. Each area has its own chapter, which opens with a *Regional Map* with a numbered list of the sights described. There is a *Road Map* and a key to symbols inside the back cover.

Each area has a colour-coded thumb tab.

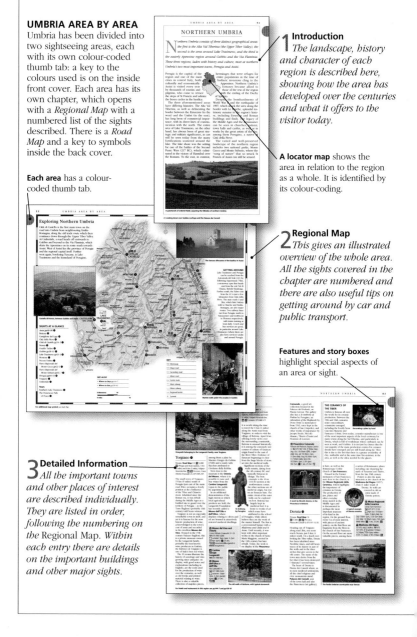

1 Introduction
The landscape, history and character of each region is described here, showing how the area has developed over the centuries and what it offers to the visitor today.

A locator map shows the area in relation to the region as a whole. It is identified by its colour-coding.

2 Regional Map
This gives an illustrated overview of the whole area. All the sights covered in the chapter are numbered and there are also useful tips on getting around by car and public transport.

Features and story boxes highlight special aspects of an area or sight.

3 Detailed Information
All the important towns and other places of interest are described individually. They are listed in order, following the numbering on the Regional Map. *Within each entry there are details on the important buildings and other major sights.*

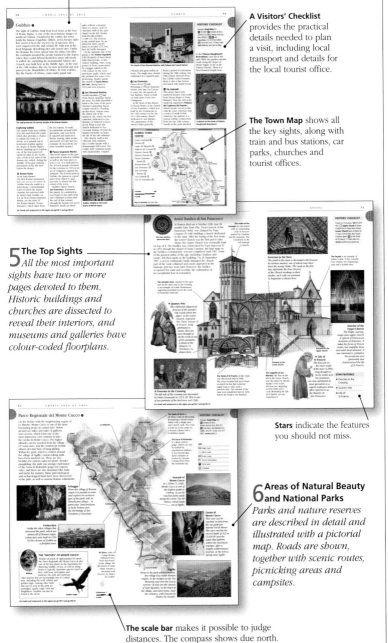

4 Major Towns

All the important towns are described individually. Within each entry there is further detailed information on all the main sights. The Town Map *shows their location.*

A Visitors' Checklist provides the practical details needed to plan a visit, including local transport and details for the local tourist office.

The Town Map shows all the key sights, along with train and bus stations, car parks, churches and tourist offices.

5 The Top Sights

All the most important sights have two or more pages devoted to them. Historic buildings and churches are dissected to reveal their interiors, and museums and galleries have colour-coded floorplans.

Stars indicate the features you should not miss.

6 Areas of Natural Beauty and National Parks

Parks and nature reserves are described in detail and illustrated with a pictorial map. Roads are shown, together with scenic routes, picnicking areas and campsites.

The scale bar makes it possible to judge distances. The compass shows due north.

Verification of the Stigmata, detail, Upper Church of the Basilica di San Francesco, Assisi ▷

stone churches. This town is also the perfect place to catch one of those pageant events that Umbria does so well: the spectacular **Corsa dei Ceri** *(see p32)* is a madcap uphill chase with participants dressed in historic garb and shouldering precariously balanced statues.

Participants in period costume for the Corsa dei Ceri in Gubbio

SOUTHERN UMBRIA

- **Trekking in the Parco Nazionale dei Monti Sibillini**
- **Spoleto's Roman past**
- **The impressive Cascata delle Marmore waterfalls**
- **Orvieto and its legendary Cathedral**

Nature enthusiasts will love the **Parco Nazionale dei Monti Sibillini** *(see pp108–9)*, with its wonderfully varied landscapes and scope for outdoor activities such as trekking, horse riding, cross-country skiing and even hang-gliding. The park's heart is the vast Plain of Castelluccio, an unusually fertile medium-altitude basin that bursts into flower in springtime.

The eastern edge of the plain is dominated by Monte Vettore, one of the Apennines' highest peaks, snow-capped well into the summer. Sheltering below the western edge is the medieval town **Norcia** *(see p116)*, which has a reputation for being the birthplace of many saints and for producing delicious cured meats.

Further west is **Spoleto** *(see pp110–15)*, a stately town with narrow winding streets and a wealth of architectural and artistic sights, such as the fortress, the Roman remains and the 12th-century duomo. Nestled in wooded hills, the Benedictine abbey of **San Pietro in Valle** *(see p115)* is perfect for a short day trip.

Close by is the nature reserve **Parco Fluviale del Nera** *(see pp122–3)*, which follows the course of the Nera River. The park is of great interest for both rafting enthusiasts and climbers, who are drawn to its steep cliffs. However, the must-see attraction here is the **Cascata delle Marmore**, a dramatic series of three linked waterfalls with a combined drop of 165 m (541 ft). Connected to a hydroelectric plant, the falls are "turned on" at set times.

Recognizable from afar thanks to the silhouette of its landmark cathedral, the atmospheric town of **Orvieto** *(see pp134–9)* stands on a soft tufa outcrop. As a result, it has long been subject to subsidence and rockfalls, recently brought to a halt by a far-reaching consolidation project. The town itself is

The Marmore waterfalls in the Parco Fluviale del Nera

honeycombed with man-made tunnels and **caves** *(see p135)* used for storing the local crisp white wine. In addition, there are intriguing deep wells, such as the famous **Pozzo di San Patrizio** *(see pp138–9)*, which ensured water supply in case of siege. Though of ancient Etruscan origin, Orvieto is best known for its Gothic **duomo** *(see pp136–7)*, which is exquisitely decorated with frescoes by Luca Signorelli, Lippo Memmi and other artists in homage to the blood-stained altar cloth testifying to the Miracle of Bolsena.

Poppies and other wildflowers in the vast Plain of Castelluccio

Putting Umbria on the Map

Of all the regions that make up the Italian peninsula,
Umbria is the only one to be totally landlocked. The
region covers 8,450 sq km (3,260 sq miles), of which
three-quarters belongs to the province of Perugia and
one-quarter to the province of Terni. Plains make up
less than one-tenth of the total area, the rest
being taken up with hills and mountains.
The main river is the Tiber (il Tevere) and the
highest peak is Monte Redentore, at 2,450 m
(8,050 ft). Lake Trasimeno,
west of Perugia, is the
largest inland lake in
central Italy.

0 kilometres 100

0 miles 100

KEY

✈ International airport

⛴ Ferry port

══ Motorway

▬▬ Main road

— Railway

--- Regional boundary

-- International boundary

---- Ferry route

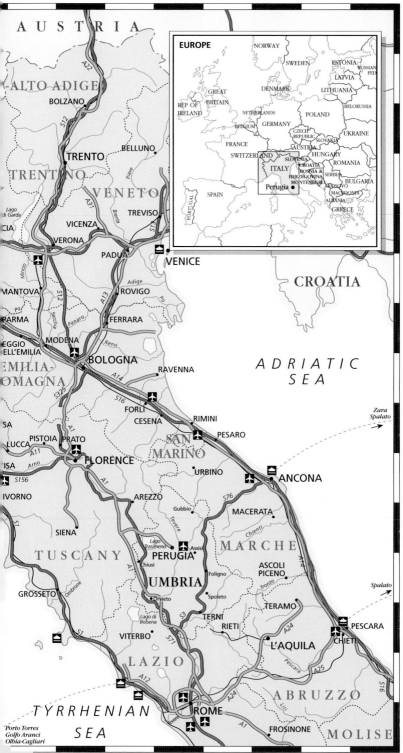

A PORTRAIT OF UMBRIA

Umbria is a land apart, with its own singular character and identity. At the geographical centre of Italy, it is known, thanks to its lushness, as the peninsula's "Green Heart"; its rolling hills and fertile plains are studded with picturesque towns, castles and monasteries, recalling millennia of human habitation.

Small in comparison to its neighbouring regions, at just 8,450 sq km (3,260 miles), with barely a million inhabitants, Umbria nevertheless radiates a powerful image, both in Italy and abroad. Elemental features of its reputation are its unspoilt landscape, its inimitable art and architecture, and, perhaps most significantly, its deeply mystical heritage. Add to that the region's famously fine cuisine and exuberant festivals and it is no wonder that Umbria has developed a cachet all its own.

Recent decades have witnessed the arrival of a breed of "New Umbrians", neo-settlers who have migrated here, maybe from Milan, Manchester or Manhattan. It is not unusual, while exploring the region's splendidly scenic roads and byways, to come across American couples enjoying the view, monks with typically Nordic features, or Italian ex-urbanites who have chosen a new, more relaxed way of life in this idyllic, largely rural setting.

St Francis, fresco in the Basilica of Assisi

TIMELESS LANDSCAPES

Umbria's pristine natural loveliness is certainly a major enticement. The landscape ranges from the great green slopes and peaks of the Monti Sibillini and the mountain chains that border Le Marche to the gentle hills and plains around Assisi and Perugia; from the roaring waters of the Cascata delle Marmore to the subtle sibilance of the wind among the

The hamlet of Castelluccio, in a spectacular spot within the Monti Sibillini

◁ Flag-wavers in medieval costume at the Corsa all'Anello at Narni

Piece of traditional Umbrian fabric

Umbria's cities and towns are among Italy's most gorgeous. Perugia, Assisi, Gubbio, Orvieto, Spoleto, Todi – the very names are synonymous with the perfection of the medieval hill town. They are approachable, human in scale, but also filled with world-class masterpieces of architecture and art in recognizably Umbrian style. Some of Italy's finest palaces and civic structures are here, as well as some of its most resplendent churches, while Umbrian painters such as Perugino helped set the standard for sheer beauty in the High Renaissance.

Lying at the crossroads between Rome and Florence, the region has been embellished by the works of many renowned artists, including Cimabue, Giotto, Piero della Francesca, Simone Martini, Fra Angelico, Filippo Lippi, Luca Signorelli, Ghirlandaio, Raphael and Gian Lorenzo Bernini. At the same time, venerable Umbrian crafts, especially ceramics and textiles, have been famous for centuries.

Nor should the ancient remains be overlooked. Throughout Umbria, the Romans left behind superb gates, towers, bridges and even a still-func-

reeds on the shores of Lake Trasimeno. Green – the colour which has, in effect, become the region's popular "trademark" – is very much a reality here and dominates the scenery. However, the beauty of the environment alone could never fully account for Umbria's undeniable mystique. The fields, the olive groves, the forests of beech, holm oak and chestnut are inevitably set off by evocative vestiges of a long-standing human presence.

Umbrian potter at work

SUBLIME ARCHITECTURE AND ART

Whether in the form of a town, a village or a medieval monastery, an ancient farmhouse, a dry-stone wall or a ruined church, architecture is essential to the region's spirit. Whether grand or rustic, Roman, Romanesque or Renaissance, such architectural heritage conveys a timeless feel that is distinctively Umbrian. It evokes a symbiosis of man and nature that has flourished since the days of the primordial Umbri and Etruscans, and later the Romans, right down to modern Italians.

The renowned Basilica di San Francesco in Assisi

A snapshot of daily life in Assisi, a city visited by millions of tourists every year

tioning theatre or two, while the archaeological finds dating back to Etruscan times and beyond are immensely rich and displayed in beautifully appointed museums.

One insightful observer of Italian life wrote, "With its millennia of infiltration, art has saturated the soul – everyone here lives art, whether they know it or not." This is nowhere more true than in Umbria.

A PLACE OF SPIRITUALITY

Most appealing to many modern newcomers is Umbria's glowing spiritual legacy. The birthplace of St Francis, St Clare and Jacopone da Todi has become the home of many spiritual centres and teachers of every persuasion. Retreats here are not only Christian, but are affiliated with all beliefs, everyone apparently drawn by the ineffable meditative power of the place. Overwhelmingly, it is a venue of peace, as embodied in the Marcia per la Pace (Walk of Peace) from Perugia to Assisi, which

takes place every other autumn. Many global spiritual leaders have promoted greater understanding here, including the Dalai Lama.

INVITING HOSPITALITY

Visitors attracted more by earthly pleasures are well satisfied, too. Umbria's robust and tasty cuisine consists of dishes that combine the best of local culinary traditions, while taking full advantage of the produce and game of the region – highlighting wild mushrooms, black truffles and wild boar *(cinghiale)*.

Hospitality is an art form here, too. Every city, town or village proudly rivals its neighbours with its age-old festivals, as well as its gastronomic specialities. In the countryside, *agriturismi* (farm lodgings) have become a reliable alternative to standard hotel accommodation, offering a delightful first-hand taste of authentic Umbrian life.

Decades of modernization have tested the traditional values of the region, and the disastrous earthquake of 1997 has left its mark in others, but the quintessential allure of Umbria remains intact.

Apparition at Arles, Upper Church, Assisi

The Landscape of Umbria

The rare red lily

The mountains of Umbria are of comparatively recent origin. The fact that the region's topography developed relatively late, together with the presence of still-active powerful tectonic forces, mean that there is a heightened risk of earthquakes in Umbria. Once cultivated up to fairly high altitudes, the mountains have now been largely abandoned by farmers. Rolling hills made up of fertile but often fragile terrain border the highest peaks; centuries of cultivation have given them their current shape. In Umbria's southwestern corner, and around Orvieto, the land is of volcanic origin. Lake Trasimeno, in the northwest, is the most important lake in Central Italy.

A bright field of sunflowers, widely cultivated in Umbria

THE MOUNTAINS

The average height of the mountains in Umbria is around 1,000 m (3,280 ft). Most of the range consists of karst limestone and is riddled with caves and subterranean galleries and rivers. The vegetation most characteristic of this environment is beech forest and upland pasture. Among the wildlife found in the mountains are birds of prey, wildcats and several kinds of wolf.

Wolves *became extinct in Umbria in the 18th century but have reappeared in the protected Monti Sibillini. There is a greater chance of seeing them in winter, when they come down to the valley.*

This Apennine edelweiss *lives on calcareous crags. Similar to alpine edelweiss, it is distinguished by its spathulate leaves (that is, wide at the tip and narrow at the base).*

THE HILLS

The climate in the hills is milder than that at higher altitudes, and is also less polluted than on the plain. For this reason, the hills of Umbria have been settled and cultivated since ancient times. In areas not given over to farmland and olive groves there are oaks, holm oaks and, lower down, mixed woodland and scrub.

The wild boar *is one of the most common mammals in the hills. Its meat is prized.*

Acorns

The olive *is one of the most important agricultural products in Umbria. Olives produced in the area around Trevi (see p107) are especially highly regarded.*

CULTIVATION OF THE PLAINS

The few areas of plain found in Umbria lie along river courses and include the Valle Umbra (between Assisi and Spoleto), the Valle del Paglia (in the southwest), and the plains of Terni and Gubbio. Reclamation in these areas in the years after World War II has created very fertile land, where farming is now carried out on an industrial scale (where possible, producing forced and cash crops), although man has been present here since ancient times. The plants found are those commonly seen in cultivated fields.

The corn cockle (Agrostemma githago) *was once widespread on cultivated land. It is now rare, owing to the use of herbicides by farmers.*

Lapwings *form flocks in cultivated fields and in pastureland during the winter season.*

THE PLAINS

In general, every area of flat ground in Umbria occupies the site of an ancient lake or marsh, and is therefore especially fertile. These plains are now primarily given over to cultivation (grapevines and olives, for example). As a consequence, the land is not known for its varied wildlife, although rodents and small predators, such as foxes, are common.

Grain *was once grown as animal fodder, while today, increasingly, it is grown in industrial quantities.*

The fox *is a highly adaptable mammal which manages to live in all kinds of habitat. In cultivated fields, foxes find shelter among the hedgerows.*

LAKES, RIVERS AND MARSHLAND

Lake Trasimeno is a place that has a fascinating history, with a tradition of fishing going back to ancient times. Rivers in Umbria include the Tiber (il Tevere), the Velino and the Nera; the last boasts the spectacular manmade waterfall, the Cascata delle Marmore, and some particularly fine scenery. Freshwater fish and other species abound in the wild.

A trout *is camouflaged among the stones on the river bed thanks to its marbled colouring.*

Freshwater crabs *live in reed beds and are active mainly at night. Their presence indicates good water quality.*

Nature Reserves in Umbria

Logo of the Sistema Parchi Umbri

Although nature plays a fundamental role in the overall image of the region, Umbria has been rather slow to set up protected parks and reserves. The creation of parks has frequently been opposed at a local level (the inhabitants are exceedingly passionate about hunting), and their establishment has been achieved largely by balancing the demands of nature with those of the development of the economy and the tourist trade.

Together with the Umbrian portion of the Parco Nazionale dei Monti Sibillini (part of a great series of protected areas in the Apennines, safeguarding the principal mountain masses in the chain), Umbrian parks today protect around seven per cent of the terrain in the region. These parks can be divided into two categories: "mountain parks", which are those along the border with Le Marche, and "water parks", which are focused around the lakes and water courses of the region.

The Parco Regionale del Lago Trasimeno (see pp92–3) *covers 13,200 ha (32,600 acres) and includes the lake shores – thereby safeguarding the water and banks – but not the tourist resorts around the lake. The perimeter of Lake Trasimeno measures around 60 km (37 miles).*

The Oasis of Alviano (see p127) is an ecosystem that serves as a breeding ground for numerous species of water birds, as well as an important source of food for rare birds such as cranes, wild geese and ospreys.

The Parco Fluviale del Tevere (see p133) *extends from the gates of Todi as far as Alviano, along the banks of the longest river in central Italy, the Tiber. The park protects some 7,925 ha (19,585 acres), over a length of 50 km (31 miles).*

Città di Castello

Umbertide

LAKE TRASIMENO

Perugia

Orvieto

LAGO DI CORBARA

Todi

Alviano

S221
S257
S219
S75bis
S599
S220
S317
S71
S397
S79bis
S448
S205

0 kilometres   15

0 Miles   15

KEY

☐ Regional Park

▨ National Park

The **Parco Regionale del Monte Subasio** (*see pp66–7*) separates but also links Assisi, Spello and Nocera Umbra, and covers an area of 7,440 ha (18,390 acres). For centuries, Monte Subasio has been a favourite destination among mystics and hermits. St Francis lived here with his fellow brothers in the Eremo delle Carceri, in the shade of a forest of ancient holm oaks.

The Parco Regionale del Monte Cucco (see pp62–3) *is in the northeast area of the province of Perugia. It extends over more than 10,000 ha (24,700 acres), and was created in 1995 to protect the peak (1,555 m/ 5,100 ft) made famous by the subterranean cave system of the Grotta di Monte Cucco; the latter is 920 m (3,017 ft) deep and extends for tens of kilometres.*

The Parco Regionale di Colfiorito (see p103), *not far from Foligno and Nocera Umbra, protects a beautiful landscape of upland plain and marshland. The area consists of a series of drained depressions, once ancient expanses of water, and a lake that has been declared a Waterfowl Habitat and is home to amphibians and many species of bird.*

The Parco Nazionale dei Monti Sibillini *(see pp108–9)* extends over more than 70,000 ha (173,000 acres), crossing regional borders. The Umbrian side of the park, along the border with Le Marche, is a typical Apennine environment. The countryside is characterized by peaks of varying height (the highest, at 2,475 m/8,120 ft, is Monte Vettore), large areas of upland pasture, river valleys and beech forests. Wolves, wildcats and porcupines live at ground level, while golden eagles and peregrine falcons circle in the sky.

The Parco Fluviale del Nera (see pp122–3) *is famous for the abundance of its waters and for the magnificent Cascata delle Marmore. The course of the Nera is protected by this 2,120-ha (5,240-acre) park, which includes the lower reaches of the river for 18 km (11 miles), as far as the famous cascade.*

Gubbio

S147
Assisi

Topino
S75

Foligno

S3

S396
Norcia

S418 Spoleto
S209

S320

Nera

Terni

S3

Outdoor Activities

Given the beauty of the landscape in Umbria, nature and the great outdoors should feature in every visitor's trip to the region. Furthermore, open-air sports are increasingly well catered for, and in every part of the region. Just as pilgrims flock to Assisi from all four corners of the globe, it is equally easy to encounter a whole range of languages among a crowd of canoeists sweeping its way down the Nera or the Tiber, or among the hang-gliding community taking off from Monte Cucco or from the windswept uplands of the Monti Sibillini.

More everyday activities should not be forgotten either, particularly as they constitute one of the best ways of seeing and appreciating this beautiful region: consider going on a long bicycle ride through the hills, past farms and ancient abbeys, or on a gentle horse-ride through one of the greenest, most fascinating and relaxing landscapes in Italy.

Hiking in one of the magnificent valleys of the Monti Sibillini

Horse-riding just outside the historic town of Spello

HORSE-RIDING

In Umbria there are many stables and farm holiday (*agriturismo*) businesses that can organize horse-riding trips. As well as being an enjoyable sport, riding offers a closer and more natural view of the countryside than is possible with conventional means of transport.

Many Umbrian horse-riding stables belong to national associations, such as ANTE (Associazione Nazionale Turismo Equestre), and can offer trekking in all the most beautiful areas of the region, including the hills around Assisi, Città della Pieve and Bettona, the shores of Lake Trasimeno, the slopes of Monte Subasio and the steep bridle paths of the Valnerina. Treks that last for several days or more are available from various equestrian clubs, or you can apply directly to ANTE.

WALKING AND CYCLING

No equipment is required to enjoy walking: all you need is a good view, decent weather, paths to follow and a destination, whether it be historical or natural.

The Monti Sibillini national park, to present the most enticing example, has always been one of the best-loved destinations among walkers in Umbria (along with neighbouring park areas in the nearby region of Le Marche). In the colder seasons, however, it is also possible to find routes at lower altitudes, such as the bridle paths that link the towns and villages.

The routes that connect Umbria's most famous towns and villages are very popular with cyclists: the gradients are not excessive and the varied landscape provides plenty of interest along the way. Bridle paths and footpaths at higher altitudes are also used by mountain bikers. There are now more than 600 km (373 miles) of mountain biking trails in the region. Brochures and information about walking and cycling are available from tourist offices.

ROCK CLIMBING, CAVES AND GORGES

Not all that long ago, all that one had to choose from was mountaineering. Today, various rock climbing sports are popular in Italy, and there are all kinds of cliff faces to use. In Umbria, any visitor in search of a vertical cliff face will feel at home on certain cliffs in the Monti Sibillini and in the village of Ferentillo, where there are numerous suitable sites: rock climbing is such a big thing here that there is even a climbing guide dedicated to the area. Umbria is also a place that finds much favour among speleologists. The biggest attraction is the cave system beneath Monte Cucco, on the border with Le Marche (not far from that region's famous caves, the Grotte di Frasassi). There are also caves worth visiting in the mountains near Terni.

A sport that has taken hold in Umbria, which developed out of speleology – the equipment used is much the same – is "torrentismo", or canyoning, the sport of navigating steep-sided gorges. The most famous and popular sites are found in the Valnerina (Fosso di Rocca Gelli and Forra del Casco), on Monte Cucco (Forra di Riofreddo), and in the hills surrounding Lake Corbara (Gole di Prodo).

It is important to make clear that all of the above are extreme sports, and that they can all be exceedingly dangerous. Anyone trying them out for the first time should ensure that they are accompanied by an expert.

An Umbrian cave, and one of many visiting speleologists

HANG-GLIDING AND CROSS-COUNTRY SKIING

Wind, unlimited vistas and serious gradients are the three ingredients necessary for hang-gliding and paragliding. Umbria has plenty of all three. Famous locations for this exciting but daredevil sport are Monte Cucco and the Monti Sibillini, where the isolated, high-altitude village of Castelluccio di Norcia is now one of the most popular destinations for hang-gliding

Hang-gliding on the slopes of Monte Vettore

aficionados, who come here from all over the world.

The topography of the Umbrian mountains does not much favour downhill skiing, however; few of the slopes are steep enough, and the lower altitudes are not suitable for the building of ski lifts or ski resorts of any great size. To compensate, the great Apennine uplands provide perfect cross-country territory. Skiers can follow the beaten tracks or, better still, ski along snow-covered bridle paths and footpaths.

Shooting the rapids on the Nera

SHOOTING RAPIDS

In spring, the many rivers and water courses that cross Umbria, almost all of them torrential, are an irresistible attraction for canoeists from all over Europe. As the water rises and the rapids swell, canoes, kayaks and rubber rafts appear as if from nowhere along the banks of the rivers Nera and Tiber.

The Nera offers a range of experiences and caters to various levels of difficulty, up to the highest level, requiring considerable skill and expertise. This river also offers the extraordinary sight of the Cascata delle

Marmore *(see pp122–3)*, which is the principal starting point for rafting trips. The stretch of the Tiber below Todi is one of the most popular routes for river rafting and other excursions, but you can also join the Tiber further north, at Città di Castello, allowing you to cross virtually the entire region.

A non-competitive descent from Todi to Rome takes place every year from the end of April to early May. It is open to everyone and is very popular. There are also good river-rafting sites from the Monti Sibillini down to the Valnerina.

SAILING ON THE LAKES

Lake Trasimeno is clearly the most obvious place for holidaymakers in landlocked Umbria to go sailing and windsurfing. Visitors can bring their own boats or make use of the craft available for hire. There are numerous regattas. Other stretches of water that are at least partially equipped for sailing, windsurfing and other water sports include Lago di Piediluco and Lago di Corbara, both in southern Umbria.

You can also go water skiing on Lake Trasimeno, but you must first apply for a permit from the office of the Provincia di Perugia.

Sailing boats manoeuvring on Lake Trasimeno

In the Footsteps of St Francis

Francis was born in Assisi in 1181–82, and grew up to be a bright, cultured and even ambitious youth. A military career was chosen as the means by which he could rise up through the social hierarchy, and he enrolled in the army that Walter of Brienne was preparing for the Crusades. However, illness brought Francis back to Assisi, where he experienced his conversion and where he began his charity work. The story of his life, marvellously illustrated in the frescoes in the upper church at Assisi, provides us with a picture of a man drawn to nature, poverty and prayer. They also inspire us to go and explore the many places in Umbria that retain the memory of St Francis's presence.

St Francis, attributed to Cimabue

Isola Maggiore, on Lake Trasimeno, was the home of one of the first communities of the Friars Minor at the beginning of the 13th century. St Francis spent a long Lenten period with them here.

CITTÀ DI CASTELLO

Tiber

AREZZO

LAKE TRASIMENO

Nestore

Chiani

Paglia

LAKE CORBARA

LAKE ALVIAN

Every church, every corner *of Assisi bears traces of the life of the saint. He was baptized in the font in the cathedral of San Rufino; next to the church of San Giorgio was his school; and the Chiesa Nuova was constructed on the very spot where Francis is thought to have been born.* Left, St Francis gives his cloak to a poor man, *with a view of Assisi in the background.*

One of the most famous episodes *in the life of the saint is undoubtedly his preaching to the birds. The stone on which the scene is said to have taken place is in the church of San Francesco in Bevagna (see p104).* Right, Francis preaches to the birds.

Near the Fonti del Clitunno (see p107), *in the church of San Pietro di Bovara, is a Crucifix which spoke to St Francis. (The more famous talking Crucifix is in the Basilica di Santa Chiara, see p70.)* Left, The Saint in Ecstasy.

KEY

▬▬	Trail of St Francis
═══	Other roads
～～	River

0 kilometres	20
0 miles	20

Francis found refuge *with the Spadalonga family of Gubbio after his departure from his father's house. The saint also spent time in the small monastery of the Vittorina (see p81), along the road between Gubbio and Assisi. It was here, according to historians, that he tamed a wolf. Right,* The saint renounces his worldly goods.

On Monte Subasio (see pp66–7), cloaked in holm oaks, the monastery of the Eremo delle Carceri was built around the little church and the caves where Francis and his companions would gather in prayer. A trail from the hermitage goes through the surrounding woods and passes a series of sites dear to the saint's tradition because they were places of prayer and meditation.

Santa Maria degli Angeli *was erected in the 15th century, in order to shelter the old monastery of the Porziuncola (see p80), in whose infirmary St Francis died on 4 October 1226. What is left of that room is kept in the Cappella del Transito. Left,* The Poor Clares mourn the dead saint.

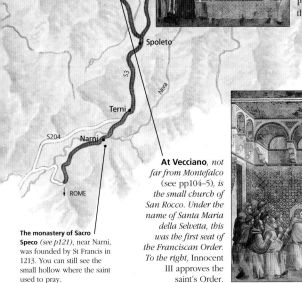

At Vecciano, *not far from Montefalco (see pp104–5), is the small church of San Rocco. Under the name of Santa Maria della Selvetta, this was the first seat of the Franciscan Order. To the right,* Innocent III approves the saint's Order.

The monastery of Sacro Speco (see p121), near Narni, was founded by St Francis in 1213. You can still see the small hollow where the saint used to pray.

Map labels: Gubbio, E45/S3bis, S298, Chiascio, Tiber, Perugia, Assisi, Santa Maria degli Angeli, S75, Cannara, Topino, Bevagna, Montefalco, Vecciano, Bovara, Spoleto, S3, Nera, Terni, S204, Narni, ROME

Art in Umbria

The region of Umbria as it is defined today was established only after the unification of Italy in 1861. In the preceding centuries, Umbria's towns and cities formed part of a political and artistic mosaic which extended from Tuscany to the Adriatic coast, without precise boundaries. In art, as in politics, there was plenty of opportunity for contacts and exchanges with other regions. Two crucial highlights stand out in the long history of art in Umbria: the founding and construction of the basilica of St Francis in Assisi – with the contribution of great artists, from Umbria and from other parts of Italy – and the golden age of the city of Perugia.

Etruscan bronze

Tempietto del Clitunno, detail of the front

Cast of stone with Umbrian inscription, 2nd century BC

ORIGINS

Umbria was populated from the sixth millennium BC. Interesting ceramic finds from that time have been discovered near Norcia and Parrano (outside Orvieto). With the passing of the millennia, a community of shepherds – part of what scholars describe as the Apennine civilization – developed in the mountains. Around the 16th century BC, they started to produce elegant pottery, decorated with geometrical motifs. The burial site at Monteleone di Spoleto dates back to these very early civilizations. Archaeologists discovered a bronze cart here, and this is now in

the Metropolitan Museum in New York. During the first millennium BC, Umbrian land was divided between two very different peoples: the Etruscans, who settled on the west bank of the Tiber, with the key towns of Perugia and Orvieto, and the Umbri, about whom little is still known, who were on the Tiber's east bank and in the Apennine mountains.

THE ROMANS

The Roman conquest of Umbria was slow but inexorable. If one had to choose a symbolic historical date for the arrival of the Romans in Umbria, it would be 219 BC, the year in which the Via Flaminia was opened. This Roman road became the main communication route through the region for centuries.

The presence of the Romans led to a great push in building and civil engineering: theatres, public works as well as roads were built. In terms of sculpture dating from the Roman age, many marble and some bronze statues survive. The latter include the extraordinary

Male statue, 1st century AD

statue of Germanicus, found in Amelia and returned there only recently after a long and controversial residence in Perugia *(see p126)*. One can also see well-preserved Roman buildings, such as the amphitheatre in Gubbio *(see p58) and the* Temple of Minerva in Assisi *(see p71)*.

Christianity reached Umbria in around the 3rd and 4th centuries AD: of particular interest from this period are the church of San Salvatore in Spoleto *(see p115)* and the little temple at the Fonti di Clitunno *(see p107)*, both of which show clearly how early Christian architecture was inspired by the Roman and classical traditions. Another important church from the early Christian era in Umbria is San Michele Archangelo, or Sant'Angelo, in Perugia *(see p91)*, which was influenced by Byzantine architecture.

THE MIDDLE AGES

Politically split between Byzantium (on the west bank of the Tiber) and the Lombard dominion (on the east bank), Umbria was subject to a range of influences in the field of art. Even though few works of art have survived from the second half of the first millennium, and even though the buildings that remain have often been extensively remodelled, it is known that the 9th century was a period of significant development in Umbria. Cathedrals were founded all over the region and were often adorned with great pictorial cycles (now mostly lost). The main centre for this boom was the Lombard stronghold of Spoleto *(see pp110–15)*, where even today you can admire the reliefs on the façade of San Pietro and the frescoes in the churches of San Gregorio and San Paolo inter Vineas.

The cloister of the abbey of Sassovivo, near Foligno, was built using Roman columns and arches.

Detail of the façade of San Pietro in Spoleto

ASSISI

In 1228, less than two years after the death of St Francis, and at the wishes of Frate Elia (who took it upon himself to hide the body of the saint), construction of the basilica of San Francesco in Assisi *(see pp 72–3)* began. This was a truly crucial moment, since the work on the basilica was to influence the art and architecture of both Umbria and nearby regions for centuries to come. The basilica in Assisi is still one of the most important monuments of Western art today.

The first frescoes were commissioned in 1254 from an anonymous Umbrian artist, known as the Maestro di San Francesco, who is regarded as having operated

GIOTTO

Presumed self-portrait

Born in 1267, Giotto di Bondone probably trained at the Florentine workshop of Cimabue. While it is thought that Giotto contributed to the frescoes in the basilica of St Francis in Assisi, it is now accepted that the cycle of the *Life of St Francis* was not his work but that of Roman painters. Giotto's great works include a *Last Judgment* and *Stories from the Life of the Virgin* in the Cappella degli Scrovegni in Padua and the bell tower for the duomo in Florence, a project that he directed up to his death in 1337.

a workshop of the highest quality. Then, from the end of the 13th century, great masters were summoned from outside the region – among them Cimabue and Giotto – to decorate the walls of the upper and lower churches. Their work would become a model for Umbrian painters later on. Work on the two basilicas continued for more than two centuries, with contributions by other great names from the history of Italian art, including Simone Martini and Pietro Lorenzetti. In parallel with the spreading of the Franciscan faith, so too

Painted Cross, Maestro di San Francesco, 1272

the pictorial style created in Assisi gained ground, and was imitated and reproduced in many new Franciscan churches all over Italy.

On 26 September 1997 this immense inheritance risked being lost forever. The entire complex was badly damaged by a violent earthquake, and parts of the vault in the upper church collapsed. Through the extraordinarily hard work of restorers, fragments of frescoes were saved and reinstalled where possible, but many vaults remain blank. The basilica remains magnificent but tarnished.

Vault of the Evangelists, Cimabue (1240–1302), Basilica of Assisi

PERUGINO

Pietro Vannucci, or Perugino, was born in Città della Pieve in 1452 and died in Fontignano in 1523. He was influenced by the work of Piero della Francesca and Verrocchio, in whose workshop the painter trained early on. Works in Rome include *Handing the Keys to St Peter* in the Sistine Chapel (1481), in the Vatican. In Florence are a *Lamentation* (Palazzo Pitti, 1494) and a *Crucifixion* (Santa Maddalena de' Pazzi, 1493). He also painted frescoes in the Sala dell'Udienza in the Collegio del Cambio, Perugia. His work can be found in several of the smaller towns of Umbria, particularly near Lake Trasimeno *(see p95).*

Epiphany, **1475–78,** detail

age came here, including: Piero della Francesca, Fra Angelico (who contributed to the decoration of the cathedral in Orvieto), Filippo Lippi (who would later be called to Spoleto to fresco the cathedral apse), and also Agostino di Duccio. A cycle of frescoes (1498–1500) painted by Perugino in the Collegio del Cambio was to exert a great influence over painters such as Pinturicchio and the young Raphael, who produced some of his early work in Perugia.

In this same period – in Perugia as well as in other cities in Umbria – a new style of architecture began to change the look of the old medieval city spaces, with new palaces being erected for noble merchant families. Influences in this field came from Rome, Urbino or from the great cities of nearby Tuscany.

An example of Umbrian art by the Maestro di Città di Castello

PERUGIA'S GOLDEN AGE

The position of Perugia, on the Via Flaminia and Via Amerina, at the junction of routes of communication between Rome and the Adriatic coast, made the city vulnerable to conquest. After invasions by the Goths and Lombards, the foundation of the cathedral (by the 10th century) marked the first stage in Perugia's rebirth in the Middle Ages.

For around three centuries, the commune of Perugia grew in power, riches and possessions. Signs of the prosperity of this age are the thick walls and city gates, though an even greater indication is the aqueduct, which brought water to the

city centre and was one of the first of its kind to be built in Italy. To celebrate this magnificent achievement a fountain was built in Piazza IV Novembre, featuring sculptures by Nicola and Giovanni Pisano *(see p87).*

THE 16TH CENTURY IN PERUGIA

Towards the middle of the 15th century, the city of Perugia was rich and cosmopolitan. The great Italian painters of the

THE UMBRIAN SCHOOL

It was because of the influence of the great artists who were attracted to Umbria in the second half of the 15th century that a regional school

Polyptych, Niccolò di Liberatore known as l'Alunno, 1471

developed in its own right, liberated from the Gothic models that had influenced art in the previous centuries. The principal artists to learn lessons from the Florentine Renaissance were, besides Perugino, Niccolò Alunno, Antonio Mezzastris, Matteo da Gualdo, from around Foligno, and Benedetto Bonfigli, of Perugia. In the first half of the 16th century, the most representative name is that of Giovanni di Pietro, or Spagna. The Umbrian school lost its originality and died out rapidly with the advent of Mannerism.

Coronation of the Virgin, 1511, Spagna

THE DOMINATION OF ROME

When the power of the communes *(see pp42–3)* gave way to papal rule, great military structures were built: Antonio da Sangallo the Younger designed Perugia's Rocca Paolina *(see p84)* and the Pozzo di San Patrizio in Orvieto *(see p138)*. Vignola worked on the Castellina in Norcia *(see p116)*.

By the end of the 16th century all the major artists of the time were working in Rome – not only Italians, but also Flemish artists such as Van Mander, Stellaert and Loots. Umbrian towns were totally dependent on the Church. In Todi, the construction of Santa Maria della Consolazione *(see pp132–3)*, worked on by

Baldassarre Peruzzi, Vignola and Ippolito Scalza, inaugurated a new concept of religious architecture. In 1569, on the plain below Assisi, work began on the great church of Santa Maria degli Angeli *(see p80)*, intended as a home for the Franciscan chapel of the Porziuncola. Designed by Galeazzo Alessi with Vignola as consultant, it was finished only in 1679.

Umbria's noble families, often important figures in administration and in the ranks of Roman power, built palazzi and villas in their native cities.

Statue in Santa Maria della Consolazione

18TH–19TH CENTURIES

The following centuries, dominated by papal rule right up to the unification of Italy in 1861, did not really produce great works of art in Umbria: the dominant influence was Rome, and the examples of Baroque and Rococo in the region are not of great importance.

A moment of regional pride came with the brief period of splendour of Perugia's Accademia di Belle Arti, which championed the Neo-Classical style. It is certainly no coincidence that the artist Canova, who stayed at San Gemini (near Todi), took up contacts with the great families of Perugia.

The 19th century saw the cities of Umbria becoming stages on the set routes followed by travellers on the Grand Tour. Admiration for the art of the Middle Ages became the cult of the time and *medievalismo* took hold in Perugia and led to the restoration – sometimes rather ingenuously – of ancient buildings.

APPLIED ARTS

Along with most of Italy, Umbria has long been famous as a treasure trove of art, sculpture and architecture. However, it has also produced a great many master craftsmen of skill and stature. In the many museums in Umbria's towns, old and new, one can find pieces of rare beauty, in particular ceramics and textiles, worked by hand over the centuries. The production of these objects continues today, and no tourist in Umbria should miss the opportunity of visiting one of the numerous handicrafts workshops in the region. Besides ceramics, for which Deruta *(see p83)* is particularly renowned, and fabrics, which are still woven by hand, look out for the embroidered tulle of Panicale (near Lake Trasimeno) and the delicate lace of Assisi, as well as painted stuccoes and woodcarving.

Majolica jug, 16th century

Antique fabric, manufactured in Todi in the 14th century

Architecture in Umbria

San Lorenzo di Arari in Orvieto

Even though the most significant impact on the towns of Umbria occurred during the centuries of the Middle Ages and the Renaissance, monuments from all periods of history are found in the region. From the time of the Etruscan city state to the era of Roman domination, from the rise of Romanesque architecture to the advent of Neo-Classicism, every people, every era, every architectural style and every artistic movement has left its traces, thanks to the work of the major artists of the time. The influence of the Roman Catholic church has been a constant.

A bas-relief, frequently used to decorate churches and palazzi

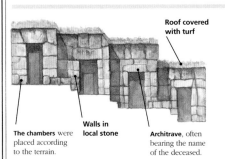

Roof covered with turf

The chambers were placed according to the terrain.

Walls in local stone

Architrave, often bearing the name of the deceased.

The necropolises *are the most tangible sign of the Etruscan presence in Umbria. In general, they consisted of a series of tomb chambers lined up along cemetery roads. Inside, the deceased lay on a funeral bench.*

ANTIQUITY

While the Umbri left few traces of the form of their cities, the imposing polygonal walls of Amelia and Spoleto owe their existence to this Italic people. The Etruscans left necropolises and tombs, such as those near Orvieto (Necropoli del Crocifisso del Tufo) or the extraordinary monumental burial site of the Ipogeo dei Volumni at Perugia. There are impressive Roman monuments such as the Temple of Minerva in Assisi, the theatres of Gubbio, Spoleto and Terni, the great cisterns of Amelia and Todi, and the city gates of Spello and Todi. Not forgetting the Via Flaminia, which still links Rome with the Adriatic coast, as it did 2,300 years ago.

THE MIDDLE AGES AND THE RENAISSANCE

After a period of Byzantine and Lombard domination, architecture was rejuvenated by the birth of the Romanesque style. Town squares lined with public buildings – a sign of temporal and communal power – were being built, as were cathedrals, a tangible and potent symbol of spiritual power.

The building of commercial towns in contact with outside markets brought about the arrival of the Gothic style during the 14th century. Especially fine examples of this style are Orvieto cathedral *(see pp136–7)* and the decoration in the Sala delle Arti Liberali e dei Pianeti in Palazzo Trinci in Foligno *(see p102)*, from the early years of the 15th century.

Palazzo dei Priori

Duomo

Fontana Maggiore

Piazza IV Novembre *in Perugia (see p86) is overlooked by both the duomo (cathedral) and the Palazzo dei Priori, a sign of the political power of the medieval commune. Between the two stands the Fontana Maggiore, decorated between 1275 and 1278 by Nicola Pisano and his son Giovanni.*

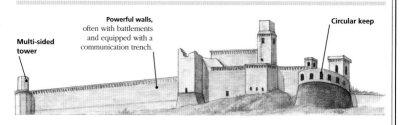

Multi-sided tower

Powerful walls, often with battlements and equipped with a communication trench.

Circular keep

The Rocca Maggiore at Assisi
(see p79) *was rebuilt in 1356 on the foundations of a feudal fortification built by Frederick Barbarossa. Its restoration was the work of Cardinal Albornoz, the papal legate who studded central Italy with these strongholds of the faith.*

THE AGE OF THE FORTRESSES

The conquest of Umbrian towns by the papacy brought about profound changes in the urban layout. The new power, aiming to increase military control and to diminish the importance of the traditional social space of the town square, commissioned a series of imposing fortresses which, although they have been modified over the centuries, have come down to us today virtually intact. These include the fortresses of Orvieto (begun in 1364 and then rebuilt in 1450), Narni (built from 1367–78), Assisi (rebuilt in 1356) and Spoleto (built in 1359).

Tympanum in classical style

Mirrored windows

Colonnade inspired by the entrance to a classical temple.

Palazzo della Regione
(see p90), *in the Fontivegge quarter of Perugia, was part of a town plan by the architect Aldo Rossi. From 1982 to 1989 he rebuilt this area of the regional capital in postmodern style, with classical references.*

MODERN ARCHITECTURE

Outside the encircling walls of Umbria's medieval towns, large and small, modern suburbs have developed, usually on the flat land just below the hilltop towns. Building styles have not always been particularly respectful of the artistic beauty of the old town, but there are some successful examples of modern architecture, such as the quarter of Fontivegge in Perugia. The countryside, too, has had to accept change. Many medieval groups of houses and farms have been converted for modern use, for example as hotels.

ROMANESQUE CHURCHES IN UMBRIA

Around the 11th century, when medieval society was developing and the Church was re-creating its own autonomy, a style of religious architecture developed which, with simple linear forms, attempted a direct link with local cultures. In the 19th century, this style was defined as "Romanesque", after its derivation from the Christian basilica of the Roman era. The Romanesque church presents a harmonious façade, featuring arches and one or more rose windows. From the three doorways access is gained to the three-aisled interior, at the end of which is a presbytery, raised to allow the construction of a crypt. Examples of the style, since reworked, are San Lorenzo di Arari in Orvieto and the cathedrals of Spoleto, Assisi and Todi.

Three-mullioned window in a square frame

Large rose window (13th century)

San Michele
(1195) in Bevagna has a beautiful doorway in which Romanesque elements and Roman finds are combined.

UMBRIA
THROUGH THE YEAR

All year round in Umbria there are feast days, religious celebrations and pagan festivals linked to the farming year, including the harvest, or to popular and historical traditions of the ancient communes. Some of these events are famous worldwide, but every small village in Umbria has

Spoleto festival logo

its own festival or saint's day worthy of wider renown. Besides the traditional events that have taken place for decades or centuries, there is also a full calendar of cultural events, such as the Festival of Spoleto and Umbria Jazz, not to mention historical re-enactments, and cinema and theatre seasons.

SPRING

Umbria has no sea coast. As a result, the spring climate can be cool and windy. On higher ground, the snow may remain until March or April, while on the hills and high plains spring flowers are emerging. The main religious events during this season are those that fall during the Easter period, but there are also important feast days in May.

Women in medieval costume at the Calendimaggio in Assisi

MARCH

Benedictine celebrations, Norcia *(20–21 Mar)*. Includes a torchlit procession and a crossbow competition.

APRIL

Antiques fair, Todi *(mid- to late Apr)*. Held in the Palazzo delle Arti.
Wine week, Montefalco *(Easter)*. Large trade fair of DOC wines.
La Desolata, Perugia *(Holy Week)*. Exciting staging of the Passion.

Opening of the Corsa all'Anello festival in Narni

Tableaux Vivants, Città della Pieve *(Holy Week)*. Scenes from the Passion.
Processione del Cristo Morto, Assisi, Tuoro sul Trasimeno and Norcia *(Holy Week)*.
Via Crucis, Alviano and Amelia *(Good Friday)*.
Processione della Rinchinata, Bastia Umbra and Cannara *(Easter)*. Staging the meeting of Christ and the Madonna.
Coloriamo i Cieli, Castiglione del Lago *(late Apr to early May)*. A colourful biennial kite festival.
Corsa all'Anello, Narni *(late Apr to mid-May)*. Costumed knights spear a ring *(anello)* with a lance.

MAY

Cantamaggio, Terni *(May)*. Folk festival celebrating the advent of spring. Parade of floats with allegorical scenes.
Festa del Calendimaggio, Assisi *(first week)*. Three days

of fun, including a costumed re-enactment of medieval stories, in which two of the town's districts compete.
Corsa dei Ceri, Gubbio *(15 May)*. Three guilds challenge each other to carry towering candlesticks *(ceri)* on their shoulders up to the basilica of Sant'Ubaldo.
Palio della Balestra, Gubbio *(last Sun)*. In Piazza della Signoria, the crossbowmen of Gubbio and Sansepolcro (Tuscany) challenge each other in a Palio.
Festa di Santa Rita, Cascia *(21–22 May)*. A torchlit procession towards the Santa Rita basilica, then a historical procession with the saint's remains and the staging of scenes from her life.
Festa della Palombella, Orvieto *(Pentecost)*. Similar to the Scoppio del Carro in Florence, in which an artificial "dove" sets light to a cart of fireworks.

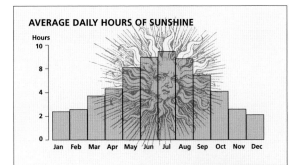

AVERAGE DAILY HOURS OF SUNSHINE

Hours
10
8
4
2
0
Jan Feb Mar Apr May Jun Jul Aug Sep Oct Nov Dec

Sunshine
In summer the days are long and sunny, and it can become very hot in the towns. In September and October the days are still sunny, and often pleasantly warm, as they are also in the spring – perhaps the best time to visit Umbria.

SUMMER

Umbria can be very hot and humid in July and August, so many summer events are held outside, and in the evening. Festivals take place in squares, parks and gardens, and attract locals and tourists alike.

JUNE

Festa della Fioritura, Castelluccio di Norcia. Ancient feast marking the return of flocks of sheep to the mountains.
Mercato delle Gaite, Bevagna *(second half of Jun)*. Medieval fair with splendid costumes and stalls.
Infiorata, Spello *(Corpus Christi)*. Procession along a flower-strewn route. Floral carpet competition.
Procession, Orvieto *(Corpus Christi)*. Procession in historical costume.
Festa del Voto, Assisi *(22 Jun)*. Re-enactment of the expulsion of the Saracens.

Piazza IV Novembre in Perugia, crowded with jazz fans

Rockin' Umbria, Perugia and Umbertide *(last ten days of Jun)*. Rock music festival, with up-and-coming bands, as well as photography and comic exhibitions.
Biennale di Scultura, Gubbio. A biennial exhibition of works by contemporary Italian artists.
Festa delle Acque, Piediluco and at the Cascata delle Marmore *(late Jun)*. Processions of boats, canoe races and fireworks.

JULY

Festival di Spoleto *(end Jun to mid-Jul)*. A major international event dedicated to theatre, dance and music.
Umbria Jazz, Perugia *(mid-Jul)*. Theatres, gardens and squares are taken over by some of the world's great jazz artists.
Gubbio Festival *(Jul–Aug)*. Chamber and symphony

music in the open air.
Palio delle Barche, Passignano sul Trasimeno *(last week in Jul)*. Town districts compete in a boat race, for which participants wear medieval costume.

Historical costume

AUGUST

Palio dei Terzieri, Città della Pieve. Archery competition and all manner of street entertainment, including acrobats and a procession featuring costumes derived from the works of Perugino.
Palio dei Quartieri, Nocera Umbra. Popular historical re-enactment in costume.
Palio di San Rufino, Assisi. Crossbow competition.
Rassegna internazionale del folklore, Castiglione del Lago. Folklore festival.
Festival delle Nazioni *(late Aug to early Sep)*, Città di Castello. Festival of chamber music.

Floral decorations in the street during the Infiorata, Spello

AVERAGE MONTHLY RAINFALL

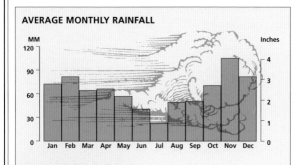

| | Jan | Feb | Mar | Apr | May | Jun | Jul | Aug | Sep | Oct | Nov | Dec |

Rainfall

Late autumn is the time of year when rainfall is at its heaviest. In winter heavy snowfalls are common in the Apennines, while storms may occur in spring and late summer.

The Joust of the Quintana in Foligno, September

AUTUMN

The end of the summer heralds the grape harvest, followed by the olive harvest. These are two very important occasions for the customs and culture of the region. Summer festivals and tourist events are usually over by this stage, and this is the start of a season of festivals linked to the gastronomy and history of the region.

SEPTEMBER

Cavalcata di Satriano, Nocera Umbra *(first Sun)*. Knights in medieval costume retrace the last journey of St Francis, from the hermitage at Nocera to his native Assisi.
Giostra della Quintana, Foligno *(second Sun)*. In this joust, competing knights attempt to spear a ring held by a wooden puppet. The streets are filled with historical processions.
Giochi delle Porte, Gualdo Tadino *(last week of Sep)*. Includes archery and catapult competitions, donkey and donkey cart races all around

the town. There are also historical re-enactments.
Festa dell'Uva *(end Sep)*, Montefalco. Celebration of the grape harvest.
Segni Barocchi, Foligno *(Sep–Oct)*. Musical and theatrical performances, all with a Baroque theme.

OCTOBER

Giostra dell'Arme, San Gemini *(late Sep to mid-Oct)*. Costumed knights from two town districts compete in a jousting tournament.
Palio dei Terzieri, **Trevi** *(1 Oct)*. Cart race and historical parade.
Festival Eurochocolate, Perugia *(mid- to late Oct)*. Chocolate stands and superb chocolate sculptures fill the historic centre.
Festa di San Francesco, Assisi *(3–4 Oct)*. Important religious celebration on the anniversary of Francis's death.
Marcia per la Pace, Perugia to Assisi *(biennial)*. Groups and movements from around the world participate in an

international march for peace.
Rassegna Antiquaria, Perugia *(end Oct to early Nov)*. Antiques fair. Includes displays of antique textiles.
Ottobre Trevano, Trevi. Gastronomic feasts and historical re-enactments performed in costume.
Mostra del Tartufo, Città di Castello *(late Oct to early Nov)*. See and taste white truffles and all sorts of other tasty woodland delicacies.

NOVEMBER

Fiera dei Cavalli, Città di Castello *(third Sun of Nov)*. Cattle markets and horse fairs.
Wine Tasting, Torgiano *(late Nov)*. World-famous wine-tasting competition of Umbrian and other Italian wines.
Festa dei Ceramisti, Deruta *(25 Nov)*. Festival of Deruta's older ceramicists, plus displays of ceramics.
Rassegna cinematografica di Assisi. Film festival dedicated to Italian cinema.

Flag waving display at the Giochi delle Porte in Gualdo Tadino

AVERAGE MONTHLY TEMPERATURE

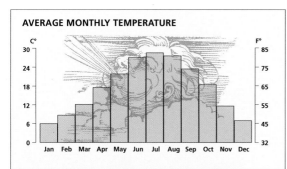

C° 30 24 18 12 6 0
F° 85 75 65 55 45 32
Jan Feb Mar Apr May Jun Jul Aug Sep Oct Nov Dec

Temperature
The Umbrian climate is temperate, though temperatures are much cooler in the Apennines. Autumn and spring, when the days are not too hot, are the most pleasant seasons. The summer months are hot and humid, especially in the towns.

The Nativity in Città di Castello, one of Italy's most important festivals

WINTER

This season can be very cold and windy, and snow often falls at higher mountain altitudes. There are festivals celebrating the chestnut harvest, for instance, but Christmas is the focus of the season. At Christmas, living nativity scenes are staged, a popular tradition dating from the Middle Ages.

NATIONAL HOLIDAYS

New Year (1 Jan)
Epiphany (6 Jan)
Easter Sunday
Anniversary of Liberation (25 Apr)
Labour Day (1 May)
Festa della Repubblica (2 Jun)
Ferragosto (15 Aug)
All Saints (1 Nov)
Immaculate Conception (8 Dec)
Christmas (25 Dec)
Santo Stefano (26 Dec)

DECEMBER

Ri Fauni or Festa delle Campane *(9 Dec)*. Commemorating the transporting of the Madonna of Nazareth to Loreto (9 December 1921).
World's largest Christmas tree, Gubbio *(from 7 Dec)*. Lights transform Monte Ingino into a giant Christmas tree.
Living Nativity, Attigliano, Alviano, Acquasparta, Calvi, Giove, Monteleone, Petrignano, Lugnano in Teverina, Perugia and Rocca Sant'Angelo *(24 Dec)*.
Christmas in Assisi. Concerts and formal celebrations in the basilica and other churches.
Monumental nativity, Città della Pieve *(Christmas to Epiphany)*. This is displayed in the Palazzo della Corgna.

JANUARY

Umbria Jazz Winter, Orvieto *(end Dec to early Jan)*. Winter version of the Perugia jazz festival. Concerts and musical events.

FEBRUARY

Carnevale. Parades and events throughout Umbria.
Festa dell'Olivo and **Sagra della Bruschetta**, Spello *(penultimate Sun of Carnevale)*. Olive and bruschetta festivals, with parades, feasts and music.
Mascherata, San Leo di Bastia *(1st Sun of Carnevale)*. A masked procession through the village.

Norcia black truffles

Festa di San Valentino, Terni *(Feb)*. Events all month, but 14 Feb is the focus. Betrothed couples exchange vows of love in the basilica of St Valentine.
Sagra del Tartufo Nero e dei Prodotti Tipici della Valnerina, Norcia *(Feb)*. Tastings and sales of produce, including truffles.

Gospel singing in Orvieto cathedral during Umbria Jazz Winter

THE HISTORY OF UMBRIA

Wedged between powerful neighbours like Tuscany, Le Marche and Lazio (especially Rome), the territory of Umbria has been an area of conquest, transit and trade for millennia. Its regional identity today dates back to the creation of a unified Italy in the 19th century, although the towns and cities of Umbria nonetheless have many characteristics in common.

The first populations date back to the Neolithic age – evidence remains of ceramics from the 6th and 5th millennia BC. Later, the Apennine civilization occupied Umbria's hills and mountains, and lived off agriculture and stock raising. They left behind decorated vases and tools of stone, bone and metal.

Black lacquer Etruscan vase, 3rd century BC

The golden age of prehistory in central Italy coincided with the development of the Villanovan culture in the 9th and 8th centuries BC. This people used iron for tools and arms, and had complex funerary rituals. The cities of many Italic peoples developed from the settlements of this era. They had a turbulent relationship with the emerging economic and military powers of the Etruscans and the Romans, and would manage to remain independent for only a few more centuries.

Until the Romans arrived, the Umbrian territory was divided into two areas of control: on the west bank of the Tiber was a series of rich Etruscan cities, while on the east bank the Umbri held control.

The little that is known about the Umbri comes from the famous Eugubine Tablets (see p60). Discovered in 1444, these seven bronze slabs were written in the 2nd century BC in the Umbrian language, using the Etruscan and then the Latin alphabet. The text describes religious rites and also Gubbio's political system. Other cities founded by the Umbri include Todi, Assisi, Spello and Gualdo Tadino.

Confrontation between Rome and the Etruscans reached crisis point in 295 BC, when Roman legions defeated the Umbri, the Sannites, Gauls and Etruscans, opening up territory for conquest. The cities changed sides quickly, and the opening in 219 of the Via Flaminia from Rome to the Adriatic confirmed Rome's power. Rome suffered one of its most bitter defeats, however, on the shores of Lake Trasimeno. In 217 BC the Roman army clashed with Hannibal and the Carthaginians to the west of the lake. The Carthaginians laid a trap to surprise the enemy on the lake shore and Hannibal's army wiped out two-thirds of the Roman forces.

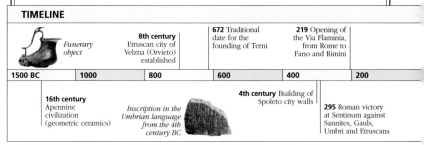

TIMELINE

Funerary object

16th century Apennine civilization (geometric ceramics)

8th century Etruscan city of Velzna (Orvieto) established

Inscription in the Umbrian language from the 4th century BC

672 Traditional date for the founding of Terni

4th century Building of Spoleto city walls

219 Opening of the Via Flaminia, from Rome to Fano and Rimini

295 Roman victory at Sentinum against Sannites, Gauls, Umbri and Etruscans

1500 BC	1000	800	600	400	200

◁ **Fortitude and Temperance**, Perugino (1448–1523), Collegio del Cambio in Perugia (detail)

Roman Umbria

Emperor Augustus

After the defeat of the Etruscans and the Italic peoples allied to the Umbri, Rome consolidated its domination of Umbria in the 1st century BC, when Emperor Augustus created Region VI (Umbria), which included all the cities and municipal towns on the west bank of the river Tiber. Region VII (Etruria) took in territory and settlements on the east bank of the river. The Romans, who were great civil engineers, undertook a series of urban projects in the 1st and 2nd centuries AD: including aqueducts, cisterns, theatres and walls that would feature in the lives of Umbrian towns for centuries. Via Flaminia and Via Amerina would become the main communication routes in the region for hundreds of years to come.

The Villa di Plinio (Pliny's Villa) at San Giustino would have been very grand at one time. This shows one of many hypothetical reconstructions.

Lake Trasimeno *was the scene of a battle between the Romans and Carthaginians* (see p93). *Today, there is little to be seen of the encounter: just the names of a river and a hill – Rio Sanguineto (bloody river) and Monte Sanguigno (Mount Blood) – and several ditches dug to cremate the corpses of Hannibal's soldiers.*

ROMAN UMBRIA
This map shows the administrative shape of Umbria under the Romans, as well as the busy network of Roman roads planned and built over the centuries. The Via Flaminia was of particular importance to Umbria. Construction began at the end of the 3rd century BC, and a number of towns of importance developed along its length, among them Spoleto. The road maintained its role in the centuries following Roman domination.

Tuoro al Trasimeno

LAKE TRASIMENO

Perusia (Perugia)

REGION VII

VIA TIBERINA

Tifernum Tiberinum (Città di Castello)

VIA ORVIETANA

VIA CASSIA

VIA NOVA TRAIANA

VIA AMERINA

Tuder (Todi)

Volsinii Veteres (Orvieto)

Paglia

River Tiber

Ameria (Amelia)

The site of Carsulae (see p128) *is one of the most important in Umbria, and many of the objects discovered here now feature in the museums of the region. The site was abandoned in 27 BC, when commercial traffic moved to the eastern side of the Via Flaminia.*

Via Amerina was the second main artery road.

The baths at Otricoli were built on the site of natural springs. Baths were an important feature of Roman civilization.

Ocriculum (Otricoli)

The Mausoleum of Pomponio Grecino, *near Gubbio, demonstrates that the city was an important political and religious place at the time of Region VI.*

The Via Flaminia was the main route through Umbria, built along the axis of the towns of Narnia, Spoletium, Carsulae and Fulginiae. Traces of the original paving stones can be seen in many towns.

The Temple of Minerva *(see p71)* in Assisi was built in the 1st century AD, on a set of terraces representing the centre of the Roman city. The temple performed different functions over the centuries until, in 1456, it finally became the church of Santa Maria sopra Minerva.

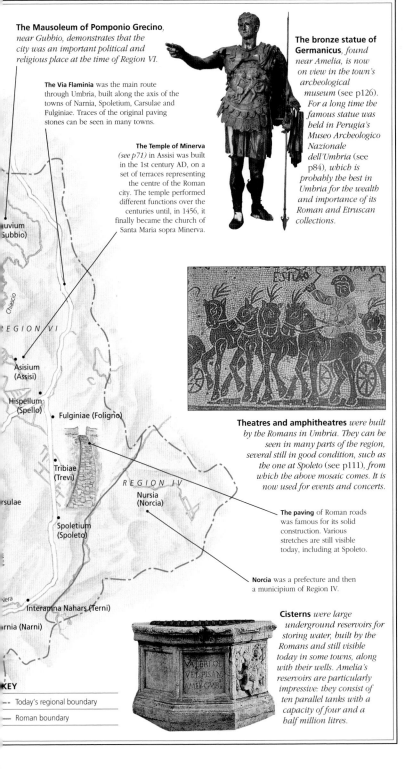

The bronze statue of Germanicus, *found near Amelia, is now on view in the town's archeological museum (see p126). For a long time the famous statue was held in Perugia's Museo Archeologico Nazionale dell'Umbria (see p84), which is probably the best in Umbria for the wealth and importance of its Roman and Etruscan collections.*

uvium
(Gubbio)

Chiascio

REGION VI

Asisium
(Assisi)

Hispellum
(Spello)

Fulginiae (Foligno)

Tribiae
(Trevi)

REGION IV
Nursia
(Norcia)

rsulae

Spoletium
(Spoleto)

Theatres and amphitheatres *were built by the Romans in Umbria. They can be seen in many parts of the region, several still in good condition, such as the one at Spoleto (see p111), from which the above mosaic comes. It is now used for events and concerts.*

The paving of Roman roads was famous for its solid construction. Various stretches are still visible today, including at Spoleto.

Norcia was a prefecture and then a municipium of Region IV.

Nera
Interamna Nahars (Terni)

rnia (Narni)

Cisterns *were large underground reservoirs for storing water, built by the Romans and still visible today in some towns, along with their wells. Amelia's reservoirs are particularly impressive: they consist of ten parallel tanks with a capacity of four and a half million litres.*

KEY

-- Today's regional boundary

— Roman boundary

THE LATE MIDDLE AGES

The ending of Roman rule in Umbria was a heavy blow to a region that depended on trade and agriculture. Communication routes ceased to be secure, apart from the road linking Rome with Amelia, Narni, Perugia and Gubbio. The townspeople had built houses on the plain in the quest for more space during the years of the *pax romana* (as can still be seen today in Gubbio), but they were forced to return to the hills to protect themselves from the aggressive barbarians – the Goths and Huns – coming from the north. The towns became crowded and unsanitary, plague and famine wrought havoc in many areas. The Umbrian population declined noticeably and the ordered farms of the Roman era rapidly became fragmented into numerous small plots of land. Feudal power held sway virtually everywhere, typically dominated by local families who ruled over small areas from a castle or a fortress. In 553, a narrow strip of Umbrian land passed into Byzantine hands, but of far greater significance was the arrival of the Lombards, who set up a principality that included much of Umbria. From the 570s onwards, the so-called Duchy of Spoleto developed into a political entity of some weight. When either historians or geographers referred to "Umbria" at this time, and indeed for centuries to come,

Frederick Barbarossa flanked by his sons Enrico il Severo and Frederick, 12th-century miniature

Lombard sword hilt

they generally meant the lands of the Duchy of Spoleto and therefore only the east bank of the Tiber. In the centuries prior to the year 1000, small monasteries and convents appeared all over the region, albeit scattered and often in inaccessible places. Under the Lombards, who adopted many of the customs of the local people, there was a flowering of art and architecture.

The end of the first millennium signalled a change in the tendency to build hill fortresses. During this phase, lower, flat ground gradually began to be reoccupied, as trade became more significant. New towns (which sometimes kept Roman elements in their names, such as Villa nova) were built, populated by ordinary peasants, now freed from their feudal obligations. This led to the birth of

TIMELINE

4th century
Construction of the basilica of Santo Salvatore in Spoleto

553 End of the war with the Goths: part of Umbria comes under Byzantine domination

756 Pepin the Short gives Perugia and the Duchy of Spoleto to Pope Stephen II

300 A.D.	400	500	600	700	800

c.480 Birth of St Benedict (San Benedetto) in Norcia

St Benedict in a miniature

6th–7th centuries Invasion of the Lombards. The Duchy of Spoleto includes Terni, Foligno, Spello and Assisi.

early forms of self-government, which would later develop into the communes of the 11th and 12th centuries.

At the request of the papacy, the Franks (under Pepin the Short and then Charlemagne), drove the Lombards and the Byzantines out of Umbria. Charlemagne won the title of Holy Roman Emperor from the papacy in exchange for territory, but relations soured. When Barbarossa, Holy Roman Emperor, arrived in Italy in the 1150s, he destroyed Spoleto and a number of other towns.

Artisans and farm labourers at work in the era of the communes

THE RISE OF THE COMMUNES

Eventually, economic progress and demographic growth made it essential to expand the towns, too restricted now inside their old walls. In 1244 construction began of the new walls in Todi, and in 1296 Spoleto enlarged its city walls. The emphasis on ambitious public works, such as town halls and cathedrals, demonstrated a lively spirit of initiative on the part of the town populations. It was certainly no coincidence that they elected to adopt a form of autonomy in the 11th and 12th centuries, leading to the rise of the communes (see pp42–3). By 1111, Pope Pasquale II was complaining that Umbrian towns did not recognize the authority of the Church of Rome. In Umbria, meanwhile, the communes flourished: Perugia's Palazzo dei Priori, Orvieto

cathedral and the basilica in Assisi date from this time. In addition, the Franciscan influence started to spread from Assisi, encouraging the use of the Gothic style in new churches. The years of architectural, social and political triumph of these autonomous towns were, however, also years of constant battles for regional or local domination, and plagues and earthquakes badly affected the towns and countryside. The end of the era of the communes coincided with a push by the papacy to regain control. Between 1350 and 1370 the figure that the Umbrians feared most was Egidio Albornoz, cardinal and papal legate, creator of the great fortresses which were to watch over Umbrian towns on behalf of Rome for the next five centuries.

Montefalco, an example of a fortified city commune, in a painting by Benozzo Gozzoli (1420–1497)

Pasquale II, pope from 1099 to 1118	**1155** Frederick Barbarossa destroys Spoleto	**1277** Cimabue starts work on the frescoes in the basilica of Assisi	**1290** Orvieto: Nicholas IV blesses the first stone laid in the building of the cathedral	
900	**1000**	**1100**	**1200**	**1300**
	11th–12th centuries The Umbrian communes are set up: in 1111 Pasquale II realizes that none of the Umbrian towns respect the authority of the pope		**1226** On 4 October, St Francis of Assisi dies	**1354** Beginning of the papal campaign to reconquer Umbria

The Communes of Umbria

The communes *(comuni)*, or independent city states, and their organizational structures spread rapidly throughout central Italy in the 11th–12th centuries. The independence of the communes – which were frequently at war with one another – developed at a time when central power was weakening. Despite the reaction of the papacy and of the Holy Roman Empire, the 12th century marked the rise of the commune, asserting the autonomy of the city state and enabling the arts and economy to flourish. The political master was no longer a feudal lord but an urban bourgeoisie growing rich through manufacturing and trade. Textile industries were established, as were the first banks (which later led to the creation of the great Italian banks of subsequent centuries). In the meantime, merchants from the communes developed trade relationships with the rest of Europe and the Mediterranean, and, thanks to the Crusades, with the Far East, too.

Palazzi Comunali (town halls), symbols of the communes, were built in Umbria during the 13th and 14th centuries. In many towns and cities, they are still the seat of the town hall.

The Torre del Popolo remains a landmark in Assisi's Piazza del Comune.

One of the first signs *of the birth of communal civilization was population growth, which required cities to increase available housing. City walls were enlarged and rebuilt in all the main town centres in Umbria, among them Spello, shown above.*

Increasingly imposing cathedrals *(left is the cathedral of Foligno) were often built facing the centres of temporal power. After centuries of fortified towns criss-crossed with narrow streets, the era of the commune saw the building of town squares that functioned as meeting places as well as centres of power.*

St Francis was the subject of a book by St Bonaventure, written in the same century that the saint died.

The Temple of Minerva, still visible in Assisi's Piazza del Comune, is clearly recognizable, even in this stylized rendering.

Population growth meant that urban centres were forced to expand upwards as well as outwards. This is how multi-storey houses and porticoes arose.

The town fountain *was a celebration of the wealth of a city – the years when the communes flourished signalled the return of water supplies to many towns. After centuries of abandonment, ancient aqueducts were restored and rebuilt. This is the famous Fontana Maggiore in Perugia (see p87).*

HOMAGE OF A SIMPLE MAN

St Bonaventure, a 13th-century Franciscan monk, tells the story that one day, in Assisi, Francis met "a simple man". Inspired by God, the man laid his own cloak down before the saint. This episode begins the story of the life of St Francis in the cycle of frescoes in the basilica in Assisi. The work is of great importance because, with great attention to detail and careful observation, the artist has created a perfect picture of the medieval centre of Assisi at the end of the 13th century. A picture that is not so different from that visible in Piazza del Comune today.

Clashes and battles *between the Umbrian communes were continual. Some cities had troops of soldiers, such as the crossbowmen, that formed exclusive companies. They are commemorated today in numerous historical processions.*

The citizen *in the era of the communes, like the one present in this scene, was expected to maintain a dignified demeanour in public squares: swords should never be unsheathed. Crimes committed in this place were severely punished.*

Impressive fortresses, *like the one at Spoleto, pictured here, dominate Umbrian towns. They were built by the papacy, from the end of the 14th century, in order to consolidate the power of the Church. The construction of such strongholds, often under the watchful eye of Cardinal Albornoz, heralded the end of communal power.*

Perugia, as depicted in a fresco by Benedetto Bonfigli in the mid-15th century

THE CENTURIES OF DECLINE

The conquest of Umbria by the papacy coincided with the effects of the great plague that had devastated Europe in 1348.

At the end of the 15th century the term Umbria began to appear in the works of scholars and academics: the clergyman Innocenzo Malvasia, in his *Italia Illustrata* drawn up for Pope Sixtus V, defined Umbria as the land of the Duchy of Spoleto, while he described the remainder of the region as being part of Etruria, and Gualdo and Gubbio as dependencies of the Duchy of Urbino.

Following centuries of development, 16th-century Umbria found itself in a tricky situation. The cities, peripheral dominions of the state gravitating around Rome, were declining, while craftsmen and industries were diminishing in number and quality.

The heads of the great aristocratic families abandoned the cities and returned to the land and agriculture.

TOWN AND COUNTRYSIDE

A fundamental instrument in the development of the new Umbrian economy was the "mezzadria", or sharecropping system, and the gradual colonization of the hills and plains, on partly reclaimed land in some cases. One very noticeable effect of the agricultural revival was the gradual de-population of the cities. The historian Cipriano Piccolpasso wrote of Assisi: "...it is a badly composed city, with many derelict and unoccupied houses next to inhabited ones, so that it seems more like the residue of a city than a completed one...". The move to the country was not the only factor to alter the appearance of the cities: during the 16th and 17th centuries, nobles invested some of the profits from their farms in town projects.

Urban VIII, pope from 1623 to 1644

Politically, the 17thcentury saw important new developments: in 1624 the della Rovere family ceded the Duchy of Urbino to the pope, and the following year Pope Urban VIII put the University of Perugia under episcopal control.

FROM PAPAL RULE TO THE UNIFICATION OF ITALY

By now an agricultural, rural region, Umbria became one of Rome's "bread baskets" and a major producer

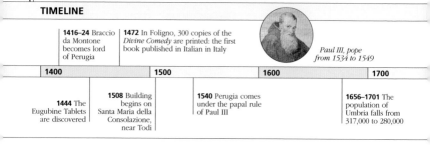

TIMELINE

1416–24 Braccio da Montone becomes lord of Perugia

1472 In Foligno, 300 copies of the *Divine Comedy* are printed: the first book published in Italian in Italy

Paul III, pope from 1534 to 1549

1400	1500	1600	1700

1444 The Eugubine Tablets are discovered

1508 Building begins on Santa Maria della Consolazione, near Todi

1540 Perugia comes under the papal rule of Paul III

1656–1701 The population of Umbria falls from 317,000 to 280,000

Perugia's Rocca Paolina, destroyed on 14 September 1860

MODERN UMBRIA

Following a plebiscite, the province of Umbria was created in 1861, as part of a unified Kingdom of Italy. It included all the current provinces (plus Rieti), with a population of 500,000. The economic situation in the closing decades of the 19th century was, however, woeful: agriculture was languishing and farmers were increasingly forced into seasonal migration towards the Maremma and the countryside around Rome. Even so, the industrial revolution did not leave Umbria behind: in 1866 the railway line that links Rome, Terni and Foligno was completed, and between 1875 and 1887 arms factories and the Terni steelworks (the first – and only – really major employer in the region) were founded. In 1881 the population of Umbria numbered 611,000, in 1911 it was 767,000.

of olive oil. Mills multiplied, as did the frequency of country fairs, which took the place of town markets in the economy of the countryside.

With the end of the 18th century came the Napoleonic revolution. As part of the Roman Republic created in 1798, Umbria was divided into the two departments of Trasimeno and Clitunno. In the imperial era the division was dissolved, and Umbria became a single territory with Spoleto as its capital. This confirmation of a common identity would be returned to without much alteration by the unified state after 1860.

In line with the Romantic movement elsewhere, the 19th century saw a rise in interest in the Middle Ages. The discovery of the remains of St Francis (1818) and Santa Chiara (1850) caused a sensation. In 1859, a great popular uprising in Perugia against the papal troops resulted in a brutal massacre, which became known as the "Stragi di Perugia". In September 1860 soldiers entered the town, and the local population immediately set about destroying the Rocca Paolina fortress, which had become a much detested symbol of the power of the Roman Catholic church.

World War II saw the bombing of Umbria's industries, and recovery in the postwar period was slow. The development of light industry, cottage industries and especially tourism has helped boost the region's fortunes, though the earthquakes that strike periodically have affected certain areas of Umbria badly. The worst happened in 1979, in Valnerina, but the quake that struck Assisi, Foligno and Nocera Umbra in 1997 received broader coverage around the world because of the damage done to the art-packed St Francis basilica.

Santa Chiara in Assisi, which holds the remains of Santa Chiara

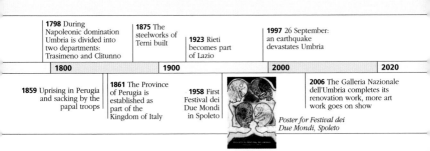

1798 During Napoleonic domination Umbria is divided into two departments: Trasimeno and Clitunno	1875 The steelworks of Terni built	1923 Rieti becomes part of Lazio	1997 26 September: an earthquake devastates Umbria	
1800	**1900**		**2000**	**2020**
1859 Uprising in Perugia and sacking by the papal troops	1861 The Province of Perugia is established as part of the Kingdom of Italy	1958 First Festival dei Due Mondi in Spoleto		2006 The Galleria Nazionale dell'Umbria completes its renovation work, more art work goes on show

Poster for Festival dei Due Mondi, Spoleto

UMBRIA
AREA BY AREA

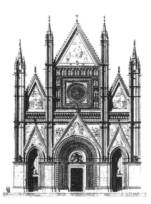

Umbria at a Glance

The region of Umbria is not particularly large, but it has numerous towns, villages, parks and other places of great interest. Northern Umbria includes the upper valley of the River Tiber (Alta Val Tiberina), the Apennine regional parks (Monte Subasio and Monte Cucco), the medieval towns of Perugia, Assisi and Gubbio and the great expanse of Lake Trasimeno. The southern half of the region revolves around the towns of Todi, Narni, Terni and Orvieto, on the border with Tuscany, within the area once occupied by the Etruscans. Completing this picture of southern Umbria are the great mountains of the Monti Sibillini national park and the Valnerina (the valley of the Nera River), with its famous waterfalls, the Cascata delle Marmore.

NORTHERN UMBRIA
(pp50–95)

Città della Pieve

Città della Pieve
Famous as the birthplace of the artist Perugino (some of his works are here), this small town near the Tuscan border is a good departure point for visiting the area south of Lake Trasimeno.

| 0 kilometres | 15 |
| 0 miles | 15 |

Todi

Todi
Perched on a hill above the Tiber, Todi was for centuries a border town between the land of the Etruscans and territory occupied by the Umbri. It has a lovely historic quarter, centred around Piazza del Popolo.

◁ **The Abbey of San Pietro in Valle (11th century), near Spoleto**

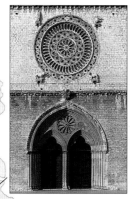

Assisi

St Francis died on 4 October 1226. Just a year later, Pope Gregory IX gave Frate Elia the responsibility of building a church to be dedicated to the saint. With the completion of the Cappella di Santa Caterina in 1367, the great basilica of San Francesco in Assisi was finally finished. The greatest artists of the age contributed to the church, including Cimabue, Giotto, Pietro Lorenzetti and Simone Martini.

Assisi

Spoleto

This city, famous for its festival, owes some of its importance to its position on the old Roman road, the Via Flaminia. In the Middle Ages, this road enabled the Lombards to come down from the north and make Spoleto the capital of their dukedom.

SOUTHERN UMBRIA
(pp96–139)

Spoleto

Monti Sibillini

This mountainous area, on the border between Umbria and Le Marche, is one of the most important protected reserves in central Italy, with important historical and artistic treasures as well as a varied natural history.

NORTHERN UMBRIA

Northern Umbria consists of three distinct geographical areas: the first is the Alta Val Tiberina (the Upper Tiber Valley), the second is the area around Lake Trasimeno, and the third is the easterly Apennine region around Gubbio and the Via Flaminia. These three regions, laden with history and culture, meet at northern Umbria's two most important towns, Perugia and Assisi.

Perugia is the capital of the region and one of the main cities in central Italy, both culturally and economically. Assisi is visited every year by thousands of tourists and pilgrims, who come to retrace the steps of St Francis and admire the fresco cycles in the basilica.

The three aforementioned areas have differing histories. The Alta Val Tiberina, as well as delineating the border between the Etruscans (to the west) and the Umbri (to the east), has long been of commercial importance, with its direct lines of communication with the north. The entire area of Lake Trasimeno, on the other hand, has always been of great strategic and military significance, as can still be seen today from the many fortifications scattered around the lake. The lake shore was the setting for one of the battles of the Second Punic Wars (217 BC), which culminated in the victory of Hannibal over the Romans. To the east, in contrast, hermitages that were refuges for entire populations in the time of barbaric invasions cling to the Appenines. Northern Umbria's fortunes became allied to those of the rest of the region with the ending of the Duchy of Spoleto.

Despite the bombardments of World War II and the earthquake of 1997, which struck the area along the border with Le Marche, splendid testimony remains to the region's history, including Etruscan and Roman buildings and finds. The legacy of the Middle Ages and the Renaissance can be seen in churches, palazzi, town halls and castles, as well as in works by the great artists of the day, among them Perugino, a native of Città della Pieve.

The varied and well-preserved landscape of the northern region includes two national parks, Monte Cucco and Monte Subasio, where the "song of nature" that so struck St Francis of Assisi can still be sensed.

A patchwork of ordered fields carpeting the hillsides of northern Umbria

◁ **Looking down over Gubbio rooftops and the Palazzo dei Consoli**

Exploring Northern Umbria

Città di Castello is the first main town on the road into Umbria from neighbouring Emilia-Romagna, along the old trade route which then continues down through the Upper Tiber Valley. At Umbertide, a road heads off eastwards to Gubbio and beyond to the Via Flaminia, which skirts the Apennines on its route south towards Assisi. West of Assisi lies the province of Perugia and the regional capital itself. Further west again, bordering Tuscany, is Lake Trasimeno and the homeland of Perugino.

Castello di Petroia, between Gubbio and Assisi

SIGHTS AT A GLANCE

Assisi *pp68–80* ❾
Bettona ⓬
Castiglione del Lago ⓰
Città della Pieve ⓱
Città di Castello *pp54–5* ❶
Deruta ⓭
Gualdo Tadino ❻
Gubbio *pp58–61* ❹
Lake Trasimeno *pp92–3* ⓯
Montone ❷
Nocera Umbra ❼
Parco Regionale del
  Monte Cucco *pp62–3* ❺
Parco Regionale del
  Monte Subasio *pp66–7* ❽
Perugia *pp84–91* ⓮
Torgiano ⓫
Umbertide ❸

Tours

Southern Lake Trasimeno ⓲
The Franciscan Path
  of Peace ❿

SEE ALSO

• **Where to Stay** pp144–7

• **Where to Eat** pp156–61

0 kilometres   10

0 miles   10

For additional map symbols *see back flap*

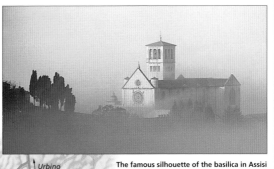

The famous silhouette of the basilica in Assisi

Pietralunga
Caicambiucci
S424
Vallécchio
Urbino
La Valdorbia
Monte Civitello
735m
S452
Schéggia
PARCO REGIONALE DEL
MONTE CUCCO
Rággio
S298
Camporeggiano
S219
Assino
GUBBIO
Costacciaro
Ponte d'Assi
S219
Sigillo
Sáonda
Pierantónio
Mengara
Fossato di Vico
Ancona
Branca
Vallingegno
THE FRANCISCAN PATH OF PEACE
Chiáscio
S318
GUALDO
TADINO
Tavernacce
Tevere
S298
Casa
Castalda
Córcia
Piccione
S3b
Osteria
di Morano
Bosco
S444
Valfábbrica
Torchiagina
S318
San Presto
PERUGIA
Piano
di Pieve
PARCO REGIONALE DEL
MONTE SUBASIO
Topino
S3
NOCERA
UMBRA
ASSISI
Monte Pennino
1571m
Bastia Umbra
Armenzano
TORGIANO
Rivotorto
di Assisi
Valtopina
Topino
BETTONA
Collepino
DERUTA
S3b
Spello
Ponte Centésimo
Foligno
S77

GETTING AROUND
Lake Trasimeno and Perugia
can be reached from the
Autostrada del Sole (A1) by
following Superstrada 75bis,
a motorway spur that heads
east from the exit Val di
Chiana, Bettole-Sinalunga.
Further south, the Fabro exit
from the A1 is just a few
kilometres from Città della
Pieve. The state roads 3 and
3bis, which link Umbria
with Le Marche and Emilia-
Romagna, are also major
routes. Two railway lines run
from Perugia: north to
Sansepolcro and northwest
to Florence respectively,
with trains running at
least daily. Coach and
bus services are good,
in particular around Lake
Trasimeno (where there are
also ferry services) and in
and around Perugia.

KEY

▬▬▬	Motorway
▬▬▬	Major road
▬▬▬	Secondary road
▭▭▭	Minor road
▬▬▬	Scenic route
▬▬▬	Main railway
----	Minor railway
▬▬▬	Regional border
△	Summit

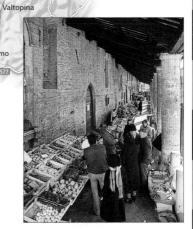

Market stalls under the arcades in Gubbio

Todi

Città di Castello ❶

The town that is today the most important centre in the Upper Tiber Valley, the gateway to Umbria for anyone approaching from the north, was originally a settlement of the ancient Umbri.

Decoration on the Palazzo del Podestà

Situated as it was between Le Marche and Tuscany, and not far from Emilia-Romagna, the town was in a perfect position as far as trade was concerned. It became a commune in the Middle Ages, when it was in almost perpetual conflict with the nearby city-states. Even so, the former "Civitas Castelli" grew in power and riches, thanks to the flourishing commercial activity, including printing, which is still an important part of the city's economic fabric today. Following a period of rule by nobles installed by the Church, Città di Castello was completely redesigned under the rule of the Vitelli family, in the 16th century, as can be seen by the various palazzi bearing its name.

Exploring Città di Castello

The town is built on the right bank of the River Tiber, at the northernmost edge of Umbria. The architecture displays Tuscan influences, thanks to the work of the Florentine architects Antonio da Sangallo and Giorgio Vasari, brought in by the Vitelli family in the 16th century.

The tour described here begins in Piazza Gabriotti. Visitors are advised to leave their cars in the car park in Viale Nazario Sauro and then take the escalator up to the piazza. The monuments seen at the beginning of the tour date from the period prior to that of the Vitelli.

🏛 Duomo

Piazza Gabriotti. ⏲ daily.
It is immediately apparent that the cathedral exterior has undergone more than one remodelling. The round bell tower formed part of the original 11th-century building, but the body of the church reveals two successive rebuildings, in the 14th and then the 15th–16th centuries. The unfinished Baroque façade dates from 1632–46. The interior has a single nave and

contains a wooden choir and a *Resurrection* by Rosso Fiorentino (1529), in the chapel on the right-hand side. In the **Museo del Duomo,** objects on display map the evolution of the church in the Middle Ages.

🏛 Museo del Duomo

Piazza Gabriotti. *Tel* 075 855 4705.
⏲ Apr–Sep: 9:30am–1pm, 2:30–7pm Tue–Sun; Oct–Mar: 10am–1pm, 2:30–6:30pm Tue–Sun. 🎟

🏛 Palazzo Comunale

Piazza Gabriotti.
In the same piazza as the Duomo (typical of a medieval town) is the Palazzo Comunale, or town hall. This 14th-century building is the work of Angelo da Orvieto and shows how the Florentine influence on the town's architecture

Paliotto, c.1144, Museo del Duomo

pre-dates the arrival of the Vitelli family: in particular, the use of rusticated stone echoes the style of the Palazzo Vecchio in Florence.

In front of the palazzo, on the other side of the piazza, stands the **Torre Civica**, also 14th-century and once called "del Vescovo" (the bishop's), because it stood next to the bishop's palace (Palazzo Vescovile). From the top of the tower (open daily, entrance fee), there are good views over the town and the surrounding countryside.

The 14th-century Torre Civica

🏛 Palazzo del Podestà

Corso Cavour.
From the east of the piazza runs Corso Cavour, home to the Palazzo del Podestà. The façade facing the street dates from the same era as the Palazzo Comunale, and it may be that the original design was also by Angelo da Orvieto. The eastern side is Baroque and leads on to Piazza Matteotti, where **Palazzo Vitelli "in piazza"** stands.

🏛 San Francesco

Via D Albizzini. ⏲ daily.
The street that cuts the city in half from north to south is made up of Via XX Settembre, Via Angeloni and Corso Vittorio Emanuele. Halfway along Via Angeloni, near the corner of Via Albizzini, stands the church of St Francis, of 13th-century origin, to which the famous Florentine painter and architect Giorgio Vasari contributed in the 1500s. He was responsible for the Cappella Vitelli as well as an altar with a *Coronation of the Virgin* (1564).

🏛 Palazzo Vitelli a Porta Sant'Egidio

Piazza Garibaldi.
A short distance from San Francesco is this Vitelli palace (1540), one of many that the family had built in the town in an effort to impose some stylistic unity. The façade is

THE WORK OF ALBERTO BURRI

Alberto Burri, a major figure in 20th-century Italian art and known all over the world, was born in Città di Castello in 1915 (he died in Nice in 1995). A doctor by profession, he turned to art during World War II. His work is often large-scale and makes use of innovative materials: particularly famous is the *Cretto* at Gibellina Vecchia, in Sicily, a huge carpet of white cement covering the ruins left by the 1968 earthquake. Città di Castello has a good collection of his work in Palazzo Albizzini and the former tobacco drying house, Ex Seccatoi del Tabacco.

Great Iron Sextant, 1982, on show in Città di Castello

Collezioni Burri *Tel 075 855 46 49.*
Palazzo Albizzini *Via Albizzini.*
Ex Seccatoi del Tabacco *Via Pierucci.*
🕐 *Apr–Oct: 9am–12:30pm, 2:30–6:30pm Tue–Sat; 10:30am–12:30pm, 3–7pm Sun & public hols; Nov–Mar: book in advance; tel 075 855 98 48.*
⬤ *1 Jan, 25 Dec.* 📷
www.fondazioneburri.org

VISITORS' CHECKLIST

Perugia. **Road Map** B2. 🚗
40,000. 🚆 *FCU Perugia–Sansepolcro line, 075 575 401.* 🚌 *from Arezzo, 800 512 141.* ℹ️ *IAT Alta Valle del Tevere, Piazza Matteotti, 075 855 4922.* **www.**cdcnet.net

symmetrical and there is a pretty garden inside.

🏛 San Domenico
Largo Monsignor Muzi. 🕐 *daily.*
Between Piazza Garibaldi and the Pinacoteca is the church of San Domenico, the largest in the town. It was built by the Dominicans in the 15th century and later reworked, although the façade remains unfinished. Frescoes from the 15th century line the nave.

🏛 Pinacoteca Comunale
Via della Cannoniera 22.
Tel *075 852 0656.* 🕐 *Apr–Oct: 10am–1pm, 2:30–6:30pm Tue–Sun; Nov–Mar: 10am–1pm, 3–6pm Tue–Sun.* ⬤ *1 Jan, 25 Dec.* 📷 🚫 🔴
The Pinacoteca, one of the region's top art galleries, is housed in the **Palazzo Vitelli**

Coronation of the Virgin, detail, Ghirlandaio workshop

alla Cannoniera, the most notable of the various Vitelli palazzi. It was built by Antonio da Sangallo (1521–32) with the assistance of Vasari, who was responsible for part of the frescoed friezes.

Among the many works are an *Enthroned Madonna and Child* by the Maestro di Città di Castello (early 14th century); a *Martyrdom of St Sebastian* by Luca Signorelli (1497–8); a *Gonfalone della Santissima Trinità* by Raphael (1499); and a *Coronation of the Virgin* attributed to the workshop of Ghirlandaio (early 1500s). There is, also, a remarkable *Assumption of the Virgin* in terracotta from the workshop of Andrea della Robbia (early 16th century).

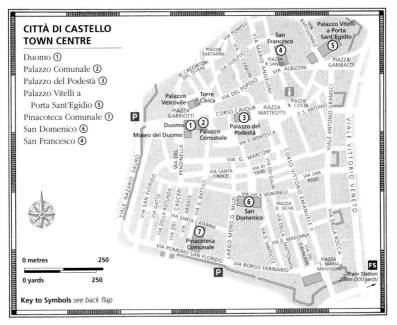

CITTÀ DI CASTELLO TOWN CENTRE

Duomo ①
Palazzo Comunale ②
Palazzo del Podestà ③
Palazzo Vitelli a
Porta Sant'Egidio ⑤
Pinacoteca Comunale ⑦
San Domenico ⑥
San Francesco ④

0 metres 250
0 yards 250

Key to Symbols *see back flap*

View of the verdant Upper Tiber Valley, from the medieval village of Montone

Montone ❷

Perugia. **Road Map** C2. 🏘 *1,500*.
FS *Umbertide, 13 km (8 miles),*
FCU Perugia–Sansepolcro line. 🚌
ℹ *Pro Loco, Piazza Fortebraccio 1,*
075 930 7019. **www**.*montone.info*

Montone, 10 km (6 miles) from Città di Castello, is built on two hill tops on the left bank of the Tiber, and is the first town of historical interest on the road running south through the Upper Tiber Valley. Founded as a fortified site in the Middle Ages (probably in the 11th century), Montone is still enclosed within a powerful circle of walls. These are pierced by three gates: Porta del Verziere, Porta di Borgo Vecchio and Porta del Monte; the names correspond to the districts into which the castle was once divided.

Montone was the birthplace of Braccio Fortebraccio, better known as Braccio da Montone (1368–1424), who became perhaps Umbria's greatest condottiere (leader of a mercenary army). He created a genuine state, with Perugia as its capital.

The medieval village is beautifully preserved and, furthermore, offers superb views. There are several buildings of interest. On the road leading up to the centre of Montone from the south is the church of the **Madonna delle Grazie** (16th century), as well as the oldest church in the village, the Romanesque **Pieve di San Gregorio**, dating from the 11th century.

Beyond the walls, it is worth visiting the Gothic church of **San Francesco** (14th century), at the top of the village. Along with the attached monastery, this is now home to the **Museo Comunale**. The fine doorway is made of inlaid wood (1519). Inside, the single-nave building contains several valuable works of art by Bartolomeo Caporali. Above the votive altar are frescoes of the Fortebraccio family and also a painting depicting the *Madonna del Soccorso*.

The church, which contains a splendid wooden choir dating from the 16th century, once housed a *Madonna in Gloria* by Luca Signorelli. This is now in the National Gallery in London. The former monastery also houses an ethnographic museum.

Students of Italian history should consider visiting the **Archivio Storico Comunale**, one of the most important historical archives in Umbria, with papal bulls and other important documents. It is housed in the former convent of Santa Caterina, at the southern end of the village.

🏛 **Museo Comunale & Museo Etnografico**
Ex Convento di San Francesco. **Tel** *075 930 6535.* ⏱ *Apr–Sep: 10:30am–1pm, 3:30–6pm Fri–Sun; Oct–Mar: 10:30am–1pm, 3–5:30pm Sat & Sun.* 📷 📹 ♿ 🚻

Environs

The countryside around Montone offers plenty of opportunities for walking, particularly along the course of the **Torrente Carpina**, which skirts the village to the east and joins the Tiber at Umbertide. On its banks, 4 km (2 miles) northwest of Montone, is the splendid **Rocca d'Aries**, a fortress with Byzantine origins. It was renovated in the Renaissance era and restored in the 1990s, and is now open for concerts and exhibitions. It offers marvellous views over the Valle del Carpina.

A narrow, paved street in the heart of Montone

Umbertide ❸

Perugia. **Road Map** C2. 🚶 *15,000.*
FCU Perugia–Sansepolcro line.
🚌 🛈 *IAT Alta Valle del Tevere, Via
Cibo 26, 075 941 7099.*
www.comune.umbertide.it

One of the principal centres
of the Upper Tiber Valley,
Umbertide is of ancient
origin, dating back to the
6th century BC, and was
probably founded by the
Etruscans. The town, skirted
to the west by the Tiber,
frequently found itself at the
centre of wars and suffered
the resulting destruction and
sackings. In 1863, the town's
traditional name of Fratta
was replaced by the name
Umbertide in honour of the
sons of Umberto Ranieri,
who rebuilt the city after
the devastation caused
by the Lombard
invasions of
AD 790.

Much more
recently, the centre
of the old town was
badly damaged by
bombardments
during World War II
(1944). Even so,
many important
buildings survive.
Two of these
overlook the vast Piazza
Mazzini, northwest of the
town centre: **La Rocca** (1385),
a fortress inserted into the
walls and now a centre
for contemporary art, and the
church of **Santa Maria della
Reggia**, begun in the second
half of the 16th century and
built on an octagonal plan.
The design was by Galeazzo
Alessi and Giulio Danti.
Inside, among the canvases

The square and circular towers of the Rocca of Umbertide

The octagonal Santa
Maria della Reggia

that decorate the tambour
(the wall below the dome),
note the one above the organ,
an *Ascension to Heaven* by
Pomarancio (1578).

Other important works
to be found in the town's
churches include a fresco
by Pinturicchio (1504),
in the lunette of the
doorway to the
church of **Santa
Maria della Pietà**
(north of the old
town, outside
the walls), and,
in particular, a
Deposition by
Luca Signorelli
in the Baroque
church of **Santa
Croce**, in the southern (and
oldest) part of the town, in
Piazza San Francesco. Due
to the importance of the
Signorelli painting – it is the
only one by the Cortona artist
still to be found in its original
setting – the church is now a
museum. In the same square
are two other churches:
San Francesco (13th–14th
centuries) and San Bernardino
(18th century).

🏛 **Santa Croce Museum**
Piazza San Francesco. **Tel** 075
942 0147. ⬚ Jun–Sep:
10:30am–1pm, 4–6:30pm Fri–Sun;
Oct–May: 10:30am–1pm, 3–5:30pm
Fri–Sun. ● 1 Jan, 25 Dec. 🛇 📷

Environs
The countryside around
Umbertide is scattered with
fortifications, lasting evidence
of the region's great strategic
military importance. Along
the road to Preggio, 15 km (9
miles) southwest of Umbertide,
is the **Rocca di Preggio**, one
of the principal strongholds
in the area, dating from the
10th century. Also of note
along this route are the castles
of **Romeggio and Polgeto**.

A short distance east of
Umbertide, towards Gubbio,
look out for the privately-
owned **Castello di Civitella
Ranieri** (15th century), which
is one of the most complete
and best preserved examples
of military architecture in the
area. Nearby, but higher up,
is the splendid **Castello di
Serra Partucci**.

Just north of Umbertide,
along the Città di Castello
road, you can see the tall
tower of another castle,
the **Castello di Montalto**.

A couple of kilometres
south of town, along the
River Tiber, a road climbs up
to the **Badia Monte Corona**,
a Romanesque abbey with a
beautiful underground crypt.
Climbing still higher, you reach
the 16th-century hermitage
and pretty village of **San
Giuliana**, set in a panoramic
position, and restored to its
medieval appearance.

The churches of Santa Croce and San Francesco in Umbertide

Gubbio ❹

The sight of Gubbio, built from local stone at the foot of Monte Ingino, is one of the most famous images of medieval Umbria. Founded by the Umbri, the town holds the famous Eugubine Tablets, seven bronze slabs that survived from the ancient city of Iguvium; they were engraved in the 2nd century BC with text in the local language describing rites and sacred sites. Under the Romans the town spread onto the plain, but after the Lombards invaded the people returned to the slopes, where they could defend themselves more effectively. A walled city, including the monumental Palazzo dei Consoli, was built here in the Middle Ages. At the end of the 14th century, the city, by now powerful and rich, passed to the Montefeltro of Urbino. In 1624 Gubbio, like the Duchy of Urbino, came under papal rule.

The well-preserved 1st-century arcades of the Roman theatre

Exploring Gubbio
The easiest route into Gubbio is by the road from the south, which also provides a chance to admire the town as a whole, as it spreads out in horizontal swathes against the slopes of Monte Ingino. Before climbing up to explore one of the best preserved medieval cities in the world, take a look at the ruins of the Roman city, which, during the stability of the *pax romana*, developed on the flat land below the slopes.

⛪ Roman Ruins
Via del Teatro Romano.
The first Roman monument that you see as you arrive in Gubbio from the south is a mausoleum, a monumental tomb of which the burial chamber has survived with its barrel vault. Further on, not far from Piazza Quaranta Martiri, are the ruins of the Roman theatre (Teatro Romano), which dates from

the 1st century. It could accommodate around 6,000 spectators, and was faced in squared and rusticated blocks. Among other works uncovered over the last two centuries of excavations are some beautiful mosaics.

🚩 Piazza Quaranta Martiri
This broad square is the principal point of arrival in Gubbio, as well as the best place to leave a car. It is dedicated to the 40 local people executed by the Germans in 1944 in an act of vengeance against the partisans. The lowest point in Gubbio, the piazza is a good place from which to gaze upwards to admire the full extent of the town.

Gubbio's finest church, San Francesco, dominates the piazza. Its construction was begun in the mid-1200s and continued at least until the end of that century (though the façade was never finished). Inside are three

aisles without a transept. There is a fresco cycle by Ottaviano Nelli in the apse chapel on the left (*Scenes from the Life of Mary*, c.1408–13). The frescoes in the central apse, by an unknown artist, can be dated to around 1275, but they are badly damaged.

On the opposite side of the piazza is the **Antico Ospedale** (Old Hospital) of Santa Maria della Misericordia, a 14th-century building, with a long portico in front, surmounted by a loggia, added in the 17th century by the wool merchants' guild, which used the premises for some of its processing. Nearby stands the church of **Santa Maria dei Laici**, dating back to 1313 and now restored.

🔒 San Giovanni Battista
Via della Repubblica. ⬭ *daily*.
From Piazza Quaranta Martiri the steep Via della Repubblica leads to the base of the great structure supporting Piazza Grande *(see p61)*. Heading up this street, visitors enter the oldest part of the medieval city, where the first cathedral, dedicated to San Mariano, is believed to have stood. What is now the church dedicated to San Giovanni Battista (St John the Baptist) probably occupies the site of the old cathedral.

This church, built in the 13th and 14th centuries, has a Gothic façade with a Romanesque bell tower. The Gothic style continues inside, with characteristic coupled

Gubbio, clinging to the lower slopes of Monte Ingino

The church of San Giovanni Battista, with Palazzo dei Consoli behind

columns and great arches in stone. The single-nave church culminates in a squared apse.

San Domenico
Piazza G.Bruno. ◯ daily.
Returning to Piazza Quaranta Martiri, turn into Via Cavour to enter the old quarter of San Martino, which is built on both sides of the river Camignano.

At the heart of this district, in Piazza Bruno, is the church of San Domenico, which was built by the Dominicans in the 14th century on the site of a 12th-century church dedicated to San Martino. The appearance of the interior dates primarily

from a period of restoration during the 18th century, but 16th-century frescoes from the Gubbio school remain; there is also a fine lectern decorated with inlaid wood.

Via Gabrielli
This street, lined with medieval houses, runs north from Piazza Bruno to Porta Metauro. Near the end is the small but impressive **Palazzo del Capitano del Popolo**, whose façade curves in line with the road. Adorned with a series of small Gothic windows, the palazzo is a typical Gubbio construction from the late 13th century. Nearby is the park attached

to the **Palazzo Ranghiaschi Brancaleoni**. Laid out in the mid-1800s, the garden extends south along the slopes of Monte Ingino as far as the Palazzo Ducale. There is a Neo-Classical temple here.

Sculpture on the tower of Palazzo Ranghiaschi Brancaleoni

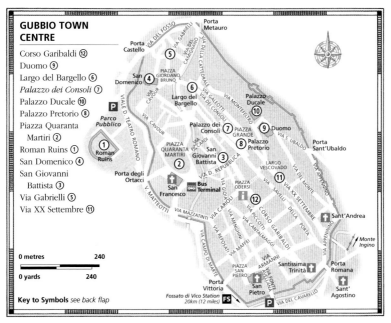

GUBBIO TOWN CENTRE

0 metres   240
0 yards   240

Key to Symbols see back flap

Gubbio: Palazzo dei Consoli

Ceramic plate, Museo Civico

This superb building, begun in 1332, lords it over Piazza Grande and is supported on the west side by an impressive row of arched buttresses. The entrance doorway, approached by a fan-shaped flight of steps, is a masterly example of the Gothic style and is decorated with a lunette representing the *Madonna and saints John the Baptist and Ubaldo*, patron saint of the city. The palazzo houses the Museo Civico and an art gallery. From the loggia there are fine views over the city and countryside around.

VISITORS' CHECKLIST

Piazza Grande. **Tel** 075 927 4298. ☐ 10am–1pm, 3–6pm (Nov–Mar: 2–5pm) daily. ● 1 Jan, 13–15 May, 25 Dec. ▨

Madonna and Child
This fresco by Mello da Gubbio from 1340–50 is one of the works on display in the Pinacoteca Civica (art gallery) on the first floor.

The tower is crowned with battlements and has four apertures echoing the form of the windows below.

Arches, supporting the palazzo on the hill

The windows are set in pairs and decorated with a toothed cornice, which runs above the arches and unifies them.

Museo Civico, situated on the ground floor

In the Sala dell'Arengo, a magnificent room which occupies the entire floor area of the building, popular assemblies were held in the 14th century. Today fragments and stone tablets are displayed here.

Eugubine Tablets
These inscriptions in the old Umbrian language are on display in the Museo Civico. They provide crucial evidence of life in the region before the Roman conquest.

The Fontana dei Matti in Largo del Bargello

🏛 Largo del Bargello

About halfway along Via dei Consoli, which connects the San Martino quarter and Piazza Grande, the street broadens out to form Largo del Bargello, the centre of the ancient quarter of San Giuliano. In front of the 14th-century palazzo, after which the square is named, is the small **Fontana dei Matti**: tradition has it that in order to be defined as mad (*matto*), people had to run around the fountain three times bathing themselves in the water.

🏛 Piazza Grande

Via dei Consoli follows the route of the old Umbrian fortifications before suddenly opening out into Piazza Grande. Quite apart from the importance of the buildings

found here, the square is an extremely impressive piece of engineering: it is, in fact, an artificial space supported by walls and embankments.

In front of the more famous and much larger Palazzo dei Consoli is the **Palazzo Pretorio** (closed to the public), which was erected in the mid-14th century and designed by the same architect, Gattapone. On the last Sunday in May the traditional Palio della Balestra (involving the crossbowmen of Gubbio and Sansepolcro, over the border in Tuscany), takes place between the two buildings.

🏛 Duomo

Via Galeotti. ◯ *daily.*

From Piazza Grande, Via Galeotti climbs in a series of steps to the cathedral. This was founded in 1229 and enlarged around a century later. The façade has an entrance with an ogival arch and an oculus with bas-reliefs which belonged to the previous church on the site. Inside, the single nave is covered by a very high and distinctive stone "wagon vault", a local architectural speciality. There are many frescoes and other paintings, as well as some fine stained-glass windows.

🏛 Palazzo Ducale

Via Federico di Montefeltro.
Tel 075 927 5872. ◯ 8:30am–7pm Tue–Sun. ◼ 1 Jan, 25 Dec. ▨

The restored Palazzo Ducale stands right in front of the cathedral. Locally known as the Corte Nuova, it was built by the Montefeltro family after they had taken possession of the town. The palazzo has an interesting archaeological area underground (where it is possible to see traces of the piazza that was here before the palazzo was built) as well as several rooms used for temporary exhibitions.

🏛 Via XX Settembre

From Piazza Grande, Via XX Settembre leads past palazzi and churches to the quarter of Sant'Andrea and the **Porta Romana**. This medieval town gate, with its high tower, houses a collection of majolica pottery and other pieces in various materials, as well as weaponry, maps and so on. Nearby, outside the walls, is the church of **Sant'Agostino**, which retains traces of frescoes dating back to the church's founda-tion (1294), as well as several works dating from the 14th century.

The medieval Porta Romana

A short walk east of the church is the terminal for the funicular up to the **Basilica di Sant'Ubaldo**, which lies high above the town on Monte Ingino. The ride takes almost eight minutes and offers lovely views on the way; there is also a path, if you prefer to go up on foot.

🏛 Corso Garibaldi

This street runs parallel with the quarter of Sant'Andrea and is the main thoroughfare through the San Pietro quarter, the busy centre of Gubbio. The narrow streets retain a village atmosphere and are lined with shops. On Corso Garibaldi itself look out for the churches of **Santissima Trinità** and of **San Pietro**, of 13th-century origin and built close to a large monastery complex.

THE FESTA DEI CERI

The Corsa dei Ceri (candle race), considered within Umbria almost as great a spectacle as Siena's Palio, takes place every year on 15 May. The finishing line is the hilltop basilica of Sant'Ubaldo. The "candles" in question, three in all, are heavy wooden and papier mâché structures in the form of superimposed prisms, 10 m (33 ft) high and 200 kg (440 lb) in weight. They bear the effigies of Sant'Ubaldo, St George and St Anthony Abbot, patron saints of masons and stonecutters, craftsmen and peasants respectively. The first drum roll is heard at dawn, but the *ceri* are not brought out until noon. The actual race, which attracts huge crowds, takes place in the evening.

The heavy wooden "candles", carried aloft over the crowd

Parco Regionale del Monte Cucco ⑤

On the border with the neighbouring region of Le Marche, Monte Cucco is one of the most fascinating peaks in central Italy. Below ground are miles and miles of galleries and caverns, which form one of the most impressive cave systems in Italy: the Grotta di Monte Cucco. The higher altitudes can be reached from the village of Costacciaro, and the windswept terrain attracts devoted fans of hang-gliding. Within the park, which is centred around the village of Sigillo, various hiking trails have been marked out. There are also facilities for various open-air sports. Besides paragliding, the park can arrange exploration of the Forra di Riofreddo gorge (for experts only), and there are also mountain bike trails and tracks for runners. Many paleontological and archaeological finds have been discovered in the park, as well as ancient Roman settlements.

Scheggia
From this village of Roman origin it is possible to enter and explore the northern part of the park, with its Benedictine abbeys – in particular, Sant'Emiliano at Isola Fossara and the Hermitage of San Girolamo a Pascelupo.

Costacciaro
Unlike the other villages that surround the park, which are almost all of Roman origin, Costacciaro was built in 1250 by the citizens of Gubbio as a fortified town.

At Scirca, ruins of a large Roman settlement have been uncovered. In the village, the old church of Santa Maria Assunta is decorated with frescoes by Matteo da Gualdo.

THE "NATIVES" OF MONTE CUCCO

Wildcat

Besides all kinds of opportunities for sport, the Parco Regionale del Monte Cucco is also one of the best places in the Apennines for observing wildlife. In fact, as well as being home to typically Apennine species (such as deer, wild boar, porcupines and martens), the park also harbours other species that are increasingly rare in Central Italy, including the wolf, wildcat and golden eagle. Among other birds that can be seen in the park are partridges, quails, eagle owls and kingfishers. Crayfish can also be found in the rivers.

Golden eagle

0 kilometres 1
0 miles 1

The Badia di Sitria is
an abbey with an interesting Romanesque church (Santa Maria) with a single nave and a barrel vault. The crypt is held up at the centre by a Roman column with a Corinthian capital.

The Forra di Riofreddo
is a deep, narrow gorge, which can only be tackled by experienced climbers. It was formed after many centuries of erosion by streams coming down from the mountain top.

Badia di Sitria

Isola Fossara

Casacce

Montebollo

PIAN DELLE MACINARE

MONTE CUCCO
1,566m

Ranco

illo

Purello

VALICO DI FOSSATO

PERUGIA

GUALDO TADINO

VISITORS' CHECKLIST

Perugia. **Road Map** D2.
🚊 *Fossato di Vico,
Rome–Ancona line, 892 021.*
ℹ️ *Ente Parco, Via Matteotti 52,
Sigillo, 075 917 7326, 075 917
9025.* **www**.parks.it

KEY

▬▬▬	Major road
═══	Minor road
▬▬▬	Scenic route
ℹ️	Tourist information
🏕	Picnic area
⛺	Campsite

Summit of Monte Cucco

At 1,566m (5,136ft), Monte Cucco is one of the highest peaks in Umbria. It can be reached fairly easily along the scenic Via del Ranco, which leads out of Sigillo.

Grotta di Monte Cucco

This cave can be reached on foot from the car park just beyond Val di Ranco. The cave reaches the record depth of 922 m (3,024 ft) and the water that gathers within the mountain emerges, after a lengthy subterranean journey, at the Scirca spring near Sigillo.

Sigillo

Home to the park administration, this village has visible Roman origins, in the bridges on the Via Flaminia and over the Scirca torrent. Of note are the church of Sant'Agostino, in the heart of the village, and Sant'Anna, near the cemetery, with frescoes by Matteo da Gualdo.

Gualdo Tadino ❻

Perugia. **Road Map** D3. 🏛 *15,000*.
🚊 *Foligno–Ancona line.* 🚌 *Piazza
Orti Mavarelli.* ℹ *Associazione Pro
Tadino, Piazza Martiri della Libertà,
075 912 172.*

Gualdo Tadino, a town of
ancient Umbrian and
Roman origins,
endured a tormented
history of defeats,
destruction and emi-
gration until the 12th
century, when it was
resettled on its
present site. The
name is a combina-
tion of the Roman
name *Tadinum* and
the Lombard word
wald, meaning forest.

As a commune, the
village took shape in
the Middle Ages, but
was heavily modified
over the course of
the centuries and today bears
only a few traces of its centuries-old history. Gualdo suffered terrible damage during
the 1997 earthquake, but has
now been almost totally
restored. The town is still, as
it was in the Middle Ages and
later centuries, one of the
principal centres of majolica
manufacture in Umbria.

The only ancient gate to
survive in Gualdo is that of
San Benedetto, on the eastern
side: from here, Corso Italia
(which becomes Corso Piave)
cuts through the whole of
the historic centre. Walking
along this street, you reach
Piazza XX Settembre, home to
the churches of **San Donato**
(12th century) and **Santa
Maria dei Raccomandati** (13th
century). The latter contains
a fine triptych by Matteo da
Gualdo of the *Madonna
with Child and saints
Sebastian and Roch*, but
is closed to the public.

Further along, on Corso
Piave, is the church of
San Francesco, built by
the Franciscans in the 13th
and 14th centuries. It has
a beautiful façade, with an
elegant Gothic doorway, and
inside are many frescoes,
most of which are the work
of Matteo da Gualdo (1435–
1507), the best-known artist

**Fresco on a
palazzo in the
centre of Gualdo**

native to Gualdo Tadino,
whose works can also be
seen in Assisi and Spoleto.
The fresco on the first pilaster
on the left, of *St Anne, the
Virgin and Child*, is said to be
the oldest work by the artist.
You soon arrive at the central
**Piazza Martiri della
Libertà**, better known to
the residents of Gualdo
as Piazza Grande, and
where the town's
most important
buildings are found.
Lording it over the
space is the **Palazzo
Comunale**. The
original, 12th-century
palazzo was rebuilt
after a terrible
earthquake in 1751,
so what is seen now
is its 18th-century
form. Most of the
town's medieval
buildings collapsed
during the same
earthquake, and the
Palazzo del Podestà
(13th century), in
front of the Palazzo
Comunale, was also
badly damaged.
An international
ceramics exhibition
and competition is
held annually in the
Palazzo del Podestà,
which brings dozens
of ceramic workers back
to Gualdo, a centre for the
manufacture of lustreware.

The cathedral of **San
Benedetto** stands on the
eastern side of Piazza Martiri.
The façade, dating from the
13th century but carefully
restored after the earthquake,
has three doors – one for
each of the aisles inside – and
a beautiful rose window.
The interior was entirely
rebuilt in the 19th

century, and has 20th-century
frescoes. Outside, to the left,
stands a lovely Renaissance
fountain. The only building
that remained intact after the
earthquake, and that is still
visible in the piazza today,
is the **Torre Civica**.

In common with many other
villages in this part of Umbria,
Gualdo Tadino has a fortress
at the top of the hill. The
origins of the **Rocca Flea** date
back to the 10th century,
when the construction of
fortifications began on the site
of a church, of which several
frescoes have been uncovered.
Today, the sizeable fortress
has more than 40 rooms – the
result of a series of enlarge-
ments and restoration work
carried out over the centuries.
In particular, the buildings
show the influence of
Frederick II, who restored and
made improvements to the
castle during the 13th century,
and also of the Perugians,
who made changes in
the following century.
The Rocca, which
has reopened after
several years of
closure, houses
a **Pinacoteca** (art
gallery), a ceramics
gallery and a
collection of
archeological finds.
The former has on display
detached frescoes by Matteo
da Gualdo as well as works
by Jacopo Palma, Antonio da
Fabriano and Niccolò Alunno.

**Detail of
a fountain**

🏛 **Rocca Flea**
Piazza della Rocca. **Tel** *075 916 078*.
🕐 *Apr–May: 10:30am–1pm,
3–6pm Thu–Sun; Jun–Sep:
10:30am–1pm, 3:30–7pm Tue–Sun;
Oct–Mar: 10:30–1pm, 2:30–5pm Sat
& Sun.* ⬤ *1 Jan, 25 Dec.* 📷 📹

The fortified bulk of Rocca Flea, guarding the town

For hotels and restaurants in this region see pp144–7 and pp156–61

Environs

About 7 km (4 miles) north of Gualdo Tadino is **Fossato di Vico**, a town that is divided into two parts: Fossato Basso, the largely modern town along the road, and Fossato Alto, the remnants of a major medieval settlement perched on a rocky spur. It is worth stopping off along the road between the two parts, at the church of San Benedetto, in order to see the frescoes by Matteo da Gualdo.

In the heart of Fossato Basso are covered walkways and the Cappella della Piaggiola, with frescoes by Ottaviano Nelli and his school (early 15th century).

Porta Vecchia, ancient entrance to the old centre of Nocera Umbra

Nocera Umbra ❼

Perugia. **Road Map** D3. 🏛 6,000.
🚉 *Nocera Scalo, 3 km (2 miles), Rome–Ancona line.* 🚶 *Pro Loco, Via San Renaldo 9, 0742 834 036.*
🎭 *Palio del Quartiere, first Tue in Aug.*

The collapse of the Torre di Nocera Umbra, now rebuilt, during the earthquake of 1997 was an enduring image of that tragic natural disaster. The town has been hit by earthquakes on a number of occasions, but never with such ferocity. The structural damage affected the whole of the historic centre, formerly one of the best-preserved in the region. Even now, only a small number of inhabitants have returned. Yet Nocera Umbra is a hive of activity – houses are being rebuilt,

Nocera Umbra, devastated by the 1997 earthquake but being rebuilt

while historic buildings are gradually being restored. The symbolic tower has already been reconstructed.

High on a rocky outcrop that looms over fertile valleys drained by the Topino and Caldognola rivers, Nocera Umbra has always occupied a strategically significant location, thanks partly to the town's position on the border of Le Marche and to its proximity to the Adriatic Sea. Originally an ancient Umbrian town (called *Nuokria*), it was an important settlement under both the Romans and the Lombards. The waters that gush from the many springs in the area are known for their curative properties.

Most of the important buildings in Nocera Umbra are still closed for safety reasons, including the **Duomo**, on the top of the hill. The same is true of the historic centre, although visitors are allowed access to the heart of the old town, Piazza Caprera. The

former church of **San Francesco**, now home to the Pinacoteca Comunale and Museo Civico, can be found on this square at No. 5. It is open Tuesdays to Sundays from April to September, and at weekends during the rest of the year. It is also worth going as far as the western walls to the church of **San Filippo**, a Neo-Gothic structure from the late 19th century. This marks the start of the Portici di San Filippo, a covered walkway within the walls, which has apertures and arrow-slits that enable visitors to admire the views.

Environs

The peak of **Monte Pennino** (1,571 m/5,155 ft), on the Le Marche border, is reachable from Nocera Umbra by car along 20 km (12 miles) of tortuous road (asphalted, apart from the last stretch). This mountain, as well as being a very scenic place to visit, has facilities for hiking and skiing.

THE WATERS OF NOCERA

The therapeutic quality of the mineral water springs in the Nocera area has been known since the 16th century; in the 18th century the water was used as a benchmark for measuring the purity of other waters. However, it wasn't until the 20th century that the spring waters began to be exploited for economic and industrial use, through the building of bottling plants and spas. The two main springs are at Bagni di Nocera and at Schiagni (Fonte del Cacciatore). Their curative powers derive from the combination of a water that is particularly pure and mineral-rich in itself, and the clay typical of this terrain.

The modern spa at Bagni di Nocera

Parco Regionale del Monte Subasio **❽**

In outline, Monte Subasio (1,290 m/4,230 ft) has a distinctively rounded form. It rises, isolated, between the historic centres of Assisi, Spello and Nocera Umbra and, since 1995, has formed the southern margin of a 7,442-ha (18,390-acre) regional park. As well as its own natural beauty, Monte Subasio offers superb views across to the high Appenines in the east. The park also includes many places of historic and religious significance. Subasio's distinctive rose-coloured stone was used to build much of Assisi, which lies right on the fringes of the park. The mountain was regarded as a sacred place in the 10th century BC, and its importance endured during the life of St Francis, who perhaps drew inspiration from these magical and mystical surroundings.

Monte Subasio
The summit of Monte Subasio is easily reached and seems to offer a view of the whole of Umbria. To the southeast are the sink-holes known as "mortaro grande" and "mortaro piccolo", cavities which were once used for collecting ice.

Eremo delle Carceri
Around 4 km (2 miles) from Assisi, this small and peaceful hermitage is surrounded by dense woodland. The name (Hermitage of the Prisons) derives from the fact that Franciscan friars used to "lock themselves away" here in order to pray: there is still a 15th-century church here, as well as a cave where St Francis would go to rest. Beyond the hermitage is a bridge that leads to a wood containing a series of caves and hermitages used in the Middle Ages by the devout and by friars.

The northern road leaves Assisi near Cà Piombino, base for the park administration. Before winding its way south towards Spello, the road goes through the small historic centres of Armenzano, San Giovanni and Collepino.

I Prati degli Stazzi, on the road between the Eremo delle Carceri and the peak, offer fine views over Assisi. In May, the fields are carpeted in flowers.

Téscio

S444

Assisi • [△]

S147

PERUGIA

San Damiano

Piar
Piev

N
S

Road to the summit
Between Assisi and Spello the road retraces the route of an ancient cart track. A lovely scenic road, it leads almost to the peak of Monte Subasio. On the descent towards Spello, the road passes the sanctuary of the Madonna della Spella.

San Vitale

| 0 kilometres | 2 |
| 0 miles | 2 |

KEY

▭ Minor road

▭ Scenic route

[△] Campsite

Rocca di Postignano
Within the park is the ancient fortification of Rocca Postignano, as well as several churches that were built on the site of places where hermits once prayed.

VISITORS' CHECKLIST

Perugia. **Road Map** C2.
🚇 Santa Maria degli Angeli, Assisi, Foligno–Terontola line, 892021. 🚌 APM Assisi–Eremo delle Carceri, 800 512 141.
ℹ️ Loc Cà Piombino, Assisi, 075 815 5290. **Fax** 075 815 307. **www**.parks.it

WILDLIFE ON MONTE SUBASIO

The slopes of the mountain are today covered with three different kinds of vegetation. Olive trees are grown on land stretching from Assisi as far as Spello. Other areas support mixed woodland, including oak, black hornbeam, ash, maple, beech and holm oak. Forests of

A pair of porcupines

resiniferous trees, the result of replanting, characterize the third type of vegetation, along with meadow pasture. This range of natural habitats does not support a wide variety of wildlife, however, despite a ban on hunting lasting several decades: the golden eagle has not been seen since the 1960s. Current wildlife sightings include the partridge, wood pigeon, magpie, jay, wildcat, squirrel, porcupine, badger, wolf, weasel, stone marten and wild boar. Birds of prey seen here include the buzzard and goshawk.

Bandita Cilleni

Santa Maria Lignano

Castello di Armenzano
During the Middle Ages, this place was fortified because it occupied a strategic position. Today, the village offers peace and fine views.

Armenzano

→ NOCERA UMBRA

The Abbey of San Silvestro dates from the 11th century. According to tradition, it was built by San Romualdo, founder of the Camaldolese order.

San Giovanni

Collepino
About 10 km (6 miles) from the peak of Monte Subasio, this walled medieval village stands isolated near the source of the river Chiona.

Madonna della Spella

Collepino

SPELLO

Assisi ❾

Even without the churches, extraordinary frescoes and associations with St Francis, it would be worth coming to Assisi simply to witness a sunset. As the sun sinks, the medieval centre of Assisi, one of the best-preserved in the world, is bathed in a warm glow. Founded by the Umbrians, Assisi was prominent during the Roman era, but the town achieved greatest fame and importance during the era of the communes in the Middle Ages. By the time the basilica of San Francesco was founded in the 13th century, Assisi, built using the reddish stone of Monte Subasio to which the town owes its distinctive coloration, had already taken shape. In the 14th century, when Assisi came under papal rule, two fortresses were built. Over the following centuries the city changed little. Even today, the town has a timeless fascination.

View of the Basilica di San Francesco

Palazzo del Capitano del Popolo

Temple of Minerva

Basilica of San Francesco *(see pp72–3)*

VIA PORTICA

PIAZZA COMU

VIA BANDA DA QUINTAVALLE

Santa Maria Maggiore
This church was Assisi's first cathedral. Its Romanesque origins are clear from its formal simplicity.

VIA PORTA MOI

Monastery of San Giuseppe

STAR SIGHTS

★ Duomo (San Rufino)

★ Basilica di Santa Chiara

Porta Moiano

Palazzo Vescovile is where Francis renounced all worldly goods. The bishop's palace was entirely rebuilt in the 17th century.

Piazza del Comune

This square has always been the heart of Assisi. Around the piazza are the Temple of Minerva (1st century BC), Palazzo del Capitano del Popolo (13th century), the Torre del Popolo (13th–14th century) and Palazzo dei Priori (14th century).

VISITORS' CHECKLIST

Perugia. **Road Map** D4.
🚶 25,000. FS Assisi (Piazza Matteotti); Santa Maria degli Angeli (Piazza Garibaldi), Foligno–Terontola line, 892021
🚌 APM 800 512 141. 🛈 Piazza del Comune 10, 075 813 8680.
📅 Calendimaggio, 4–6 May.

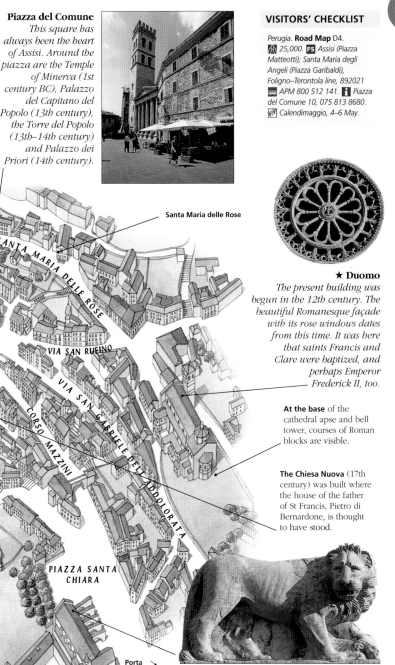

Santa Maria delle Rose

SANTA MARIA DELLE ROSE

VIA SAN RUFINO

VIA SAN GABRIELE DELL'ADDOLORATA

CORSO MAZZINI

PIAZZA SANTA CHIARA

Porta Nuova

★ Duomo
The present building was begun in the 12th century. The beautiful Romanesque façade with its rose windows dates from this time. It was here that saints Francis and Clare were baptized, and perhaps Emperor Frederick II, too.

At the base of the cathedral apse and bell tower, courses of Roman blocks are visible.

The Chiesa Nuova (17th century) was built where the house of the father of St Francis, Pietro di Bernardone, is thought to have stood.

The convent alongside the basilica still contains the crypt of the ancient little church of San Giorgio, in the cloister.

★ Basilica di Santa Chiara
This church was built shortly after the Basilica di San Francesco. As well as the remains of St Clare, it contains prized works of art and the famous Byzantine Crucifix of San Damiano.

Exploring Assisi

Duomo, detail of the façade

The draw of Assisi's famous basilica can be overpowering, but there is much else to explore in the town. Motorists would do best to leave their car in the huge car park in Largo Properzio, just outside the walls, and to enter the historic centre through Porta Nuova, on the southeastern side of town. From here, Via Borgo Aretino leads to Assisi's first great building, the basilica of Santa Chiara. This lies in the heart of a medieval quarter, which is linked by steep streets to the upper town, dating from Roman times and home to the duomo and Piazza del Comune. From this central piazza, continue along Via Seminario and Via San Francesco, lined with medieval buildings, to reach the great basilica of St Francis (see pp72–3).

Baptismal font in the cathedral of San Rufino

The door and rose window of the basilica of Santa Chiara

🔒 Santa Chiara

Piazza Santa Chiara.
Tel 075 812 282.
⏱ 6:30am–noon, 2–7pm (6pm in winter).

Assisi's second great church was begun in 1257, and consecrated eight years later by Pope Clement IV: the body of St Clare (declared a saint in 1255), founder of the order of the Poor Clares, was buried here in 1260.

The façade has a simple doorway with a rose window above, while the side that faces the street is supported by three vast buttresses. The church is distinctive because of the use of alternating layers of white and red stone, as seen in some Tuscan churches.

The interior is in the form of a Latin cross, simple and spare. In the right transept there is a cycle of frescoes

depicting *Scenes from the Life of St Clare*, by an unknown artist called the Master of Santa Chiara (late 13th century). Other interesting frescoes, from the 14th century, can be found on the left wall, while on the right, in the Oratorio delle Reliquie, there is the late 12th-century wooden Crucifix of San Damiano. According to the hagiography, this is the crucifix that famously spoke to Francis in San Damiano, asking him to "repair his church" (see p80).

🔒 Duomo (San Rufino)

Piazza San Rufino. **Tel** 075 816 016, 075 812 283. ⏱ summer: 7am–12:30pm, 2:30–7pm daily; winter: 7am–12:30pm, 2:30–6pm (Aug & the day before public hols: 7am–7pm).

From Santa Chiara, a climb up stepped streets leads to the duomo, built on a Roman religious site in around 1029 by archbishop Ugone, and then rebuilt in the 12th–13th centuries. The church was consecrated in 1253, the year

construction was completed, by Pope Innocent IV.

Less well known than the other basilicas of Assisi, the cathedral is worth a visit just for its splendid façade, a masterpiece of Umbrian Romanesque. It is divided into three horizontal sections. At ground level are three doors decorated with lions, with bas-relief lunettes; above, divided from the lower level by a band of sculpted corbels, are three rose windows with symbols of the evangelists. At the top is a triangular tympanum with a Gothic arch. To one side, rising above the scene, is the bell tower, part of the 11th-century church and with double-mullioned windows.

The interior, laid out on a rectangular plan, dates from the 16th century. It still has the old baptismal font where both St Francis and St Clare were baptized, a wooden choir dating from the 16th century and the underground Franciscan oratory, where the

View of Assisi, with its walls and fortifications, from Monte Subasio

saint would withdraw before preaching to the crowd. The Cappella del Sacramento, by Giacomo Giorgetti, is a Baroque composition on the theme of the Eucharist.

Adjacent to the church is the **Museo della Cattedrale** (cathedral museum), which contains pieces from the original church, a series of frescoes from the Oratorio di San Rufinuccio and paintings from various churches in Assisi. To the left of the church are the ruins of a Roman theatre and, a little further north, those of an amphitheatre. In the church courtyard a plaque shows the site of the house where St Clare was born.

⌖ Piazza del Comune

From the cathedral, heading along Via di San Rufino, you reach the square that has always been the true heart of the city. It was created in its current form in the 13th century. The main focus of the piazza is the **Temple of Minerva**, built in the 1st century BC on a set of terraces that once marked the centre of the town. This beautifully preserved Roman temple has changed function at various times over the centuries: first a church, then a group of shops, then seat of the town hall until, in 1456, it finally became a church again, with the name of Santa Maria sopra Minerva.

On the left of the temple portico is the **Palazzo del Capitano del Popolo**, built in the 13th century and extensively restored in the

The late Renaissance façade of the Chiesa Nuova

20th century. At the foot of the bell tower (Torre del Popolo), you can see the 14th-century measures for bricks, tiles and fabrics then in use in Assisi, set into the wall. On the opposite side of the piazza is the **Palazzo dei Priori**, begun in 1275 and completed in the late 15th century. On the right is the Arco della Volta Pinta, with 16th-century frescoes. The Fonte di Piazza, at the far end of the square, is an 18th-century fountain built on the foundations of a 13th-century water basin.

A brief descent through the Arco dei Priori leads to the 17th-century **Chiesa Nuova**, which was commissioned by Philip III of Spain to mark the spot where St Francis was said to have been born.

🏛 Temple of Minerva
Piazza del Comune.
Tel *075 812 268.*
⬜ *7:15am–7pm Mon–Sat; 8:15am–7pm Sun & public hols.*
◑ *2–5:15pm Tue, Fri.*

🔒 Chiesa Nuova
Piazzetta Chiesa Nuova.
Tel *075 812 339.* ⬜ *8:30am–noon, 3–6pm (5pm in winter).*

🏛 Museo and Foro Romano
Via Portica 2. ***Tel*** *075 815 5077.* ⬜ *daily. mid-Mar–May, Sep & Oct: 10am–6pm; Jun–Aug: 10am–7pm; Nov–mid-Mar: 10:30am–1pm, 2–5pm.* 🎟

On the corner of Piazza del Comune, beyond the Arco del Seminario – the ancient limit of the walled city in the Roman era – is a museum of Roman finds. From the museum, visitors can gain access to the ruins of what may have been the Roman forum, beneath the Piazza del Comune.

🔒 Via San Francesco

Heading towards the Basilica di San Francesco, you cover the whole length of Via del Seminario, which becomes Via San Francesco. Along the way you pass the **Palazzo Giacobetti** (17th century) and, opposite,

The Loggia dei Maestri Comacini, on Via San Francesco

the delightful **Oratorio dei Pellegrini** (15th century), once part of a pilgrim's hospice, followed by the arches of the Portico del Monte Frumentario, part of a 13th-century hospital. Next comes the Palazzo Vallemani, which is temporary home of the **Pinacoteca Comunale**; the art gallery's most important work is probably the *Madonna in Maestà* (Giotto school), found near the entrance. A little further along is the **Loggia dei Maestri Comacini**, a 13th-century palazzetto which, according to tradition, was the seat of the Lombard rulers; it is adorned with 15th-century coats of arms.

Madonna in Maestà

Nearby, the steep Vicolo di Sant'Andrea climbs up to the Piazza di Santa Margherita, from where there are classic views towards the Basilica di San Francesco. It is especially moving at sunset or at dawn.

🔒 Oratorio dei Pellegrini
Via San Francesco 13.
Tel *075 812 267.*
⬜ *10am–noon, 4–6pm Tue–Sat.*

🏛 Pinacoteca Comunale
Palazzo Vallemani, Via San Francesco 10. ***Tel*** *075 815 5234.*
⬜ *mid-Mar–May, Sep & Oct: 10am–6pm daily; Nov–mid-Mar: 10:30am–1pm, 2–5pm; Jun–Aug: 10am–7pm.* 🎟

The rose window above the door

Assisi: Basilica di San Francesco

St Francis died on 4 October 1226. Just 18 months later Frate Elia, Vicar-General of the Franciscan Order, was charged by Pope Gregory IX with building a church dedicated to the saint. After the laying of the first stone, the Lower Church was the first part to take shape; the Upper Church was eventually built on top of it. The basilica was consecrated by Pope Innocent IV in 1253, though the chapel of Santa Caterina, the final stage in the basilica's construction, was not completed until 1367. Some of the greatest artists of the age, including Cimabue and Giotto, left their mark on the building. On 26 September 1997, a severe earthquake badly damaged the church: part of the vault collapsed and cracks appeared in the transept. Just two years later, however, the basilica re-opened for visits and worship, the culmination of an exceptional feat of restoration.

The walls of the transept are decorated with an outstanding cycle of frescoes painted by Cimabue and his assistants. The Crucifixion in the left transept is superb.

The wooden choir, situated in the apse and on the sides next to the crossing, is an example of Gothic Renaissance engraving and inlaid wood, the work of Domenico Indovini.

★ **Quattro Vele**
The celebrated allegorical frescoes of the Quattro Vele (vault above the altar), in the Lower Church, represent The Three Virtues of St Francis. *Long attributed to Giotto, they are now thought to be the work of one of his assistants. A detail of the* Allegory of Obedience *is shown here.*

The Tomb of St Francis, in the crypt, was discovered only in 1818. The exact location had never been revealed for fear that someone might want to seize such a precious relic. The remains of the saint were transferred here in 1230, before the basilica was finished.

★ **Frescoes in the Crossing**
The left side of the crossing was decorated by Pietro Lorenzetti in 1515–20. This is one of two portraits of the Madonna and Child.

For hotels and restaurants in this region see pp144–7 and pp156–61

Frescoes in the Nave
The vault in the nave is decorated with frescoes by various masters, one of whom may have been the young Giotto. The vault in the first bay represents the Four Doctors of the Church working in their studies, each with an assistant. St Augustine is shown here.

The façade is an example of Italian Gothic. It has a double rose window in Cosmatesque style and a double door.

VISITORS' CHECKLIST

Piazza San Francesco. **Tel** 075 819 001. ◯ **Upper Church** 8:30am–6:45pm (to 5:45pm Nov–Easter). **Lower Church** 6am–6:45pm (to 5:45pm Nov–Easter). ✝ at the Tomb of St Francis: 7:15am Mon–Fri (075 819 0084 for bookings). **www**.sanfrancescoassisi.org

Interior of the Upper Church
The bright, soaring, single-nave upper church is typical of Franciscan monastic architecture. It takes the forms of French Gothic but simplifies them and adds local elements. It was intended to symbolize the asceticism and spirituality that characterized the life of St Francis.

Entrance to the Upper Church

Entrance to the Lower Church

The Cappella di San Martino, the first on the left in the Lower Church, was decorated by Simone Martini (1312–1320). His frescoes, depicting several saints and a cycle illustrating the *Life of St Martin*, are true masterpieces.

★ **Life of St Francis**
The frescoes on the lower walls of the nave (1290s), long thought to be by Giotto and his assistants, are now attributed by most specialists to a superb unknown artist, often referred to as the Maestro di San Francesco.

STAR FEATURES

★ Frescoes in the Crossing

★ Quattro Vele

★ Life of St Francis

Assisi: The Frescoes in the Basilica

Apotheosis of St Francis, Giotto, detail

It was not without controversy that Frate Elia erected such a grandiose building to hold the relics of a saint who had preached poverty. It appears that two buildings, one above the other, were envisaged from the very beginning, although the exact date of the commencement of work on the Upper Church is not known. The Lower Church, both smaller and simpler, was to function as the saint's burial place and to accommodate pilgrims, while the Upper Church was for regular worship. The speed with which the work was carried out evidently did not allow for much sculptural decoration, and the vast plain walls seemed designed for impressive cycles of frescoes, on which the greatest painters of the age could work. Together they created one of the finest and most loved monuments in the history of Western art.

LOWER CHURCH

Austere and rather gloomy, the Lower Church shows the influence of the Romanesque style.

Detail from the *Deposition*, Pietro Lorenzetti

The solemnity is lightened by the wonderfully rich pictorial decoration, which is less famous than the decoration in the Upper Church, but more representative of Italian art of the time, given the number and quality of the artists who worked here.

MAIN FRESCOES IN THE LOWER CHURCH
Walls
Maestro di San Francesco.
Left: *Stories from the Life of St Francis*; Right: *Scenes from the Passion* (c.1260, much damaged, only half visible).
Quattro Vele (vault above the altar)
Maestro delle Vele.
Apotheosis of St Francis; Allegory of Obedience; Allegory of Poverty; Allegory of Chastity (c.1315–20).
Right Transept
Vaults:
Workshop of Giotto.
Infancy and Adolescence of Jesus (c.1315–20).
West and north walls:
Workshop of Giotto.
Posthumous Miracles of

St Francis (c.1320).
East wall:
Cimabue. *Enthroned Madonna with Angels and St Francis* (c.1280); Giotto (?), *Crucifixion* (c.1320); Simone Martini, *Madonna with Child and two Magi Kings* (c.1321–6).
Cappella di San Nicola:
Simone Martini.
Saints Francis, Louis of Toulouse, Elizabeth of Hungary, Clare and an unknown saint (c.1321–6).

Left Transept
Entirely frescoed by Pietro Lorenzetti and workshop (c.1315–20).
Barrel vault:
Entry into Jerusalem; the Last Supper; Washing of the Feet; Expulsion from the Temple; Ascent to Calvary; Flagellation; Crucifixion.
South wall:
Descent from the Cross; Deposition; Descent into Limbo; Resurrection.
East wall:
Crucifixion; Madonna and Child; St Francis and St John the Evangelist.
West wall:
Death of Judas; St Francis receives the stigmata.
Cappella di San Giovanni Battista:
Madonna with Child and Sts Francis and John the Baptist.
Cappella di San Martino di Tours (first on the left)
Entirely frescoed by Simone Martini (c.1321–6).
Figures of saints and cycle of frescoes depicting the *Life of St Martin.*

UPPER CHURCH

The Upper Church is as airy and light as the Lower Church is low and dark. Its pictorial decoration is divided substantially into two main blocks: the frescoes of the apse, transept and the crossing, by Cimabue and his school, and those of the nave and vaults, where the life of St Francis and episodes from the Old and New Testament are portrayed in one of the world's great masterpieces.

Madonna and Child, Pietro Lorenzetti, detail, Lower Church

◁ The interior of the Upper Church, Basilica di San Francesco, Assisi (pre-1997 earthquake)

FRESCOES IN THE APSE AND THE TRANSEPTS

Cimabue and his school (1280).

Left Transept
Crucifixion; Scenes from the Apocalypse; Michael and the Angels.

Main Apse
Scenes from the Life of the Virgin Mary.

Right Transept
The Apostles.

Crossing
The Evangelists.

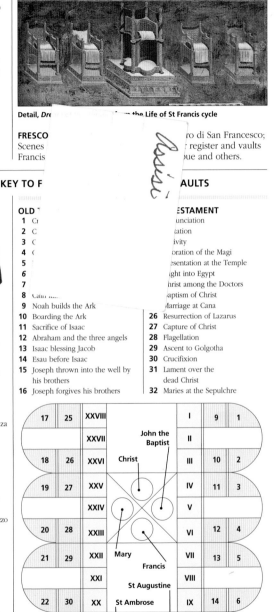

Detail, *Dre...* ... *...* the Life of St Francis cycle

FRESCO... ...ro di San Francesco;
Scenes ... register and vaults
Francis ... ...ue and others.

KEY TO F... ...AULTS

Detail from *Miracle of the Spring*,
14th scene, Giotto cycle

OLD T...
1 Cr...
2 C...
3 C...
4 C...
5 ...
6 ...
7 ...
8 Cain...
9 Noah builds the Ark
10 Boarding the Ark
11 Sacrifice of Isaac
12 Abraham and the three angels
13 Isaac blessing Jacob
14 Esau before Isaac
15 Joseph thrown into the well by his brothers
16 Joseph forgives his brothers

...ESTAMENT
...unciation
...tation
...ivity
...oration of the Magi
...esentation at the Temple
...ight into Egypt
...hrist among the Doctors
...aptism of Christ
...Marriage at Cana
26 Resurrection of Lazarus
27 Capture of Christ
28 Flagellation
29 Ascent to Golgotha
30 Crucifixion
31 Lament over the dead Christ
32 Maries at the Sepulchre

LIFE OF ST FRANCIS

I Francis honoured in the piazza
II Gift of the Cloak
III Dream of Arms
IV Prayer in San Damiano
V Renounces worldly goods
VI Dream of Innocent I
VII Approval of the Order
VIII Apparition in Chariot of Fire
IX Dream of the Throne
X Expulsion of Demons from Arezzo
XI Francis before the Sultan
XII Francis in ecstasy
XIII Celebration of Christmas
XIV Miracle of the Spring
XV Preaching to the birds
XVI Death of the Knight
XVII Prayer before Honorius III
XVIII Apparition in Arles
XIX Francis receives the stigmata
XX Death of Francis
XXI Apparition of the saint
XXII Girolamo accepts the truth of the stigmata
XXIII Poor Clares mourn the saint
XXIV Canonization
XXV Dream of Gregory IX
XXVI Healing of the man from Ilerda
XXVII Revival of the devout woman
XXVIII Liberation of Pietro di Alife

Monastic Orders

Anyone visiting Umbria, and in particular Assisi, will be aware immediately of the many convents and monasteries belonging to different religious orders, direct descendants of the ministry of St Francis and St Clare. Monastic orders in Europe were born officially in the 6th century, with the drawing up of St Benedict's Rule. Reforms to the Benedictine Order instigated at Cluny in the 10th century gave a great boost to the monastic movement, as did the

Franciscan arms

development of the Cistercian Order two centuries later. St Francis (1182–1226) broke new ground by reacting against the luxury and seclusion of old-fashioned monasticism, with its great abbeys, and instead invited his followers to live a life of poverty and renunciation, ministering to the urban poor. It was very hard to apply such a severe precept to a group, even of monks, which led to the the birth of other Franciscan orders. Three exist today.

A rosary hangs from the white cord tied around the waist.

Cape, detached from the habit, which covers the shoulders.

The rosary is made up of 70 beads.

Brown habit

THE FRIARS MINOR

Founded in 1223, the Order of Friars Minor numbers just under 20,000, mainly priests. The monks do not normally have a beard, which is reserved for lone missionaries.

Habit has two vertical pockets at rib level.

Friars wear socks and shoes.

Friars wear leather sandals or wooden clogs.

Cape covering the shoulders, chest and back.

Black habit

A conventual is never bearded.

Stiff white collar

FRIARS MINOR CONVENTUALS

After a lengthy controversy concerning the literal observance of the Rule of St Francis, in 1517 Pope Leo X decided to group together all the small orders that had been generated by Franciscanism. Following this reform, only two orders were recognized: the Friars Minor and the Conventuals. Around 4,500 belong to the latter Order, divided into 675 houses scattered throughout the world.

The cloister of the convent of San Damiano

POOR CLARES, FRANCISCAN NUNS AND CAPUCHIN NUNS

The origin of the Order of Poor Clares (Clarisse) dates back to when St Clare (Santa Chiara) took the veil, celebrated by St Francis in 1212 at Santa Maria degli Angeli *(see p80)*, when Clare was just a teenager. Having entered a traditional Benedictine convent, she left with a group of sisters and went to the church of San Damiano *(see p80)*, where she decided to follow in the footsteps of St Francis by establishing a female Franciscan order. The Rule of the Poor Clares was drawn up in 1224 by Francis himself and was observed with rigour by St Clare. Over time, the severity of the original Rule was slightly relaxed. In the 15th century, the establishment of the Reformed Franciscan Order of nuns signalled a return to the earlier, stricter observance, and in 1525 a female branch of the Capuchin Order was founded. The three orders survive to this day.

Robe of St Francis
Traditionally regarded as the first robe worn by St Francis, this item of clothing reflects the saint's own rules of poverty and is in keeping with the description that history provides of his renunciation of worldly goods.

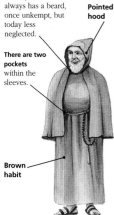

The Capuchin
always has a beard, once unkempt, but today less neglected.

Pointed hood

There are two pockets
within the sleeves.

Brown habit

CAPUCHIN FRIARS
Seeking a return to the rigour of the traditional Rule of St Francis, in 1525 Matteo da Bascio founded the first house of the Capuchins at Camerino. The Order spread throughout Italy as well as abroad, but its members suffered persecution because of the character of the Friars' rule, which was considered to be too rigid and extreme. Currently, around 11,000 belong to this Franciscan Order (including 70 bishops, 7,300 priests and 3,500 lay members).

Exterior view of San Pietro showing its clean lines

🔒 San Pietro
Piazza San Pietro. *Tel 075 813 331.*
summer: 7:30am–7pm daily.
It is just a short walk from Basilica di San Francesco along Via Frate Elia to the church of San Pietro, which was founded, along with the adjacent monastery, by the Benedictines in the 10th century. The existing church dates from the same period as the basilica of St Francis, and was consecrated in 1254.

The striking Romanesque-Gothic façade was originally decorated with a pediment, taken down in the 19th century. The interior, mainly Romanesque, contains no works of art of note. Its distinguishing features are its sober simplicity and the height of its nave.

🔒 Santa Maria Maggiore
Piazza del Vescovado.
Tel 075 813 085.
8:30am–12:30pm, 2:30–7:30pm daily.
Walking east from San Pietro, you eventually emerge into Piazza del Vescovado. This square was an important site in the Middle Ages, shown by the presence of the Palazzo Vescovile (Bishop's Palace) and the church of Santa Maria Maggiore, the city cathedral until 1020. The church was probably founded in the 10th century, but was rebuilt in Romanesque form around 1163. From the crypt, which is original, there is access to what is supposed to be the House of Propertius (Casa di Properzio) – "supposed", since the origins of the great Roman poet (c.50–16 BC) are anything but clear. In fact, at least three Umbrian cities – Assisi, Spello and Bevagna – have claimed to be the poet's birthplace.

🏰 Rocca Maggiore
Via Portica 2. *Tel 075 813 053.*
10am–dusk daily. 1 Jan, 25 Dec.
This well-preserved fortress stands at the northern edge of the city, reached by walking up Via di Porta Perlici from Piazza San Rufino. The panorama, overlooking the Valle del Tescio, the Valle Umbra and Assisi itself, with the façade of the duomo in the foreground, more than compensates for the effort of the climb.

The fortress was built in the 12th century and was used by duke Corrado di Urslingen (who was tutor to the future emperor Frederick II). It was destroyed and rebuilt more than once, including by Cardinal Albornoz in 1367, from which period most of what is now visible dates. Later additions include the polygonal tower (1458) and the round tower by the entrance (1553–8).

The fortress of the Rocca Maggiore, on the skyline above Assisi

San Damiano, its formal simplicity suited to such a mystical place

🔒 Sanctuary of San Damiano

Via Padre Antonio Giorgi. **Tel** 075 812 273. ⬜ summer: 10am–noon, 2–6pm (winter: 4:30pm); Vespers at 7pm and 5pm respectively.

From Porta Nuova, a walk of around 15 minutes leads to the Franciscan church of San Damiano, one of the most significant places in the life of St Francis. It was here that, in 1205, the saint said he heard the words: "Francis, go and repair my church which is falling down". According to the great chronicler of Francis' life, Tommaso da Celano, the words were spoken by the Crucifix which is now in Basilica di Santa Chiara (see p70). The building indicated by the crucifix was that of the church of San Damiano. Francis himself, together with a few faithful followers, undertook the restoration.

St Francis brought St Clare to San Damiano; she and her first followers congregated here, and founded the convent in which St Francis composed his *Canticle of the Creatures* (1225). Today, the convent is run by the Order of the Frati Minori Osservanti (Friars Minor).

Besides the spiritual value of the place, the sanctuary is worth a visit from both an architectural and artistic point of view, especially for the old convent rooms: the Oratorio di Santa Chiara, the cloister with frescoes by Eusebio da San Giorgio (1507) and the refectory. A good part of the 13th-century structure of the building can still be seen.

🔒 Santa Maria degli Angeli-Porziuncola

Santa Maria degli Angeli. **Tel** 075 805 11. ⬜ 6:15am–12:50pm, 2:30–7:30pm Mon–Fri (Jul–Oct: also 9–10:30pm for silent prayer).

Another place that was dear to Francis is at the bottom of the hill (through Porta San Pietro). Built at the end of the 16th century, the church of Santa Maria degli Angeli (the seventh-largest church in the world) was, in fact, designed to accommodate the buildings of the 11th-century Porziuncola ("the little portion"), the

The little oratory of the Porziuncola

chapel where St Francis lived and which was the centre of the early Franciscan Order. In 1569, Pope Pius IV laid the first stone of the vast Santa Maria, constructed to receive hordes of pilgrims. The project was given to Galeazzo Alessi, and work was concluded more than a century later with the building of the great cupola (1667) and one of the two bell towers. Inside the vast church, beneath the dome, is the old oratory, known as the Cappella della Porziuncola; on the right is the Cappella del Transito, the old infirmary cell where the saint died on 4 October 1226; the door is original. This chapel contains a majolica statue of St Francis by Andrea della Robbia. Also of note is the Cappella del Roseto (chapel of the rose garden), with early 16th-century frescoes by Tiberio d'Assisi. The chapel takes its name from a legend, according to which St Francis rolled naked on the roses in the garden (to mortify his body), only to find that all the thorns immediately vanished.

In the convent there is a small museum, with a painted *Crucifix* by Giunta Pisano (mid-13th century) and a *St Francis* by an unknown artist who later passed into history as the Maestro di San Francesco.

Environs

About 5 km (3 miles) south of Assisi, on the road to Foligno, is the imposing **Santuario di Rivotorto**, built in 1854 in Neo-Gothic style on the site of a stone hut where the first community of Franciscan friars lived briefly, in 1209; St Francis wrote the first set of rules for his Order here. On the façade are the symbols of the Basilica di San Francesco. Also in Rivotorto is the peaceful British and Commonwealth "Assisi War Graves" cemetery.

🔒 Santuario di Rivotorto

Rivotorto di Assisi, 5 km (3 miles). **Tel** 075 806 5432. ⬜ 6:45am–12:30pm, 2:30–7pm daily (from 7:30am Sun).

Crucifixion, 1561, fresco by Dono Doni in the duomo of San Rufino

The Franciscan Path of Peace ⑩

The logo of Umbria Mistica

There are many trails in the Umbrian hills, among them this one, established in the Jubilee year (2000). It retraces the journey taken by St Francis in 1206. Along the way, the saint decided to abandon his lay life and discovered the force of his spiritual conversion. The route, which is reasonably easy to walk, links Assisi and Gubbio and not only follows the physical paths trodden by Francis, but also recaptures the future saint's spiritual journey.

VISITORS' CHECKLIST

ℹ️ *Piazza del Comune 10, Assisi, 075 813 8680.*
Length: *c.40 km (25 miles).*
Time needed: *Two days.*
Stopping-off points: *Assisi, Valfabbrica, Gubbio. Lodgings at Vallingegno abbey, 075 920 158.*
www.sentierofrancescano.org

Abbey of Vallingegno ⑥
Another notable spiritual stopping place is the abbey dedicated to San Verecondo, a Benedictine centre from the 11th century, still in good condition. The church, cloister and crypt can be visited.

Gubbio ⑦
Just before the town is the "Vittorina", the church dedicated to Santa Maria della Vittoria, where it is said that Francis tamed the wolf. In Gubbio, the trail ends at the church of San Francesco.

Church of Caprignone ⑤
Foremost among all the churches that Francis built, stone by stone, during his life, this simple church sums up the austerity of the order and marks the start of the history of the Franciscan movement.

Pieve di Coccorano ④
This is one of many chapels that Francis must have encountered on his journey, giving him the chance to stop and pray. The countryside here is particularly beautiful and tranquil.

Abbey of Valfabbrica ③
This may well have been the place where Francis stayed before continuing to Gubbio. Only the little church of Santa Maria remains today, with frescoes of the Umbrian school.

Pieve San Nicolò ②
After a hilly journey from Assisi, you reach this village, which marks the divide between Assisi and Valfabbrica. Both towns can be seen from here, and, when the weather is good, you can even see as far as Gubbio.

Assisi ①
The trail starts from Porta San Giacomo, probably the gate through which Francis passed when he left Assisi. It is near the Basilica di San Francesco, where the body of the saint now lies.

KEY

▨ Tour route

═ Other roads

Map labels:
UMBERTIDE
Ponte d'Assisi
Castiglione
Santa Maria di Colonnata
Mengara
S298
Chiascio
S219
Biscina
S318
S318
Pianello
Rocca Sant'Angelo
Palazzo
PERUGIA
S147
SPELLO

0 kilometres 3
0 miles 3

Vineyards belonging to the Lungarotti family, near Torgiano

Torgiano ⑪

Perugia. **Road Map** C4.
🚶 5,000. 🚆 Perugia and Assisi stations, 5 km (3 miles) and 8 km (5 miles), Foligno–Terontola line. 🚌
ℹ Pro Loco, Corso Vittorio Emanuele 23, 075 985 297.

The small town of Torgiano, 15 km (9 miles) south of Perugia (just east of the main road 3bis), occupies a lovely position at the confluence of the Tiber and Chiascio rivers. Inhabited since the Roman era, it was rebuilt during the Middle Ages as a fortified site to guard over the territory of Perugia – as the Torre Baglioni (probably 13th century) still bears witness.

Torgiano is not an especially remarkable town in itself, and yet it is famous for the now historic production of wine, acknowledged in the town's coat of arms and recorded in the excellent **Museo del Vino and Osteria**. Housed in the 17th-century Palazzo Baglioni, this is a private museum owned by the Lungarotti family, probably the best-known wine producers in Umbria; the Rubesco Riserva di Torgiano is one of Italy's best red wines.

The 19 rooms illustrate the history of oenology and vine-growing since antiquity: on display, with good notes and explanations (including in English), are the tools used for the production of wine over the centuries, as well as old books and printed material relating to wine. There is also a valuable

collection of majolica pieces, among them a plate by Maestro Giorgio da Gubbio (1528) and a tondo with Bacchus which is attributed to Girolamo della Robbia.

Next door to the museum is the **Osteria del Museo**, where it is possible to taste and buy wines from the **Cantine Giorgio Lungarotti** (open to the public by appointment).

In an additional demonstration of the high esteem in which local agricultural products are held, the Lungarotti Foundation has also added a **Museo dell'Olivo e dell'Olio**, where displays relating to olives and oil are housed in attractively restored medieval dwellings. High-quality olive oils and balsamic vinegar produced on the estate are offered for sale in the winery shop.

🏛 **Museo del Vino and Osteria**
Corso Vittorio Emanuele 31–33.
Tel 075 988 0200.
🕐 summer: 9am–1pm, 3–7pm (winter: to 6pm). 🔴 25 Dec.
🖥 www.lungarotti.it

🍷 **Cantine Giorgio Lungarotti**
Tel 075 988 661.

🏛 **Museo dell'Olivo e dell'Olio**
Via Garibaldi 10.
Tel 075 988 0300.
🕐 summer: 10am–1pm, 3–7pm (winter: to 6pm). 🔴 25 Dec.

Bettona ⑫

Perugia. **Road Map** C4.
🚶 3,700. 🚆 Perugia and Assisi stations, 7 km (4 miles) and 4 km (2 miles), Foligno–Terontola line.
🚌 ℹ Piazza Cavour 8, Comune: 075 988 571.

It is worth taking the time to travel the 6 km (4 miles) along the Assisi road from Torgiano, in order to visit the village of Bettona. Apart from offering lovely views over the surrounding countryside, Bettona is unusual historically: it is among the extremely rare centres of culture of Etruscan origin found to the east of the River Tiber. Evidence of Etruscan beginnings is clear from the huge blocks of stone set into the medieval walls.

Significant sections of the walls remain, dating from the 4th century BC and typically Etruscan in design. The best example is the 40-m (131-ft) section at the northwestern corner; the other sections are of medieval origin, but rest on an Etruscan base. The entire circuit of the outer walls can be explored on foot.

Bettona has largely kept its medieval feel. It is home to works of art which some have attributed to the school of Perugino, while others believe they are the work of the master himself. The first is a processional banner with a *Madonna and Child and St Anne*. Until recently, it was kept with other important

St Anthony, by Perugino

Bettona's village wall, with Etruscan and medieval stonework

works in the church of Santa Maria Maggiore, erected in the 13th century but later rebuilt. Today, the work is on display in the **Pinacoteca Comunale**, a good art collection housed in the Palazzo del Podestà, on Piazza Cavour.

The gallery also has a *St Anthony of Padua* by Perugino, an *Adoration of the Shepherds* by Dono Doni (a masterpiece from 1543, once kept in the church of San Crispolto), and other works of importance by Jacopo Siculo, Niccolò Alunno, Tiberio d'Assisi and Fiorenzo di Lorenzo.

🏛 **Pinacoteca Comunale**
Palazzo del Podestà, Piazza Cavour 3. *Tel* 075 987 306.
⏰ *Mar–May, Sep, Oct: 10:30am–1pm, 2–6pm daily; Jun–Aug: 10:30am–1pm, 3–7pm daily; Nov–Feb: 10:30am–1pm, 2:30–5pm Tue–Sun.* ● *1 Jan, 25 Dec.* 📷

A work by Niccolò Alunno, in the Pinacoteca in Bettona

Deruta ⑬

Perugia. **Road Map** C4.
🏠 *7,900.* 🚌 ℹ *Pro Loco, Piazza dei Consoli 4, 075 971 15 59.*

Heading out of Torgiano along road 3bis, you soon reach Deruta, just 6 km (4 miles) south. On a knoll overlooking the Tiber valley, Deruta has been inhabited since Neolithic times, and still bears traces of its history in part of the walls and in the three arches that give access to the old centre. The town's name may derive from the fact that it has been destroyed ("distrutta") several times.

The heart of Deruta is Piazza dei Consoli where, as in most medieval settlements, all the chief religious and civic monuments stand.

THE CERAMICS OF THE TIBER

Umbria is famous all over the world for its ceramic production. Between the 15th and 16th centuries some extraordinary ceramicists emerged, including the locally born Giacomo Mancini and

Decorating a plate by hand

Francesco Urbini. Even today, ceramics manufacture is one of the most important aspects of the local economy for many towns along the Val Tiberina, and particularly in Deruta, which is full of workshops where craftsmen can be seen at work, and Gubbio. It is not just by chance that the vast majority of the main production centres for ceramics should have emerged and are still found along the Tiber: this is due to the fact that there is a greater availability of clay, malleable and at the same time fire-resistant, in the area, as well as the silica needed for the glazes.

Palazzo dei Consoli, housing the town hall and also the excellent Pinacoteca (art gallery), is here, as well as the Romanesque-Gothic church of **San Francesco**.

Residing in the former monastery of San Francesco, next door to the church, is the **Museo Regionale della Ceramica**, which highlights the importance of ceramics in Deruta. The production of jars, plates and other everyday items started in the Middle Ages and is documented in perhaps the most important museum of its kind in the region. On the ground floor, room 5 is of most interest, with pieces of ancient pottery; on the first floor are fragments from the floor in the church of San Francesco. On the second floor are more valuable pieces, among them a series of Renaissance plates including one depicting the

myth of Pyramus and Thisbe, from the late 16th century.

The production of ceramics is still a thriving industry in the town, and there are many workshops making and selling majolica pieces. Pottery is also the main attraction at the church of the **Madonna dei Bagni** (1657), 2 km (1 mile) south of Deruta. Its walls are covered in old *ex votos* made of Deruta pottery.

🏛 **Museo Regionale della Ceramica**
Largo San Francesco. *Tel* 075 971 10 00. ⏰ *Apr–Jun: 10:30am–1pm, 3–6pm daily; Jul–Sep: 10am–1pm, 3:30–7pm daily; Oct–Mar: 10:30am–1pm, 2:30–5pm Wed–Mon.* ● *1 Jan, 25 Dec.* ♿

⛪ **Madonna dei Bagni**
SS E45, exit Casalina.
Tel 075 973 455.
⏰ *summer: 8am–12:30pm, 2:30–7pm; winter: 8am–12:30pm, 3:30–6:30pm.* ♿

The fertile Umbrian countryside near Deruta

Perugia ⑭

Now with almost 160,000 inhabitants, Perugia has always been the largest city in Umbria. The historic centre of the city has a medieval appearance but is based on an Etruscan layout. The old city occupies a strategic position on a hill dominating the Tiber valley, while the modern city, with flourishing clothing and food industries, developed down below. The Etruscans settled *Perusia* in the 5th century BC or earlier, and it was conquered by the Romans in 309 BC. Perugia saw its greatest splendour in the 13th and 14th centuries, after which civil strife undermined the city's stability; it came under the jurisdiction of the papacy in 1531. Modern Perugia has a distinctly young, cosmopolitan and artistic population and outlook that sets it apart from other cities in the region. It has a thriving Università per Stranieri (University for Foreigners), and hosts Italy's top jazz festival, Umbria Jazz *(see p33)*.

Porta Marzia, set into the eastern bastion of the Rocca

Exploring Perugia

Visitors arriving by car are advised to leave their vehicle in the underground car park at Piazzale Partigiani, and from here to take the escalators, which take about ten minutes to reach the historic centre, passing by the ruins of the Rocca Paolina and emerging in Piazza Italia.

🏛 Rocca Paolina and Porta Marzia

Built in 1543 and virtually destroyed in 1860, this fortress is a

Embossed bronze plate

symbol of papal domination over Perugia. It was built on the orders of Pope Paul III Farnese, who sacked the city in 1540 and annexed it to the Church. Construction of the fortress was entrusted to Antonio da Sangallo, the great exponent of military architecture of the age. To make way for the Rocca, many other buildings were razed. This only increased the hatred of the people of Perugia towards the edifice, which was destroyed as soon as the city gained independence from the pope in the mid-1800s. The gap created was filled with Piazza Italia.

Parts of the fortress survive, including the Porta Marzia, an astonishing Etruscan archway which Sangallo liked so much that he incorporated it into the wall of his own building. Beneath the archway is the entrance to the bizarre Via Baglioni Sotterranea, a medieval street once buried beneath the Rocca Paolina.

🏛 Museo Archeologico Nazionale dell'Umbria

Piazza G Bruno. **Tel** *075 572 7141.*
◯ *8:30am–7:30pm Tue–Sun, 10am–7:30pm Mon (ticket office closes 6:30pm).* ◯ *1 Jan, 1 May, 25 Dec.* 🎫 🚻 ♿ *partial.*

Along Corso Cavour is the Church of San Domenico and its attached monastery, now home to the Museo Archeologico. The collection underwent a major renovation and there is now much more to see than the original Etruscan and Roman finds. The Carri Etruschi di Castel San Marino is a particularly fine exhibit of 6th century BC bronze chariots. Another must-see is the Cippus Perusinus, an Etruscan boundary stone which bears one of the longest inscriptions in Etruscan ever found.

PERUGIA TOWN CENTRE

🏛 San Domenico

Piazza G Bruno. *Tel 075 572 7141.*
◯ *8am–noon, 4pm–dusk daily.* 🎨
♿ 🚻 *Sat, Sun am; 075 573 1635.*

This huge church was built in the 14th century, to a design reminiscent of the Florentine churches of Santa Croce and Santa Maria Novella. It was

VISITORS' CHECKLIST

Road Map C3. 🏠 *158,000.* 🚉
Cortona–Foligno & Rome–Perugia lines, 892021; FCU line, 075 575 401. 🚌 *APM, 800 512 141.* ℹ
Piazza Matteotti 18, 075 573 6458.

elevated site, there were underground passages. These rooms were used for burial first by the Etruscans and then by the Romans, before being converted into a building dating from the early Christian era (6th century AD).

San Pietro is strikingly original, particularly in its wonderfully sumptuous decoration, which is more reminiscent of the Venetian than the local tradition. There are numerous works of several notable artists, including Perugino, Guercino, Guido Reni and Sassoferrato.

An impressive amount of the original Romanesque church survives, including the partially frescoed façade. The exuberant decoration inside is late Renaissance, and includes cycles of large paintings reminiscent of those done by Tintoretto. There is also a painted coffered ceiling and wonderful wooden choir stalls, the work of various artists in the 16th century. The vault is frescoed with *Stories from the Old Testament*. In the sacristy are five small canvases by Perugino depicting the saints. Visitors should ask the sacristan for permission to view the artworks.

🏛 San Pietro

Borgo XX Giugno. *Tel 075 337 53.*
◯ *8am–12:30pm Mon–Fri (also 3–6pm Tue & Thu).*

Further along Via Cavour, beyond Porta San Pietro (14th–15th centuries, built with some help from Agostino di Duccio), is one of the oldest religious buildings in Perugia, the Benedictine church of San Pietro. The church was founded in the 10th century, but there is some evidence to suggest that, in this slightly

The 16th-century entrance to the church of San Pietro

Perugia: Palazzo dei Priori

Piazza IV Novembre is home to two of the most important monuments in Perugia, the Palazzo dei Priori and the Fontana Maggiore. The imposing palazzo, topped by crenellations, was built to hold the town council's administrative offices, and was constructed in stages between 1293 and 1443, during an era of great splendour in the city. Though sombre outside, this is one of the most impressive medieval buildings in Italy, with truly gorgeous interiors. The palazzo is, in fact, composed of several buildings which face onto either Corso Vannucci or the piazza. These house four separate visitors' attractions, including the splendid Galleria Nazionale dell'Umbria (see pp88–9).

Il Collegio della Mercanzia is a room on the ground floor of the palazzo which was placed at the disposal of the Merchants' Guild in 1390, for meetings. The ceiling and walls are lined with inlaid wood and date from the middle of the 15th century.

Belfry

The Guild of Money-Changers acquired the right to establish its headquarters in the Palazzo dei Priori between 1452 and 1457.

The Arco dei Priori marks the start of Via dei Priori, which, it is said, flowed with rivers of blood as a result of civil strife during the Middle Ages.

★ **Collegio del Cambio**
In the Sala dell'Udienza of the Collegio del Cambio (1452–7), where money-changers operated, there is a cycle of frescoes by Perugino, painted from 1496 to 1500. The iconography brings together religious themes and figures with secular ones, a hallmark of Renaissance Humanism.

★ **Portale delle Arti**
Framed by rounded arches, the doorway dates from 1346 and is adorned with sculptures and reliefs representing vices and virtues, as well as symbolic animals.

★ **Sala dei Notari**
The lawyers' meeting hall, with its magnificent vaulting, is one of the oldest parts of the palazzo, dating from the late 1290s. The rich decoration includes frescoes by local artists, dating from the same period.

STAR FEATURES

★ Sala dei Notari

★ Portale delle Arti

★ Collegio del Cambio

VISITORS' CHECKLIST

Piazza IV Novembre. **Sala dei Notari Tel** 075 577 23 39. ☐ 9am–1pm, 3–7pm Tue–Sun. **Collegio della Mercanzia Tel** 075 573 03 66. ☐ Mar–Oct, 20 Dec–6 Jan: 9am–1pm, 2:30–5:30pm Tue–Sat, 9am–1pm Sun & pub hols; Nov–Feb: 8am–2pm Tue, Thu, Fri, 8am–4:30pm Wed, Sat, 9am–1pm Sun & pub hols. 🎫 combined ticket with Collegio del Cambio. 🎫 **Collegio del Cambio Tel** 075 572 85 99. ☐ 9am–12:30pm, 2:30–5:30pm Mon–Sat, 9am–1pm Sun & pub hols. 🎫 combined ticket with Collegio della Mercanzia. ♿ 🚫 all sites: 1 Jan, 1 May, 25 Dec (Collegio del Cambio also Mon pm Nov–15 Mar).

A stone gryphon (a copy of the 1274 original), high above the entrance, is the symbol of Perugia.

The fan-shaped flight of steps in Piazza IV Novembre leads up to the Sala dei Notari.

Fontana Maggiore
This is a superb piece of work, featuring many exquisite bas-reliefs and sculptures by Nicola and Giovanni Pisano.

THE FONTANA MAGGIORE

Built from 1275 to 1278, and recently restored, this fountain was designed by a monk called Fra Bevignate, and decorated by Nicola Pisano and his son Giovanni. It is both a magnificent architectural creation (one of Italy's top Romanesque monuments) and a complex feat of hydraulic engineering. It was thanks to the engineer Boninsegna da Venezia that waters from a new aqueduct from Monte Pacciano converged here.

Detail of the fountain

The fountain is built on three levels: two polygonal basins in marble, one above the other, with 25 and 24 sides respectively, and a third basin in bronze. The series of bas-reliefs is exceptional: on the lower basin are three consecutive cycles depicting episodes from the Old Testament, the Liberal Arts and the Labours of the Months. On the upper basin are 24 sculptures representing biblical figures (David, Moses, Solomon, Salome), saints, mythological figures or allegories from the history of the city, as well as the Perugian *condottiere* Ermanno di Sassoferrato, Capitano del Popolo in 1278.

Stylistically, all kinds of influences converge in the reliefs (including classical, Byzantine and medieval), making it difficult to attribute individual panels to one or other of the two artists.

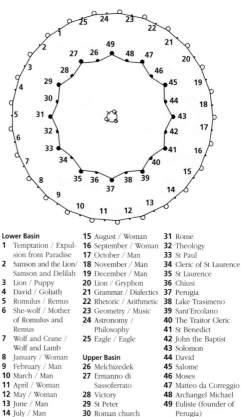

Lower Basin		
1 Temptation / Expulsion from Paradise	**15** August / Woman	**31** Rome
2 Samson and the Lion / Samson and Delilah	**16** September / Woman	**32** Theology
	17 October / Man	**33** St Paul
3 Lion / Puppy	**18** November / Man	**34** Cleric of St Laurence
4 David / Goliath	**19** December / Man	**35** St Laurence
5 Romulus / Remus	**20** Lion / Gryphon	**36** Chiusi
6 She-wolf / Mother of Romulus and Remus	**21** Grammar / Dialectics	**37** Perugia
	22 Rhetoric / Arithmetic	**38** Lake Trasimeno
	23 Geometry / Music	**39** Sant'Ercolano
7 Wolf and Crane / Wolf and Lamb	**24** Astronomy / Philosophy	**40** The Traitor Cleric
8 January / Woman	**25** Eagle / Eagle	**41** St Benedict
9 February / Man		**42** John the Baptist
10 March / Man	**Upper Basin**	**43** Solomon
11 April / Woman	**26** Melchizedek	**44** David
12 May / Woman	**27** Ermanno di Sassoferrato	**45** Salome
13 June / Man	**28** Victory	**46** Moses
14 July / Man	**29** St Peter	**47** Matteo da Correggio
	30 Roman church	**48** Archangel Michael
		49 Euliste (founder of Perugia)

Perugia: Galleria Nazionale dell'Umbria

This is the most important museum not only in Perugia but in Umbria as a whole, featuring works of art dating from the 13th to 19th centuries. Created partly out of Napoleon's seizure of works of art held by religious orders, the gallery was established in 1863. It was moved to the Palazzo dei Priori in 1879 and has been state-owned since 1918. A major renovation project has increased the number of rooms to 40 spread over two floors, mostly grouped to cover various eras, including the 15th-century Cappella dei Priori, which features some splendid Perugian scenes. While the emphasis is clearly on Umbrian art, Sienese masters are nevertheless dominant in the early rooms.

Donna alla Fonte (1278–81)
In Room 1 there are five statues which were originally part of a fountain, including the Donna alla Fonte, *by Tuscan Arnolfo di Cambio (1240–1302). There are also two bronzes of a griffin and a lion.*

★ St Anthony Polyptych (1459–68)
In this work by Piero della Francesca, on show in Room 11, innovative use of perspective blends with a structure and colours that are still medieval.

Room 6 is dedicated to the International Gothic style, of which Gentile da Fabriano (1370–1427) was one of the major Italian exponents.

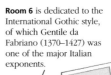

3rd Floor

16 · 17 · 18 · 19 · 15 · 14 · 9 · 8 · 13 · 11 · 10 · 12 · 7 · 5 · 6 · 4 · 20 · 21 · 1a · 1 · 2 · 3

2nd Floor

25 · 24 · 23 · 26 · 27 · 22 · 33 · 32 · 31 · 28 · 30 · 29 · 36 · 34

★ San Domenico of Fiesole Altarpiece (1437)
This work by Fra Angelico (1395–1455) is one of the major Renaissance masterpieces in the museum. Also known as the Guidalotti Polyptych, *it is displayed in Room 8.*

STAR FEATURES

★ St Anthony Polyptych

★ San Domenico of Fiesole Altarpiece

KEY

☐	6th and 7th centuries
▨	8th century
▨	13th and 14th centuries
☐	Late Gothic period
▨	Early Renaissance
☐	15th century
▨	Treasury and Decorative Arts
☐	Cappella dei Priori
▨	Renaissance masterpieces
☐	Perugian and Umbrian art
▨	Luigi Caratolli collection

To rooms 22–40

Entrance and ticket office

39   **40**

38

Room 15 displays this *Adoration of the Magi* by Perugino (1450–1523). There are also splendid paintings from the Umbrian school. More works by Perugino can be found in rooms 22–4, including the *Madonna della Consolazione*.

The duomo's Gothic doorway, the unfinished pulpit and papal statue

🔒 Duomo

Piazza Danti. *Tel 075 572 3832.* ◯ *7:30am–12:30pm, 4–7pm daily.* ♿

The duomo, dedicated to San Lorenzo, was built on the site of a 10th-century basilica. The first stone of the new building was laid in 1345, but the Black Death (1348) delayed progress for many years, with work starting again properly only in 1437. Even then, the façade was left unfinished.

The façade, which gives onto Piazza Danti, is undoubtedly of much less interest than the left-hand side of the duomo, which overlooks Piazza IV Novembre. This is covered in distinctive pink and white marble, and features an impressive monumental Gothic doorway, designed by Galeazzo Alessi in 1568. In a niche above the doorway is a cross, beneath which the Perugians symbolically laid down the keys to the city following their defeat by Pope Paul III Farnese in the Salt War of 1540. In contrast, a statue of Pope Julius III, sculpted by Vincenzo Danti in 1555, to the left of the doorway, was commissioned by the people of Perugia to celebrate the pope who had restored some communal liberty to the city. On the right is an unfinished, 15th-century

Detail from the cathedral

pulpit, from which St Bernardino of Siena preached to vast crowds of Perugians in the 1420s. The saint was so popular with Perugians that they built a church in his honour (*see pp90–91*).

Also on the side of the duomo that overlooks the piazza is a loggia with an arched portico, built for Braccio Fortebraccio, the celebrated condottiere from Montone, in 1423.

The interior is bare and solemn, unusual in Italy, being more reminiscent of the great churches of northern Europe. Inside is the Virgin's "wedding ring", housed in the Cappella del Sant'Anello and said to change colour according to who wears it. On the left, just past the entrance, is the Cappella di San Bernardino da Siena, home to one of the two major works of art in the building, a *Descent from the Cross* by Federico Barocci, dated 1567–9. The other is a masterpiece by Luca Signorelli, *Enthroned Madonna with Saints*, which was painted in 1484 and has been beautifully restored to show off its original brilliance.

Another restored feature worth seeing is the choir, featuring inlaid wooden stalls: the work of Domenico del Tasso and Giuliano da Maiano.

POSTMODERN PERUGIA

The quarter of Fontivegge is in the new part of Perugia, southwest of the historic centre, near the railway station. It stands out from the other quarters of the modern city because it was designed as a completely new district between 1982 and 1989 by the architect Aldo Rossi and his colleagues. It is one of the most successful examples of postmodern architecture in Italy, featuring buildings that are both futuristic and full of classical references (see

in particular the Palazzo della Regione, in Piazza Nuova), and also include elements from the past; a 17th-century fountain and a chimney from the old Perugina factory have both been incorporated into the new architectural context.

View of the Fontivegge quarter

🏛 Etruscan Well
Piazza Danti 18. **Tel** 075 573 3669.
⏰ 10am–1:30pm, 2:30–6pm (Nov–Mar: 11am–1:30pm, 2:30–5pm).
🚫 Mon (except in Apr & Aug), 1 Jan, 25 Dec. 🎟

The Etruscan Well (Pozzo Etrusco) in the basement of Palazzo Bourbon-Sorbello, next to the cathedral façade in Piazza Danti, is an astonishing feat of engineering: it was capable of providing a constant supply of water to the entire city. The well (the bottom of which is accessible) is partially covered in vast blocks of travertine, from which the original cover was also made. You can still see the furrows left by the ropes that the Etruscans used to pull the buckets of water to the surface.

Behind Piazza Danti is the district of Rione di Porta Sole, where the Rocca del Sole fortress was built in 1372. It was the largest fortification of its time, but was destroyed shortly after its completion.

🏛 Piazza Matteotti
This long square, which runs parallel to Corso Vannucci, is home to two notable 15th-century buildings. The first is **Palazzo del Capitano del Popolo** (1472–82), designed by the Lombard architects Gasparino di Antonio and Leone di Matteo, and the seat of the judiciary in the era of

the communes. Its traditional medieval town hall design has been embellished with Renaissance elements. The palazzo was originally built on three floors, but the third was demolished following the earthquake of 1741. Behind the porticoes alongside the palazzo is a 1930s' covered market, from where you can see the piazza foundations.

The other building of note is **Palazzo dell'Università Vecchia**, mostly from the same era as the Palazzo del Capitano del Popolo (the same Gasparino di Antonio collaborated in its construction); the building was made the seat of the university by Pope Sixtus IV in 1483.

🔒 San Severo
Piazza Raffaello. **Tel** 075 573 3864.
⏰ 10am–1:30pm, 2:30–6pm (Nov–Mar: 11am–1:30pm, 2:30–5pm).
🚫 Mon (except in Apr & Aug), 1 Jan, 25 Dec. 🎟 🔆

Following the narrow streets up through the Porta Sole quarter, you reach the church of San Severo, famous as the home of one of Raphael's earliest frescoes (1507–8), of the *Holy Trinity and Saints*. Perugino finished the work in 1521, adding the saints lower down on the same wall. Also look out for the 16th-century terracotta group of a Madonna and Child by an unknown Tuscan sculptor.

Justice, detail

The church is of ancient origin: it certainly existed in the 11th century, and the site was probably used for sacred buildings before that. Its current appearance dates from the mid-18th century.

🏛 Arch of Augustus
Piazza Fortebraccio.
A scenic descent signals the end of the Porta Sole quarter, marked by the splendid 3rd-century BC Arch of Augustus (Arco di Augusto). This civic gate is also known as the Etruscan Arch since it was, in fact, of Etruscan origin, and was later modified by the Romans. The still-legible inscription, "Augusta Perusia", was placed here by Octavius Caesar (later Emperor Augustus); having destroyed and then rebuilt the city, he renamed it after himself.

Façade of the Oratorio di San Bernardino

🔒 Oratorio di San Bernardino
Piazza San Francesco al Prato.
Tel 075 573 3957. ⏰ 8am–12:30pm, 3:30–5:30pm daily.
Passing under the Arco dei Priori, part of the palazzo of the same name (see pp86–7), and heading down Via dei Priori, you cross what was once a main road through medieval Perugia. Beyond the city walls, the street widens into a piazza with the church of **San Francesco al Prato**, built in the mid-13th century on a particularly subsidence-prone piece of ground; it is now partially ruined. To the left of the church is the small and elegant **Oratorio di San Bernardino** (1452), whose

fine multicoloured bas-reliefs on the façade make it a masterpiece of the Umbrian Renaissance. The sculptures, by Agostino di Duccio, are remarkable for the realism of the undulating lines and of the drapery.

Inside, in the first chapel on the left, are a 15th-century gonfalon (banner) showing the Madonna sheltering Perugia from the plague, by Benedetto Bonfigli, and the tomb of Braccio Fortebraccio da Montone. The altar was made from an ancient early Christian sarcophagus.

The early Christian church of Sant'Angelo

🪧 Borgo Sant'Angelo

Corso Garibaldi, running north from Piazza Fortebraccio, is the principal medieval street, along which the area of Borgo Sant'Angelo developed. Now the seat of Perugia's university, this district grew up around an Augustinian monastery and has the city's most important monastic

buildings, including the monastery of San Benedetto, the former hospital of the Collegio della Mercanzia, the convent of Santa Caterina and the monastery of Beata Colomba. It is in this last monastery that, according to popular tradition, St Francis met St Dominic in 1220.

At the end of the road, in the shelter of the walls and in a pretty setting, is the circular

church of **San Michele Arcangelo (Sant'Angelo)**, whose origins date back to the late 5th century. Thanks to excellent restoration work, which included the removal of Baroque additions, major parts of the original church are now visible, along with a 14th-century Gothic doorway. The interior is rich with frescoes, also 14th century.

🔒 San Michele Arcangelo
Via Sant'Angelo, Corso Garibaldi.
Tel 075 572 2624.
⏰ 9am–1pm, 3:30–6:30pm daily.

Environs

Around 7 km (4 miles) south-east of the city, along road 75bis, is one of the most interesting burial sites among many in the area: the **Ipogeo dei Volumni**. Built into the side of a hill, it consists of a great tomb chamber where, in the 2nd century BC, the nobles of the Etruscan Velimna family were buried. Their Latin name of Volumni gives its name to their mausoleum.

A festival stage just before a concert

UMBRIA JAZZ

First held in 1973, Umbria Jazz is – the experts say – Europe's top jazz festival. After the first concerts, held in different towns through-out the region, the event went into crisis and was suspended. The festival was then transferred to Perugia, where it now takes place every July, and enjoys a fame and success second only to the famous Montreal festival. Concerts take place in different venues: from fields and open-air sites (where events are generally free) to the Morlacchi and Pavone theatres, for which audiences buy tickets. Every evening, stretched out on the grass, thousands of young people listen to music for free: a flashback to a time when Umbria Jazz was briefly the setting for mass youth gatherings. Historic open-air venues include the Giardini del Frontone, used since 1984 for the jazz festival's most important evening concerts. The gardens have hosted some of the most historic events, from Stan Getz to the get-together between John Scofield and Pat Metheny, from Bobby McFerrin to Phil Woods and Dizzy Gillespie hugging each other in the rain. As well as the main festival there are other events, including a jazz festival at Orvieto (Umbria Jazz Winter), and a gospel and soul festival (at Terni, at Easter). (www.umbriajazz.it)

Since 1937, another annual event has been staged in Perugia: the Sagra Musicale Umbra, a festival of sacred music, draws artists from all over the world in September.

Inside the burial chamber of the Ipogeo dei Volumni

Lake Trasimeno ⓯

The fourth largest lake in Italy, Lake Trasimeno covers an area of 126 sq km (48 sq miles). The perimeter is almost 60 km (37 miles) long, and the lake lies at the fortified heart of medieval Umbria. No matter where you gaze among the low hills that surround the lake, you will inevitably catch sight of a castle, a tower or a fortified village. In fact, Lake Trasimeno has been the scene of battles since antiquity, and it was on these shores that Hannibal defeated the Romans on 21 June 217 BC. Although the water levels rise and fall, and the lake periodically floods the surrounding land, the area has always been inhabited. Over the centuries villages grew up on the shores of the lake, and the islands became home to monasteries and convents, later active fishing communities.

★ Isola Maggiore
Briefly a refuge for St Francis, this island is inhabited by fishermen who still stretch out their nets to dry between the churches of Sant'Angelo and San Salvatore.

Tuoro sul Trasimeno
Near the town are the battle sites where the Carthaginians fought the Romans. A historical-archaeological trail of the battle has been created, with maps and information points along the route. There is a modern sculpture park, the Campo del Sole, at Lido di Tuoro.

Vernazzano

Terontola   Tuoro

Borghetto

Ferretto

BOSCO DEL FERRETTO

Piana

Castiglione del Lago

STAR SIGHTS

★ Isola Maggiore

★ Isola Polvese

Borghetto is a small village among olive groves, with a 16th-century parish church, San Martino.

Pucciarelli

Panicarola

0 kilometres   5

0 miles   5

Castiglione del Lago
This is the main town on the shores of Lake Trasimeno, a departure point for ferries (see p94).

Isola Minore is private and the smallest of the three islands.

The southern shores are characterized, more so than the others, by marshy terrain, fringed with reed beds.

Passignano sul Trasimeno

This town of Etruscan origin is built on a chalk promontory. The most important monument in the town is the church of San Cristoforo, with 15th-century frescoes.

Magione is a town in the hills behind the most populated stretch of shore, and moderately developed in terms of tourism. There is a castle here, the Castello dei Cavalieri di Malta, and, at nearby San Feliciano, a Museo della Pesca (Museum of Fishing).

★ **Isola Polvese**
This is the largest island on the lake. The Province of Perugia has created an oasis for wildlife here, among gardens and parks. The ruins of the monastery of San Secondo and a 15th-century castle can also be seen.

La Valle is the name given to this stretch of lake, where there are vast reed beds and an area of protected fish-breeding grounds.

Passignano sul Trasimeno

Torricella

Magione

Monte del Lago

San Feliciano

San Savino

Sant'Arcangelo

Monte Buono

KEY

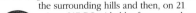

🚢	Ferry embarkation point
🔆	Place of natural beauty
----	Ferry route

The Badia di Sant'Arcangelo, in a lovely setting by the lake, is a castle of medieval origin with a Romanesque church.

The Castello di Montalera is one of many fortified sites along the lake shore. It was at one time the property of the Baglioni family.

THE BATTLE OF LAKE TRASIMENO

After defeating the Romans at the battles of Ticino and Trebbia, Hannibal was informed that his adversaries, led by Caius Flaminius, were directing part of the Roman army towards Lake Trasimeno. The Carthaginian leader distributed his men around the surrounding hills and then, on 21 June 217 BC, aided by foggy weather, he gave the order to attack the enemy forces. Trapped between the lake and the hills, the Roman soldiers suffered a crushing defeat: Hannibal lost 1,500 men, compared with the Romans' 15,000.

Portrait of Hannibal

View across Lake Trasimeno from Castiglione

Castiglione del Lago ⑯

Perugia. **Road Map** B3.
🏛 14,000. 🚆 Florence–Rome line.
📧 ℹ Piazza Mazzini 10, 075 965 2484. 🎏 Festa degli Aquiloni, Apr.

The town of Castiglione del Lago occupies a promontory which dominates the western shore of Lake Trasimeno, and which, during floods, used to be cut off from the surrounding area, in effect becoming an island.

The area was fortified by both the Etruscans and the Romans because of its strategic position. Fought over by Perugia and by the Tuscans, the site was often destroyed and rebuilt. It was following the reconstruction ordered by Frederick II Hohenstaufen in the 13th century that the place acquired the name Castello del Leone, from which its current name derives.

In the 16th century, the village was given by the papacy to the della Corgna family, who built the town's most important building, the **Palazzo della Corgna**. It may have been designed by Galeazzo Alessi and the frescoes were done by Pomarancio.

Linked to the palazzo by a covered walkway, backing on to the lake and with a fine view, is the **Rocca del Leone**, an interesting example of medieval military architecture. In the 16th century it was considered to be one of the most impregnable fortresses in Italy. From the palazzo,

the street leads towards the real heart of the town, which is centred around Piazza Mazzini. Here, the church of **Santa Maria Maddalena** is worth a visit: the building is Neo-Classical, built by Giovanni Caproni from 1836, but houses a 16th-century altarpiece (*Madonna and Child, St Anthony Abbot and St Mary Magdalene*). This was formerly identified as a youthful work by Raphael, but is now known to be by Eusebio da San Giorgio, one of Perugino's circle.

Fresco by Pomarancio, Palazzo Della Corgna

🏛 **Palazzo della Corgna and Rocca del Leone**
Piazza Gramsci. **Tel** 075 951 099.
🕐 Daily: Apr & May: 9:30am–1pm, 3:30–7pm; Jun–Aug: 10am–1:30pm, 4–7:30pm; Sep: 9:30am–1:30pm, 3:30–7pm; Oct: 9:30am–1pm, 2:30–6pm. Sat & Sun: Nov–Feb: 9:30am–4:30pm; Mar: 9:30am–1pm, 2:30–6pm (also open the day before public hols). 🚫 1 Jan, 25 Dec. 📷

🏛 **Santa Maria Maddalena**
Via Vittorio Emanuele.
Tel 075 951 159.

Città della Pieve ⑰

Perugia. **Road Map** A4.
🏛 7,000. 🚆 Chiusi–Chianciano, 10 km (6 miles), Florence–Rome line.
📧 ℹ Piazza Matteotti 0578 299 375. 🎏 Palio dei Terzieri, Aug.
www.cittadellapieve.org

The fame of Città della Pieve, on the Tuscan border, is due primarily to the fact that it was the birthplace of the great Renaissance painter Pietro Vannucci. Known as Perugino (1450–1523) and famous in his own right, he also taught the young Raphael. Città della Pieve is worth a visit above all because it houses several major works by this artist.

Adoration of the Magi, Perugino, detail

An Etruscan colony of Chiusi (in nearby Tuscany), and later Roman, Città della Pieve suffered frequently from barbarian invasions. It finally developed as a fortified town in about 1000, around the church of Santi Gervasio e Protasio. The distinctive red coloration is due to the use of bricks – there was no stone available locally.

Città della Pieve is known for its very narrow streets, including what some claim to be the narrowest in Italy – vicolo Baciadonne, which is just 80 cm (31 in) wide. The central Piazza del Plebiscito is home to **Palazzo della Corgna** (with 16th-century frescoes by Pomarancio), the Biblioteca Comunale (library) and, most importantly, the cathedral of **Santi Gervasio e Protasio**. This was rebuilt on the site of the original parish church, perhaps in the 8th century, and then remodelled and restored at intervals between the 12th and 17th centuries. Inside, among various precious works of art (by Domenico Alfani, Giannicola di Paolo and Pomarancio), there are two paintings by Perugino – a *Baptism of Christ* and a *Madonna and Child and Saints Peter, Paul, Gervasio and Protasio*.

In the church of **Santa Maria dei Servi** (included in the ticket for Palazzo della Corgna), just south of the centre, there were once some spendid frescoes by Perugino; only a *Deposition* survives, dating from 1517. Visitors will find a far more beautiful fresco by Perugino in the church of **Santa Maria dei Bianchi**, in Corso Vannucci, just off Piazza del Plebiscito. This depicts the *Adoration of the Magi* (1504), and is perhaps the best of all the works by Perugino found in his native city; the scene includes the view from Città della Pieve towards Lake Trasimeno, as well as a party of elegant Renaissance figures.

Southern Lake Trasimeno ⑱

Self portrait by Perugino

In the mountains that rise to the south of Lake Trasimeno lies a series of villages where art and history have always played an important role. The painter Pietro Vannucci, better known as Perugino, was born and worked here. This tour partly retraces the steps of the great artist and partly seeks out small medieval hill towns, among the great treasures of Umbria.

VISITORS' CHECKLIST

Piazza Mazzini 10, Castiglione del Lago, 075 965 2484.
Length of tour: 55 km (34 miles). **Time needed:** one day. **Stopping-off points:** in villages along the route.

Corciano ⑤
Almost intact 13th-century walls, protected by tall towers and a castle, extend for a kilometre around this pretty village. Corciano has both Etruscan and Roman origins, as do other villages on this tour.

Panicale ②
This fortified town is perched on a rocky spur. Perugino's *Martyrdom of St Sebastian* (1505) can be seen in the church of San Sebastiano.

Paciano ①
Encircled by walls and in a lovely hilly setting of woods and olive groves, this is one of the best-preserved of the medieval villages in the area.

Lake Trasimeno

Magione

PERUGIA

Citta della Pieve

↓ *ORVIETO*

Tavernelle ③
Just north of this village is the Santuario della Madonna di Mongiovino, a 16th-century church with frescoes from the same period.

Fontignano ④
This medieval village, built on a hillside, was where Perugino died in 1523. He left his last work of art here: a *Madonna and Child* in the church of the Annunziata.

KEY

 Tour route

Other roads

0 kilometres 5

0 miles 5

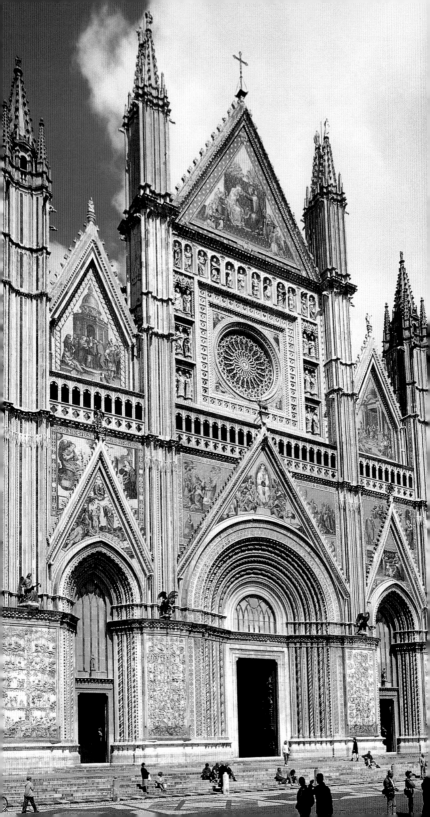

SOUTHERN UMBRIA

*T*he countryside of Southern Umbria is very hilly, rising to the peaks of the Monti Sibillini towards the eastern fringes. Rocks and water are constant features of the landscape, as at the spectacular Cascata delle Marmore and the springs of Clitunno. Most of the towns are medieval in appearance, but were once part of the Etruscan world. Even the language spoken has affinities with Tuscan.

In the past, this part of the region was dominated by the Duchy of Spoleto, whose lands were regarded by geographers as the real heart of Umbria until the 16th century. Also part of this territory, culturally and politically, were Todi, of ancient Italic and Etruscan origin, and the Roman town of Narni, while Orvieto was viewed as an independent commune.

Despite the vicissitudes of history, here, as in the rest of Umbria, the sense of local identity derived from a long-standing communal spirit is strong and heartfelt. Every town has its own artistic and historical treasures, and each cherishes and takes pride in its own ancient past, manifested in numerous feast days and secular festivals. Southern Umbria's cultural calendar, which includes the Festival di Spoleto and events in Orvieto and Terni, is varied and popular, and draws people from all over the world.

Hills, and especially water, feature large in the natural landscape of southern Umbria. The River Tiber forms the Lago di Corbara, while the River Nera flows along the edge of the splendid valley known as the Valnerina. In the west, pale tufa soil and the high ridges of Orvieto signal the land of the Etruscans. The wilder peaks of the Apennines, on the other hand, occupy the south-eastern corner of the region. Here, Cascia, Piediluco and Norcia are the last towns before the steep rise towards the windswept plateaux of Castelluccio, just a stone's throw from Le Marche and Lazio.

The cultural and gastronomic traditions of this corner of Italy, although similar in many ways to those of the neighbouring regions, are still quite individual, successfully uniting flavours and ideas from different areas. Norcia, in the Valnerina, is a byword for good food all over Italy.

Detail of the *Coronation of the Virgin*, by Filippo Lippi (1467), apse of Spoleto cathedral

◁ **The dazzling and colourful façade of Orvieto's cathedral**

Exploring Southern Umbria

Orvieto, Todi, Terni, Spoleto: a string of historical towns unravels from east to west in Southern Umbria. In between is fertile countryside, with farmhouses and cultivated fields, and important stretches of river, including the lower course of the River Tiber and the River Nera. There are also thermal springs and archaeological areas, as well as nature reserves, chief of which is the spectacular national park of the Monti Sibillini, superb territory for walking, mountain-biking and hang-gliding.

Tourists on horseback in the centre of Spello

GETTING AROUND

The Autostrada del Sole (A1) motorway skirts the western side of Southern Umbria, with exits at Orvieto and at Orte, from where Superstrada 204 runs east towards Terni. The other two principal artery routes are, as for Northern Umbria, state roads 3 and 3bis, which serve Spoleto and Todi respectively and divide the region from north to south. The main railway line connects Rome to Ancona, passing through various Umbrian towns en route. There is also a private line linking Perugia and Terni. Most smaller villages are linked by road.

SIGHTS AT A GLANCE

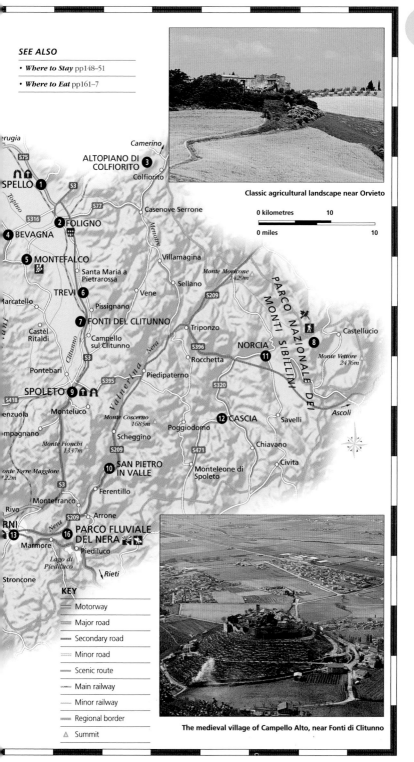

Classic agricultural landscape near Orvieto

0 kilometres   10

0 miles   10

erugia

SPELLO **1**

Camerino

ALTOPIANO DI COLFIORITO **3**

Colfiorito

2 FOLIGNO

4 BEVAGNA

Casenove Serrone

Villamagina

5 MONTEFALCO

Santa Maria a Pietrarossa

Monte Moricone
1429m

TREVI **6**

Vene

Sellano

Marcatello

Pissignano

7 FONTI DEL CLITUNNO

Triponzo

Castèl
Ritaldi

Campello
sul Clitunno

NORCIA **11**

Castelluccio

Rocchetta

Monte Vettore
2476m

Pontebari

Piedipaterno

SPOLETO **9**

enzuola

Monteluco

Monte Coscerno
1685m

Ascoli

mpagnano

Scheggino

12 CASCIA

Savelli

Monte Fionchi
1337m

Poggiodomo

Chiavano

onte Torre Maggiore
22m

10 SAN PIETRO IN VALLE

Monteleone di
Spoleto

Civita

Ferentillo

Rivo

Montefranco

Arrone

RNI **13**

16 PARCO FLUVIALE DEL NERA

Marmore

Piediluco

Lago di
Piediluco

Rieti

Stroncone

PARCO NAZIONALE DEI MONTI SIBILLINI **8**

KEY

	Motorway
	Major road
	Secondary road
	Minor road
	Scenic route
	Main railway
	Minor railway
	Regional border
△	Summit

The medieval village of Campello Alto, near Fonti di Clitunno

Spello ❶

Spello lies on a hillside in the shadow of Monte
Subasio and is built, like nearby Assisi, out of
the same pink stone. A settlement founded here
by the Umbri grew in size under the Romans,
when it was known as Hispellum. The town walls,
pierced by six gates, were built in the Augustan
era. Later, the town was sacked by the Lombards,
who made it part of the Duchy of Spoleto, and
then, in 1238, crushed again by Frederick II. In
1389, by now a papal possession, Spello was
given to the Baglioni family as a feudal estate.
They ruled until the mid-16th century, after
which Spello followed the fortunes of the rest
of the region. The evident reminders of the
town's past make it a fascinating place today.

*Dispute in the
Temple, detail*

**Porta Consolare, one of the
Roman gateways to the town**

Exploring Spello

From Piazza Kennedy, access
to the walled town is through
Porta Consolare, a well-
preserved Roman gateway.
Heading north into the centre,
Piazza della Repubblica marks
the real centre of Spello.

🔒 Santa Maria Maggiore
Piazza Matteotti.
Completed in 1285, this fine
church is the most important

monument in Spello. Its
façade was reconstructed,
using the original materials,
in the 17th century.

The single-nave church
owes its fame to the presence
of the Cappella Baglioni,
where there is a series of
frescoes by Pinturicchio,
perhaps the finest ever done
by the artist. Painted from
1500–1501, the frescoes
depict the *Four Sibyls* (on the
vault) and *Scenes from the Life
of Christ* (on the walls). The
most important frescoes are
an *Annunciation* (under
which hangs a self-portrait of
Pinturicchio), an *Adoration
of the Magi* and a *Dispute in
the Temple*. The floor of the
chapel was made of majolica
tiles from Deruta. More
Pinturicchio frescoes can be
found in the Cappella del
Sacramento, reached from the
left transept. In the right
transept is the Cappella del
Sepolcro, which at one time
housed the town art gallery.
Also of interest are a pulpit in
sandstone and a tabernacle
on the high altar.

🏛 Pinacoteca Civica
Piazza Matteotti 10.
Tel *0742 301 497.*
⬜ *Apr–Sep: 10:30am–
1pm, 3–6:30pm Tue–Sun;
Oct–Mar: 10:30am–noon,
3–5pm Tue–Sun.*
Since 1994 the civic
art gallery has been
housed in the Palaz-
zo dei Canonici (15th
century), to the right
of Santa Maria
Maggiore. Among
the varied works in
the collection,
one highlight is a
splendid *Wooden Madonna*
dating from around 1240,
brightly coloured and yet
serene and stately. Also of
note are several polyptychs
of the 14th and 15th centuries
and other significant works of
the local school.

🔒 Sant'Andrea
Via Cavour.
Near the Pinacoteca, the
church of Sant'Andrea (13th
century) has a rather gloomy
interior; and yet in the right
transept is a superb fresco by
Pinturichio of the *Madonna
and Child with Saints*. In the
left transept look out for the
mummified body of Andrea
Caccioli, one of the first
followers of St Francis.

🏤 Piazza della Repubblica
In this not particularly notable
square at the end of Via
Cavour is the 13th-century
Palazzo Comunale (now
restored), which contains the
Library and the Town Archive.

Heading north along Via
Garibaldi, you pass **Palazzo
Cruciani**, seat of the town
council, and then the 12th-
century church of **San
Lorenzo**, an architectural
hotch-potch. Of interest
inside is the carved wooden
pulpit, the work of Francesco
Costantini (1600).

🏛 Porta Venere
Via Torri di Properzio.
A short detour west from
Piazza della Repubblica takes
you to Porta Venere, a Roman
gateway flanked by two
imposing 12-sided towers
dating from the Middle Ages.
The gate, heavily restored
over the centuries, dates from

View of the town of Spello, on a hillside above the Valle Umbra

Roman Porta Venere, with its two characteristic 12-sided towers

the Augustan era: the structure that you see today originally had a double curtain giving way to an internal courtyard. The gate offers good views over the surrounding countryside.

🏛 Porta dell'Arce
Via Arco Romano.
One of the oldest entrances to the town, this gate is an example of how Roman buildings were integrated into the medieval fortifications. Nearby is the terrace of the Belvedere, from which the Topino valley, as well as the outline of Assisi's Santa Maria degli Angeli, can be admired.

🏛 San Claudio
Via Fontevecchia.
From the Belvedere, you can descend to the plain via the narrow Via dei Cappuccini and then the long Via Fontevecchia. Here, you'll find the delightful church of San Claudio, dating from the 12th century. Perhaps Spello's most interesting church architecturally, it has retained intact its Romanesque decoration and layout. The simple façade is topped by the original belfry.

🏛 Roman Ruins
Via Centrale Umbra.
The Roman city was built at a lower level than the medieval town, which was constructed more defensively on the hill. The amphitheatre, near the church of San Claudio on the main road to Foligno, dates from the 1st century AD, but little survives.

A kilometre from Spello towards Perugia is **Villa Fidelia**, once at the centre of the Roman city, and where an epigraph, known as the "Rescritto di Costantino" (rescript of Constantine), was found in 1733. According to this ordinance, the great emperor, in the years between 324 and 337 AD, authorized the Umbrians to hold their celebrations at Spello and not in Orvieto.

The Romanesque façade of San Claudio

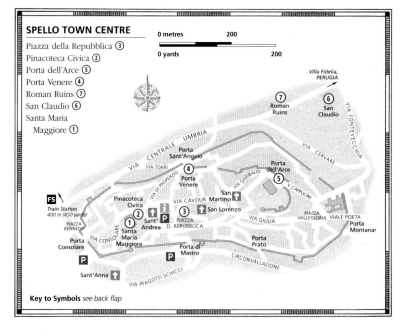

SPELLO TOWN CENTRE

Piazza della Repubblica ③
Pinacoteca Civica ②
Porta dell'Arce ⑤
Porta Venere ④
Roman Ruins ⑦
San Claudio ⑥
Santa Maria
  Maggiore ①

0 metres   200
0 yards   200

Key to Symbols see back flap

Foligno's Piazza della Repubblica with the cathedral's south façade

Foligno ❷

Perugia. **Road Map** D4. 🏠 56,000.
FS *Rome–Ancona line.* 🚌
i *Corso Cavour 126, 0742 354
459.* 🎪 *Giostra della Quintana,
2nd Sun in Sep.*

The town of Foligno, of
Roman origin, lies in the
plain of the river Topino,
which skirts its
northern edge.
One of the few
Umbrian towns
to be built on
flat land,
Foligno was
sited at the
crossroads of
two commercial
roads of great
importance: the
Via Flaminia and the road
from Perugia to Assisi.

A 15th-century fresco in
Foligno's Palazzo Trinci

The principal manufacturing
and commercial centre in the
region, with the exception
perhaps of Perugia, Foligno
is a lively, dynamic city.
Because of its location, the
city has been able to sprawl
out onto the plain, helped by
the destruction of the 14th-
century walls after the
unification of Italy. While the
original oval layout can still
be discerned, the historic
centre features a mix of old
and modern architecture.

The railway station, east
of the centre, is both a good
point of reference and a good
place from which to start a
tour. From here, passing by
streets where walls once
stood, you rapidly reach the
historic centre along Via
Ottaviani and Via Umberto I.
Halfway along Via Umberto I

is Via Piermarini, named after
the famous Foligno architect
who designed La Scala opera
house in Milan. Opposite
is the entrance to Via dei
Monasteri, where you'll find
the **monastery of Sant'Anna**.
While still in possession of
several precious works of
art, the monastery is most
famous as the former home
(until 1798)
of Raphael's
celebrated
*Madonna di
Foligno*,
removed by
Napoleon's men
and now on
display in the
Vatican museum
in Rome.

Back on Via
Umberto I, at the corner with
Via Garibaldi is the little brick
church of the **Nunziatella**
(late 15th century), of interest
to visitors because of two
works by Perugino. Above
the right-hand altar is a
Baptism of Jesus and, in the
lunette, a *God the Father*.
Both works date from 1507.

From here it is just a short
distance to the central **Piazza
della Repubblica**, the heart of
the city and home to the main
centres of religious and civic
power, as was traditional in
the Middle Ages. These
include the **duomo**, built and
modified between 1133 and
1512 and restored to its
original Romanesque form in
the early 20th century. The
cathedral is unusual for
having two façades. The main
façade faces the small Piazza
del Duomo. The building's
better side, however, is the

south front, with its richly
decorated lateral façade
adorned with a splendid
doorway (1201), which looks
onto Piazza della Repubblica.

Opposite is the **Palazzo
Comunale**, with a Neo-
Classical façade. Originally
built in the 13th century, the
palace was rebuilt several
times and altered completely
following the earthquake of
1832. The only historic
element to be kept was the
battlemented tower, which,
however, succumbed to the
earthquake of 1997.

The palace is linked to
Palazzo Orfini, which is
famous because it was
probably the former home of the
printing house of Orfini. This
was among the earliest of all
Italian printing houses (1470),
and the first to publish a
work in Italian, Dante's
Divine Comedy (1472).

On the northwestern side of
Piazza della Repubblica is
another important building,
Palazzo Trinci, home of the
Pinacoteca Comunale and the
Museo Archeologico. Among
many works of art in the
gallery are pictures by three
notable painters born
in Foligno: Ottaviano Nelli,
Niccolò Alunno and Pier
Antonio Mezzastris.

Via Gramsci, which leads
west off the piazza, contains
several palaces dating from
the 16th to 18th centuries,
some constructed over older
medieval buildings. Of these,
the Renaissance **Palazzo Deli**

Nativity, Niccolò Alunno, church of
San Niccolò

For hotels and restaurants in this region see pp148–51 and pp161–7

Well from 1340 in the Romanesque cloister of the abbey of Sassovivo

(Via Gramsci 6) is the most beautiful. It features a medieval tower that was once part of Palazzo Trinci.

In Piazza San Domenico, at the end of Via Gramsci, is the Romanesque church of **Santa Maria Infraportas**, whose exterior portico dates from the 11th or 12th century. Inside is the Cappella dell'Assunta (12th century), which has Byzantine-like frescoes that are of interest even though they are in a rather bad state. Another fine work in the church is a *St Jerome and Two Angels* by Mezzastris.

The façade of Santa Maria Infraportas

The church of **San Niccolò**, nearby on Via della Scuola di Arti e Mestieri, was rebuilt in the 14th century by Olivetan monks, remodelled in the following century and then completely rebuilt again in the 18th century. Inside are several works by Niccolò Alunno, among them the *Polyptych of the Nativity*, one of his best-known works. The School of Arts and Crafts, after which the street is named, was based in the monastery alongside.

In Piazza XX Settembre, reached from San Niccolò along Via Mezzalancia, is one of the most beautiful private palazzi built in the 17th century, **Palazzo Monaldi-Bernabò**, now a school.

🏛 **Museo di Palazzo Trinci**
Piazza della Repubblica. **Tel** 0742 357 989. ⬜ 9am–1pm, 3–7pm Tue–Sun. ⬛ 1 Jan, 25 Dec. 📷

Environs
Heading east out of Foligno along the main road no. 77, then taking a fork to the right after about 2 km (1 mile), drivers will come to a scenic road that leads up to the **Abbazia di Sassovivo** surrounded by a dense forest of holm oaks. Founded in around 1000, the Benedictine abbey was an important political and cultural centre at least until the 15th century. The abbey church is of much less interest than the 13th-century Romanesque cloister, which is the finest of its kind in the region. It features 128 variegated double or spiral columns supporting 58 round arches, decorated with coloured marbles and two bands of mosaics. There is a 13th-century fresco, too. Also of note is the Loggia del Paradiso in the monastery.

Altopiano di Colfiorito ❸

Perugia. **Road Map** E4.
🚆 *Foligno, 24 km (15 miles), Rome–Ancona line.* 🚌 ℹ️ *Corso Cavour 126, Foligno, 0742 354 459.*

Heading east from Foligno along main road no. 77, shortly before the border of Le Marche you reach the Altopiano of Colfiorito. This upland plain, which reaches over 700 m (2,300 ft) above sea level, consists of seven broad basins, once part of a lake which was drained in the 15th century. Of the original natural formation, a marsh called the Palude di Colfiorito remains. The 100-ha (250-acre) wetland is of great interest for its aquatic vegetation and associated wildlife.

Various calcareous plains alternate with steep slopes, in a fascinating undulating landscape. Silhouetted around the fringes are the Apennine peaks of Monte Pennino, Monte Acuto, Monte Le Scalette, Monte Profoglio and Col Falcone.

This upland plain and the surrounding area now form part of the Parco Regionale di Colfiorito, a protected area that was set up to preserve this unique region. Now that the park is well established, visitors can explore the Altopiano using a series of signposted routes. There are also traces of ancient human habitation, the most obvious of which are the so-called *castellieri*, pre-Roman villages. The most visited is that of Monte Orve.

The slopes of Monte Pennino and the marsh of Colfiorito

Piazza Silvestri, in the heart of Bevagna

Bevagna **4**

Perugia. **Road Map** D4. 🏛 4,600.
🚉 Foligno, 9 km (6 miles), Rome–
Ancona line. 🚌 ℹ️ Pro Loco,
Via Santa Maria Laurentia, 0742 361
667. 🎭 Mercato delle Gaite, Jun.

Situated at the western margins of the Valle Umbra, Bevagna has long been at the centre of a busy road network, Inhabited probably since the 7th century BC, ancient *Mevania* experienced its most afflluent period under the Romans, thanks largely to its position on the Via Flaminia. Many illustrious citizens of ancient Rome built their country houses here. Following a period of decline during the Lombard era, when this branch of the Via Flaminia lost importance, the town experienced a revival in the 12th century, and this was when Bevagna acquired its current appearance. Town walls, incorporating part of the Roman walls, were built, with a main square at the centre. Not only are the walls still a feature, but remarkably little has been built outside them since the Middle Ages.

Porta Foligno is the main entrance into the town, from where Corso Matteotti leads to the heart of the city, Piazza Silvestri. Around this clearly medieval piazza stand the Gothic **Palazzo dei Consoli** and three churches: **San Silvestro, San Michele Arcangelo** and **Santi Domenico e Giacomo**.

Corso Matteotti follows the route of the *cardo* – one of the main streets through the Roman settlement. In the northern part, where the Forum stood, various traces of the Roman era still survive, among them the ruins of a temple (incorporated into the church of the Madonna della Neve), a theatre and baths. In the same district, off Piazza Garibaldi, is the 13th-century church of **San Francesco**. Inside are frescoes by an artist known as Fantino. This painter was born in Bevagna at the end of the 16th century and left works of art in many local towns. The church also contains a stone which is said to have been mounted by St Francis when he preached to the birds *(see pp24–5)*, an event which happened nearby.

Also worth a visit is the **Museo Comunale**, which has many Roman and pre-Roman finds, as well as the fine *Ciccoli Altarpiece* (1565–70)

Artemis, Museo Comunale

by Dono Doni. There is also a section devoted to the local 16th- and 17th-century artists.

🛈 **Museo Comunale**
Corso Matteotti 70. **Tel** 0742 360
031. ⬭ Apr, May, Sep: 10:30am–
1pm, 2:30–6pm daily; Jun & Jul:
10:30am–1pm, 3:30–7pm daily;
Aug: 10:30am–1pm, 3–7:30pm
daily; Oct–Mar: 10:30am–1pm,
2:30–6pm Tue–Sun (to 5pm Nov–
Mar). ⬤ 1 Jan, 25 Dec. 🎫

Ciccoli Altarpiece, 1565–70, by Dono Doni, Museo Comunale

Montefalco **5**

Perugia. **Road Map** D4. 🏛 5,592.
🚉 Foligno, 12 km (7 miles), Rome–
Ancona line. 🚌 ℹ️ Corso Cavour
126, Foligno, 0742 350 493.
🎭 Agosto Montefalchese, Aug.

Perched high on a hill dominating the valleys of the rivers Topino and Clitunno, Montefalco offers superb views over central Umbria, and has been nicknamed "the balcony of Umbria". It is also famous for its Sagrantino wine.

The small medieval comune, known as Coccorone, was badly damaged in 1249 in the course of bitter battles fought between the pope and emperor Frederick II. When the latter rebuilt the town, he decided to call it Montefalco, in honour of his imperial eagle insignia. The town's artistic high point came in the 14th century, followed by decline once Montefalco came under papal jurisdiction.

Montefalco retains some elements of Roman origin,

Historic Bevagna, at the fringes of the Valle Umbra

but the atmosphere is, above all, medieval, focused on the circular Piazza del Comune. This feudal nucleus is enclosed within a circle of medieval walls with five gates, from which five main streets lead, in the shape of a star, to the central piazza.

The main access to the town is via the 14th-century Porta Sant'Agostino, which has a tower on top. From here, Via Umberto I and then Corso Mameli lead up to the main square. Along the way is the church of **Sant'Agostino**, (late 13th century), whose façade is adorned with slender columns and a rose window. Inside the church are a number of interesting frescoes, among them one attributed to Ambrogio Lorenzetti. You also pass palazzos Tempestini, Langeli and Moriconi.

Laid out during the 14th century, the central Piazza del Comune is home to the **Palazzo Comunale**, heavily reworked in the 19th century, the former church of San Filippo Neri (now a theatre) and the **Oratorio di Santa Maria**, which was used as a public meeting place during the Renaissance.

Just north of Piazza del Comune, along Via Ringhiera Umbra, is the most important monument in the town, and indeed one of the most famous in the entire region – the former church of **San Francesco**. The attached monastery houses the **Museo Comunale**. The highlight of a

Scenes from the Life of St Clare, detail, church of Santa Chiara

visit to the deconsecrated 14th-century church are the frescoes painted by Benozzo Gozzoli (1420–97), a pupil of Fra Angelico and famous above all for his exquisite frescoes in the Palazzo Medici in Florence. Gozzoli's frescoes in San Francesco are found in the Cappella di San Girolamo and, more importantly, in the central apse, where the magnificent and colourful *Life of St Francis* (1452) is the most important pictorial cycle dedicated to the saint after the one in the Basilica di San Francesco in Assisi.

The church-cum-museum also contains works of art salvaged from other local churches, as well as other objects: note, in particular, a *Crucifix* by the Maestro Espressionista di Santa Chiara (late 13th–early 14th centuries), a *Madonna and Child* from the workshop of Melozzo da Forlì (late 15th century), a *Nativity* painted by Perugino (1503) and, among the sculptures, a *Coronation of the Virgin* from the workshop of Andrea della Robbia (16th century).

From Piazza del Comune, a flight of steps leads southwards down to the medieval church of **San Bartolomeo**, and to the town gate of the same name. Beyond is Viale Federico II (named in honour of the emperor who stayed in the town in 1240 during his battles against the pope), which leads on to the quarter called Borgo di San Leonardo.

Crucifix,
Museo Comunale

Walking westwards, outside the old walls, you reach the convent and church of **Santa Chiara**. These are dedicated not to the famous Clare of Assisi, but to Chiara di Damiano di Montefalco (1268–1308), who had the complex built here in the 13th and 14th centuries, on the site of the older Cappella di Santa Croce. The chapel (opened on request by the nuns who still live in the convent) is now the apse of the church. It is completely covered in 14th-century frescoes by Umbrian artists, narrating the lives of the saints Chiara, Caterina (Catherine) and Biagio (Blaise), and of the Virgin. On the wall of the altar a *Calvary* includes more than 45 figures.

A short distance south, along Via Giuseppe Verdi, is the Renaissance church of **Santa Illuminata**, which was built from 1491 on the site where Santa Chiara and her sister were locked up by their father.

The Franciscan convent of **San Fortunato**, about 1 km south of the town, has frescoes by Benozzo Gozzoli (1449) in the church.

🔒 **San Francesco and Museo Comunale**
Via Ringhiera Umbra.
Tel 0742 379 598. ⬤ Nov–Feb: 10:30am–1pm, 2:30–5pm Tue–Sun; Mar–May, Sep & Oct: 10:30am–1pm, 2–6pm daily; Jun & Jul: 10:30am–1pm, 3–7pm daily; Aug: 10:30am–1pm, 3–7:30pm daily. ⬤ 1 Jan, 25 Dec. 📷 ♿

Porta Sant'Agostino (or dello Stradone), gateway to Montefalco

Trevi ❻

Perugia. **Road Map** D4.
🚉 7,000. 🚆 Rome–Ancona line,
FCU Perugia–Terni line. 🚌
ℹ️ Piazza Mazzini 5, 0742 781 150.

The historic centre of Trevi "unwinds" in a stunning spiral fashion around a steep conical hill, Monte Serano, which dominates the plain of Spoleto. Flooding from the nearby river Clitunno used to be a constant threat and forced the inhabitants of Roman Trevi to move to higher ground. Once this threat was averted, however, the modern city – the so-called Borgo Trevi – was free to develop down on the plain, among the fields and olive groves.

Trevi converted early to Christianity; according to legend, this was because of the presence of the martyr Emiliano. In the 4th century, after a brief period of liberty, the town became part of the papal states and remained so until the unification of Italy.

The central Piazza Mazzini is home to the **Palazzo Comunale**, built in the 14th century but with important later additions, such as the 15th-century portico. From here, Via San Francesco passes the monumental **Palazzo Valenti** en route to the enormous church of **San Francesco**.

This church, together with the adjacent **Raccolta d'Arte di San Francesco**, is the principal artistic attraction in the town. The church itself, which dates from the 13th

Coronation of the Virgin, detail

century, contains interesting works, including a fine organ from 1209. However, Trevi's most important works of art are on display in the Raccolta, which has been housed in the church monastery since 1997. The finest work is the *Coronation of the Virgin* (1522), by Giovanni di Pietro, known as Spagna, which was commissioned by the friars of the church of San Martino *(see below)*; the predella includes two scenes from the lives of the saints: *St Martin gives away his Cloak* and *The Stigmata of St Francis*. The art collection also includes paintings from the Umbrian

Painted cross (15th century), Raccolta di San Francesco

school from the 14th century, among the most complete anywhere; in particular, do not miss the *Life of Christ* by Giovanni di Corraduccio (first half of the 14th century).

The cathedral of **Sant'Emiliano** stands at the summit of the hill. It was extensively restored in the 20th century, but still has the three original apses (12th century), which are among the best examples of Romanesque in the region. Next door is the Palazzo Lucarini, which houses the **Flash Art Museum**, with a small permanent collection of contemporary art by Italian and foreign artists, as well as changing exhibitions.

A ten-minute walk along pedestrian Viale Ciuffelli takes you to the 14th-century parish church of **San Martino**, built in a panoramic position on the northeastern edge of town. Inside the church are works by Tiberio d'Assisi and Fantino *(see p104)*, among the most famous artists of the Umbrian school. It is also worth visiting the **Santuario della Madonna delle Lacrime**, just south of the centre (not far from the train station), where there is a lovely *Epiphany* by Perugino (1512), as well as an important cycle of frescoes by Lo Spagna, in the chapel of San Francesco.

🏛 **Flash Art Museum**
Via Lucarini 1. **Tel** 0742 381 021.
⏰ 3–6pm Sat & Sun,
10am–1pm, 3–6pm Tue–Fri.
www.treviflashartmuseum.org

Environs

Around 5 km (3 miles) north of Trevi rises the 14th-century church of **Santa Maria a Pietrarossa**. Its name derives from the red stone (*pietra rossa*) in the presbytery, to which miraculous powers were attributed. The church has an extensive portico, beneath which is a vast cycle of votive frescoes dating from the 15th century. A few metres from the church is the San Giovanni spring, whose water is said to be therapeutic.

Interior of the church of San Martino

The pool formed by the Fonti del Clitunno springs, framed by weeping willows and poplars

Fonti del Clitunno ❼

Perugia. **Road Map** D4.
FS *Campello sul Clitunno, Rome–Ancona line, Trevi, 10 km (6 miles), FCU Perugia–Terni line.*

These famous springs emerge alongside the Via Flaminia, at Vene, and have been known since antiquity. The cool, limpid waters of this series of karst springs create a large pool dotted with small islands, as well as a river of the same name.

On a literary level, the historic reputation of the springs derives from the oracular skills attributed to the god of the river Clitunno (Clitumnus, the messenger god). The oracle was often cited by poets through the ages, from Virgil to Byron. This does not mean that drinking the water makes you a good orator. The waters' main effect, some say, is to remove the urge to imbibe alcohol.

The site really owes its fortune to the fertility of the soil and the sheer abundance of water, which rises in such quantity that at one time the river was navigable. The Romans exploited the site and created a holiday area here, using the springs to create public baths. Numerous buildings were constructed, including several villas dotted along the river banks, although today they have almost totally disappeared. Votive buildings include the **Tempietto**, which many experts now believe was built in the 8th century, using the materials from an earlier Christian building. About one kilometre north of the Fonti, the temple has a crypt and a room for worship.

The Roman Tempietto

The latter is decorated with 7th-century frescoes, thought to be the oldest paintings with sacred subjects in Umbria.

🏛 **Fonti del Clitunno**
Tel *0743 521 141.* ⭘ *daily from 8:30am, 9am or 10am (check website for details); closed between 1–2pm Oct–Feb.* ⬤ *25 Dec.*
www.fontidelclitunno.it
🏛 **Tempietto**
Tel *0743 275 085.* ⭘ *Apr–Oct: 9am–7:45pm daily; Nov–Mar: 8:45am–5:45pm daily.*

Environs

Just south of the springs is **Campello sul Clitunno**, whose church of the Madonna della Bianca has fine 16th-century frescoes. Follow the steep road up from the village to **Castello di Pissignano**, where Barbarossa once stayed.

A trapezoid tower, part of the Castello di Pissignano

UMBRIAN OLIVE OIL

Olive oil made in Umbria can bear the label "denominazione di origine controllata" (denomination of controlled origin) if it conforms to the high quality standards set for the product. Umbria has been divided into five producing districts, each with differing quality criteria. The strictest rules are applied in the district centred around Trevi, one of the most important olive-growing areas.

Parco Nazionale dei Monti Sibillini ❽

The park logo

Established as a national park in August 1993, the mountainous Sibillini park is exceptional. Extending over 70,000 ha (173,000 acres), the park is divided between Umbria and Le Marche and offers a bewitching combination of nature and history. There are numerous abbeys and medieval hill towns as well as rich natural diversity. Trails cover the entire park and are suitable for both walkers and mountain bikes. The windy upland plains are popular for hang-gliding, and in winter the mountains attract skiers. Among the refuges higher up are Rifugio Città di Ascoli (Passo di Forca Canapine), Capanna Ghezzi (above the plains of Castelluccio) and Rifugio San Severino Marche.

Abbazia di Sant'Eutizio
The buildings of this abbey date from the late 12th century, but the area drew hermits from the 6th century onwards, and was important politically and culturally during the early Middle Ages.

Visso, now the park headquarters, was said to have been founded 907 years before Rome. From the Middle Ages to the 18th century its territory was divided into five districts called "guaite" (guards). Castles and look-out towers are visible.

Marcite di Norcia
These irrigated meadows benefit from the water that flows from karstic springs.

Map labels:
Collesanto
Cicconi
Lago di Fiastra
Fiastra
ACQUA
Sasso
Calcara
SPOLETO
S209
Nera
MONTE MORICONE
1,429 m/4,687 ft
Castelsantangelo
Passo di Gualdo
MONTE PATINO
1,884 m/6,180 ft
Norcia
MONTE VENTOSO
1,719 m/5,638 ft

WILDLIFE IN THE MONTI SIBILLINI

The park is an ideal habitat for many species. In terms of mammals, the wolf and wildcat are present in small numbers, but there are healthy populations of roe deer, marten and especially wild boar (to the degree that they are becoming a problem). Lynx have been seen, but doubt has been cast on sightings of the Marsican bear. The birdlife in the mountains is very varied. Foremost is the golden eagle, an elegant predator which is easily spotted in the area. Some rarer species such as the peregrine falcon and the goshawk are also present. Alpine choughs and wall creepers are common.

Golden eagle

Park Flora

Rare species of plant can be observed in flower on the northern slopes, including alpine orchids and daisies like these.

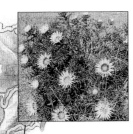

Monte Sibilla is the peak that gave its name to the park. There is a grotto here: according to legend this was the home of the mythical Sibyl (*sibilla*), capable of predicting the future.

Lago di Pilato

According to legend, Pontius Pilate was buried in this lake after the buffaloes pulling his hearse refused to go any further; though another story says that a remorseful Pilate drowned himself here.

KEY

⊟	Park road
▨	Scenic route
∼	River
▲	Peak

0 kilometres   3

0 miles   3

Monte Vettore

At 2,476 m (8,121 ft), this is the highest peak in the park and one of the major mountains in the Apennine chain. From the summit there are fine views over the entire massif: the dark waters of Lago di Pilato dominate the scene below.

Plains of Castelluccio

There are three high plains at over 1,300 m (4,264 ft) on the western slopes of the park above the isolated village of Castelluccio (famous for its lentils). In spring, the ground here is carpeted in a breathtaking abundance of flowers, known as the fioritura.

MONTE AMANDOLA
1,706 m/5,600 ft

MONTE PRIORA
2,332 m/7,650 ft

GOLA ELL'INFERNACCIO

CIMA ALLELUNGA
?21 m/7,285 ft

Foce

Ambro

Tenna

izzo di Meta

S78

stelluccio

PIANO GRANDE

Spoleto ❾

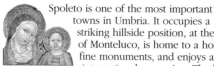

Spoleto is one of the most important towns in Umbria. It occupies a striking hillside position, at the foot of Monteluco, is home to a host of fine monuments, and enjoys an international reputation. The last started with the travellers on the Grand Tour and continues today

Detail of a lunette, San Nicolò

with the cosmopolitan crowd that has flocked to the famous Festival di Spoleto since 1958.

The first settlement here was founded, probably by the Umbri, high up where the fortress was later built: traces of the massive 4th-century-BC walls are still visible. Spoletium, founded in 241 BC, became a major Roman colony, thanks partly to its proximity to the Via Flaminia, used by people travelling to Rome from the north. Spoleto later became the seat of a Lombard dukedom and then an important commune. Numerous monastic orders were established here and the town maintained its prosperity over the centuries.

View of the city of Spoleto, dominating the Spoletine valley

Exploring Spoleto

The main approach into the city is from the northern side, over the Ponte Sanguinario, a Roman bridge. From here, the route of the tour climbs upwards, via several sites of importance, to the highest and oldest part of the city, where both the duomo and the Rocca d'Albornoziana, essential sights on a visit to Spoleto, are found.

🔒 San Gregorio Maggiore
Piazza Garibaldi.
Just over Ponte Sanguinario, the gateway to the town, is Piazza Garibaldi, home to the church of San Gregorio Maggiore. It was founded in the 4th century, in the early Christian era, outside the walls, as were all the oldest churches in the city. It was renovated in the 12th century, incorporating materials from various Roman remains. The façade is adorned with statues and a huge campanile

(notice the Roman blocks used in the lower half) and has a portico modelled on that of the duomo *(see p113)*. Despite frequent restoration and embellishment, the Romanesque interior still bears traces of interesting medieval frescoes.

The façade of San Gregorio with portico and bell tower

The entrance to San Nicolò, framed by Gothic arches

🔒 San Nicolò
Via Cecili.
From Piazza Garibaldi, Via dell'Anfiteatro heads towards the centre, past the meagre ruins of a 2nd-century-AD Roman amphitheatre. Continuing up Via Cecili you reach the deconsecrated church of San Nicolò.

What looks like a single church is, in fact, a complex of religious buildings placed one on top of the other over the course of the centuries. The imposing Gothic church, which played host to Martin Luther in 1512, is now used for plays and concerts.

🔒 San Domenico
Via Pierleoni.
Via Cecili leads to Piazza della Torre dell'Olio, with the 14th-century tower of the same name. Taking Via Pierleoni, which runs south, you reach the large monastic church of San Domenico (13th century), with its distinctive pink and white striped design.

Restored to its original Gothic form in the 1930s, the church has a single, unusually long nave. Here, you can admire interesting frescoes dating from the 14th and 15th centuries, some of which have come to light only in recent decades. In particular, linger over the Cappella di San Pietro Martire (the first on the left), the Cappella di Santa Maria Maddalena, on the right-hand side of the apse, and the Cappella Benedetti di Montevecchio, on the left of the presbytery.

The Roman theatre in Spoleto, dating from the 1st century AD

🏛 **Teatro Romano**

Piazza della Libertà.
Corso Mazzini eventually
widens out into Piazza della
Libertà. This is the site of a
much-restored Roman theatre,
built in the 1st century AD
with a capacity of 3,000.
excavated only in the
20th century. It is used
for festival performances.
The nearby monastery of
Sant'Agata, one of the oldest
religious buildings in the city,
houses the **Museo Archeologico
Nazionale**, with important
Roman finds.

🏠 Santi Giovanni e Paolo

Via Filitteria.
Heading up Via Sant'Andr...
from San Domenico, you ...
the **Teatro Nuovo**, a grand...
theatre built over the ruins...
a monastery and inaugurat...
in 1864. A little further on...
is the deconsecrated church...
dedicated to saints John an...
Paul in 1174. It is worth a v...
for the frescoes inside: the
oldest is the one depicting
the *Martyrdom of Thomas
Becket*, painted after his
canonization in 1173.

... temporary
Italian artists, participants in
the "Premio Spoleto" (Spoleto
Prize), among them Arnaldo
Pomodoro and Giulio Turcato.

🏛 Museo Archeologico Nazionale

Via Sant'Agata 18. **Tel** 0743 223
277. 🕐 8:30am–7:30pm Mon–Sat.
⚫ 1 Jan, 1 May, 25 Dec. 🎫

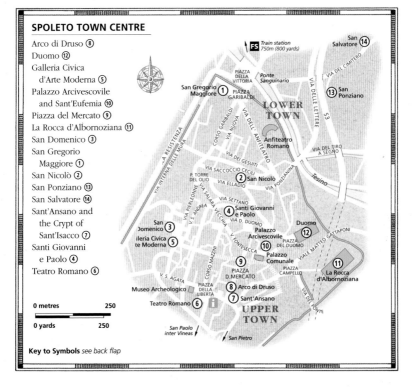

SPOLETO TOWN CENTRE

Arco di Druso ⑧
Duomo ⑫
Galleria Civica
    d'Arte Moderna ⑤
Palazzo Arcivescovile
    and Sant'Eufemia ⑩
Piazza del Mercato ⑨
La Rocca d'Albornoziana ⑪
San Domenico ③
San Gregorio
    Maggiore ①
San Nicolò ②
San Ponziano ⑬
San Salvatore ⑭
Sant'Ansano and
    the Crypt of
    Sant'Isacco ⑦
Santi Giovanni
    e Paolo ④
Teatro Romano ⑥

0 metres   250
0 yards   250

Key to Symbols see back flap

🏛 Sant'Ansano and the Crypt of Sant'Isacco

Via Brignone.

Climbing up towards the oldest part of Spoleto, you follow the route of the "cardo maximus", one of the main roads through the Roman settlement. The church of Sant'Ansano is, in fact, built on the ruins of a 1st-century temple. What you see today dates from the 18th century, but the church has a complex architectural history. The crypt of Sant'Isacco (St Isaac) provides evidence of a 12th-century church dedicated to both saints. It contains Roman columns and striking Byzantine-style frescoes. The church above contains a *Madonna* by Spagna (first half of the 16th century).

The Crypt of Sant'Isacco, beneath Sant'Ansano

🏛 Arco di Druso

Piazza del Mercato.

The Arch of Drusus, one of many arches scattered around the town, marked the point where the *cardo maximus* entered the forum (now Piazza del Mercato). It was erected in AD 23 in memory of the son of Emperor Tiberius.

🏛 Piazza del Mercato

This square lies at the heart of the oldest part of Spoleto. With an open market, shops and bars, it is always busy.

In terms of monuments, of particular note is a fountain built in the mid-18th century with material taken from other buildings, among them four coats of arms and a slab commemorating Pope Urban VIII. In the northwestern corner is one side of the **Palazzo Comunale**, originally medieval but rebuilt in the late 1700s, after earthquake damage. The **Museo del Tessuto e del Costume** contains over 2,500 pieces spanning the 14th to

The fountain in Piazza del Mercato, built in 1746–8

the 20th centuries, including liturgical vestments, clothing, fans, hats and folk textiles.

Nearby is a **Casa Romana** (Roman house), dating from the 1st century BC, which has some lovely mosaic floors.

🏛 Casa Romana

Via di Visiale. **Tel** 0743 234 250.
⏱ *mid-Mar–mid-Oct: 10am–7pm daily; mid-Oct–mid-Mar: 10am–5pm daily.* ⬤ *Mon (Oct–Mar).* 🖼

🏛 Museo del Tessuto e del Costume

Via delle Terme 5. **Tel** 0743 459 40.
⏱ *4–6pm Mon–Thu, 4–7pm Fri–Sun.* 🖼

🏛 Palazzo Arcivescovile

Via Saffi 13. **Tel** 0743 231 022.
⏱ *Apr–Oct: 11am–1pm, 3–6pm Mon, Wed & Thu, 11am–1pm Tue, 11am–6pm Fri, Sat & Sun; Nov–Mar: 11am–1pm, 2:30–5:30pm Wed–Mon.* 🖼

The architectural history of this palace, in front of Palazzo Comunale, constitutes a virtual narrative in stone of the history of Spoleto. It began with the construction of a Roman building (still partially visible), above which it is thought that the Palazzo dei Longobardi was built when Spoleto was a duchy. In the 12th century the building was incorporated into a monastery, and became the bishop's palace in the 16th–17th centuries.

Inside is a good collection of works of art and, in the courtyard, the 12th-century church of **Sant'Eufemia**. This church is Romanesque but more Lombard than Umbrian in style. It is famed for its rare women's galleries above the nave.

🏛 La Rocca d'Albornoziana

Piazza Campello 1. **Tel** 0743 224 952. ⏱ **La Rocca and Camera Pinta** *9am–5:30pm Tue–Sun.* **Museo Nazionale del Ducato di Spoleto** *9am–1:30pm Tue–Sun.*

In 1359, when the city was an outpost of a Church intent on reconquering Umbria, Cardinal Albornoz, papal legate for Innocent VI, ordered the construction of a military fortress (*rocca*) at the highest point of the city. It was linked to the hill behind, Monteluco, by the impressive Ponte delle Torri, which still straddles the Valle del Tessino (*see p113*). La Rocca can only be visited by bus (buses run hourly from Piazza Campello) and with a guide.

The fortress is built on a rectangular plan around two courtyards, the Corte d'Armi

The Rocca, seen from the far side of the Ponte delle Torri

and the Cortile d'Onore, both surrounded by towers. Over the centuries, La Rocca has been home to various notable figures, among them Lucrezia Borgia, whose caprices were perhaps responsible for the naming of the tower called "della Spiritata" (the spirited one). Converted into a prison for over a century, in 1984 the Rocca underwent restoration.

The highlights inside are the frescoes in the **Camera Pinta** (in one of the main towers). These chivalric scenes were painted by artists from the school of Terni in the 14th–15th centuries. Also inside is the **Museo Nazionale del Ducato di Spoleto**.

Behind La Rocca is the masterly, ten-arch **Ponte delle Torri**, crossing the river Tessino. It is 230 m (755 ft) long and over 70 m (230 ft) high: the date of construction is uncertain and it is probable that today's bridge evolved from a Roman bridge-cum-aqueduct. In the middle of the bridge is an opening offering lovely views.

Mosaic by Solsternus on the façade of the duomo

Duomo
Piazza del Duomo.
8:30am–12:30pm, 3:30–7pm (Nov–Feb: to 6pm) daily.

A short climb from Piazza del Mercato leads to the sloping Piazza del Duomo, home of Spoleto's cathedral. As a backdrop to the Festival di Spoleto, this church's image is now world-famous.

The cathedral, built and consecrated at the end of the 12th century, is dedicated to Santa Maria Assunta, and rises on a site where there were at least two earlier religious buildings. The façade, one of

The duomo's façade, backdrop to the annual Festival di Spoleto

the most superb examples of Umbrian Romanesque, is divided into three orders and is the result of at least three successive phases of construction.

The original project resulted in the basilica layout, and the bell tower probably dates from the same era (12th century). A second phase of construction (early 13th century) saw the building of the façade, with the mosaic of Solsternus (1207) and the three upper rose windows, which frame the original Cosmatesque one underneath, one of the most beautiful in central Italy. The portico, with its magnificent central door, was added at the end of the 15th century. The bronze bust of Urban VIII above the central door was sculpted by Gian Lorenzo Bernini in 1640.

The interior of the church, rebuilt in Baroque style in 1648, is built on a Latin cross plan, divided into three aisles separated by a colonnade. There are various important works of art here. Just past the entrance, on the right, is the Cappella del Vescovo Costantino Eroli, built in 1497 and entirely decorated with frescoes by Pinturicchio. Don't miss those in the chapel altar niche, depicting *God the Father and Angels*, *The Madonna and Child* and

John the Baptist and St Stephen. There is also a fine series of figures from the Old Testament on the vault. The other important cycle of frescoes (1467–9), by the artist Filippo Lippi, is found on the walls of the apse. The subject is the life of Mary. Among the scenes are an *Annunciation*, a *Transition of the Virgin*, a *Nativity* and a *Coronation of the Virgin*. The sarcophagus of the Tuscan artist is also kept in the church, although his remains are no longer here.

On the two sides of the apse, extending outwards from the main body of the church, are two chapels, the Cappella della Santissima Icona and the Cappella del Sacramento. In the first is an image of the Virgin in the form of a icon, much venerated because it is attributed to St Luke. On the left, to the side of the transept is the lovely Cappella delle Reliquie. Besides some fine frescoes and painted panels, this chapel contains a 14th-century wooden statue of a *Madonna and Child* and a letter written by

Transition of the Virgin, Filippo Lippi, detail

St Francis to his disciple Fra Leone. On the first altar on the left, in the nave, hangs a *Crucifix* by Alberto Sotii, painted on parchment applied to board, dated 1187. Other similar treasures are kept in the Archivio Capitolare.

Detail of a Pinturicchio fresco in the duomo's Cappella Eroli

Detail of a bas-relief on the façade of the church of San Pietro Fuori le Mura

🔒 San Paolo inter Vineas

Via San Paolo.

The first of four important churches, which form a curve around the eastern side of the historic centre of Spoleto, lies south of the city, beyond the Giardino Pubblico (public gardens) and the stadium.

San Paolo inter Vineas was built on the site of an early Christian religious building, mentioned by St Gregory the Great in the 6th century. The present Romanesque church, flanked by a cloister, dates from the 12th and 13th centuries, and was skilfully restored in the latter half of the 20th century. The most important feature inside is the fresco cycle, which was painted in the early 13th century and is considered to be among the oldest in the region. It depicts the *Prophets* and *Scenes from the Creation of the World*.

The Romanesque church of San Paolo inter Vineas

🔒 San Pietro Fuori le Mura

Via Matteotti, then via Roma, beyond main road SS Flaminia.

Whereas at San Paolo inter Vineas it is the interior frescoes which are the most important feature, here it is the decorations on the façade.

San Pietro Fuori le Mura ("outside the walls"), which lies south of the town centre, stands at the top of a flight

of steps on a plateau from where there are fine views.

The building has ancient origins, probably dating back to the 5th century, when the relics of the chain of St Peter were moved here. The current church dates mainly from the 12th century. The carved stone reliefs on the façade are regarded as one of the most prized examples of Umbrian Romanesque. The reliefs on the lower, older part of the structure, produced in the 12th and 13th centuries, tell complex stories rich in symbolism. They relate lay episodes, taken from medieval encyclopedias, and other religious stories linked to the life of Christ.

Façade of San Pietro Fuori le Mura

🔒 San Ponziano

SS Flaminia, road to the cemetery.

This church lies northeast of the centre, alongside Via Flaminia, and at the foot of the Cinciano hill. It occupies the site of the tomb of the martyr Ponziano, patron saint of Spoleto, who is commemorated on 14 January. This is a convent church, first the home of Poor Clares and later Augustinian nuns, with a Romanesque exterior and an interior which was completely restructured in 1788 by Giuseppe Valadier. (He also designed the doors and altars of the cathedral.)

The main feature of interest is the crypt, which is original. Divided into three aisles, like the church above, and with

THE FESTIVAL DI SPOLETO

The most important event in Spoleto's recent history occurred when it was chosen by the Italian-American composer Gian Carlo Menotti as the venue for the Festival dei Due Mondi, which was to become a major international arts event. The choice fell on Spoleto because of its central location within Italy, its historic appeal and its plentiful theatres and cinemas. In 1958 a performance of Verdi's *Macbeth*, directed by Luchino Visconti, inaugurated the first festival. Since then, despite the controversy with which the festival has always been associated and the change of name (today it is called the "Festival di Spoleto"), every summer the event attracts an enthusiastic audience, as well as artists from all over the world, to this splendid city.

A closing concert at the Festival

five apses, this contains Roman fragments and some pretty votive frescoes, which include one showing the *Archangel Michael* with a globe and staff, in the right-hand apse. On the left is an *Enthroned Madonna*.

The formal interior of the church of San Salvatore

🔒 San Salvatore

Via del Cimitero, off SS Flaminia. From San Ponziano, the road goes up the Cinciano hill and brings visitors to the last, and perhaps the most historically interesting, of all the religious buildings close to Spoleto.

The church of San Salvatore is an exceptional example, perhaps unique in Umbria, of a building constructed using mainly salvaged material, almost all dating from the Roman era. The columns, decorative elements, capitals, architraves – most of the architectural features in the three-aisled basilica church, in fact – date from the Roman period. For this reason, it has been difficult for art historians to date San Salvatore with any great precision, although it is undoubtedly one of the oldest churches in the country. Two theories circulate currently. According to the first, the church dates from the early Christian period, and bears witness to the heights of splendour achieved in late Roman art in this area (the Tempietto del Clitunno would be of the same era). According to the second theory, however, the building was probably designed in the 8th and 9th centuries.

San Pietro in Valle ❿

Perugia. **Road Map** D5. 🚆 *Rome–Ancona line, Terni, 20 km (12 miles); FCU Perugia–Terni line.* 🚌 **Tel** *0742 380 011.* **Abbey Tel** *0744 380 018 or 0744 780 129 (hotel).* ☐ *summer: 9:30am–12:30pm, 2–6pm daily; winter: 10am–noon daily (call ahead).* **www**.sanpietroinvalle.com

It is difficult to try to rank Umbrian abbeys in order of importance, but clearly no classification could omit the Benedictine abbey of San Pietro in Valle, situated in the lower part of the Valnerina, just north of the village of Ferentillo *(see p123)*.

Set against a backdrop of wooded hills, San Pietro in Valle is of significant artistic and religious interest. The abbey's roots lie deep in legend. Its foundation, as one of the frescoes in the left-hand transept of the church testifies, traditionally dates from the 5th century AD, when the Lombard duke of Spoleto, Faroaldo II, met the Syrian hermit Lazarus. St Peter had suggested to the duke in a dream that he should transform the hermit's small chapel into a powerful abbey, and so San Pietro in Valle was built. Faroaldo later decided to stay here, becoming a monk, and he rests here still: his splendid sarcophagus can be seen in the right-hand transept.

Capital, San Pietro in Valle

The abbey was severely damaged by the Saracens in the 9th century, but was restored in around 1000 by Ottone III and then by his successor Enrico II. In the 1930s, extensive renovation revealed the medieval linear forms which the building had managed to retain, despite all the alterations. Today, the abbey is privately owned, and has been converted into an appealing, sought-after hotel and restaurant, part of the Relais & Châteaux chain, though parts are open to the general public.

The abbey church is owned by the state and is well worth a visit. Long and formal, with a single nave ending in a short transept and three apses, the church contains some superb works of art. On the walls is a cycle of frescoes, which ranks among the finest examples of Romanesque painting in Italy in its complexity and in the precision of its execution. On the left-hand wall and on the upper right-hand side are *Stories from the Old Testament*, while in the remaining space on the right-hand side are *Scenes from the Life of Christ*. The inner façade and the transept are decorated with works from later eras.

Look out for the beautifully preserved Lombard altar (8th century), which bears the self-portrait and signature of the sculptor: "Ursus".

The medieval Benedictine abbey of San Pietro in Valle

The broad Piazza San Benedetto, in the centre of Norcia

Norcia ⓫

Perugia. **Road Map** 5F. 🏠 *5,000.*
🚌 ℹ️ *Piazza San Benedetto, 0743
828 173.* 🗓️ *Mostra Mercato del
Tartufo Nero, Feb.* **www**.norcia.net

At the foot of the Monti
Sibillini, on the edge of the
plain of Santa Scolastica, and
on the borders of the ancient
duchies of Spoleto and
Benevento, Norcia was a
trading city and a staging post
for centuries. Today, the town
is known above all for its
local produce, in particular
for its black truffles and
for the production of
high-quality meat,
sausages and
salami. (The word
"norcino" – from
Norcia – is now
synonymous with
superior meat
products.) Browsing around
the wonderful *salumerie* and
other food shops is a highlight of any visit to the town.

The walls built by the
Romans (who conquered the
city in 290 BC) were replaced
by another, heart-shaped set
in the 13th century. These
walls, and the city itself, have
been damaged by disastrous
earthquakes over the years.
Along the perimeter, however,
the ancient gates (eight in all)
can still be seen.

One of these gates, Porta
Romana, marks the start of
Corso Sertorio, which leads
to Piazza San Benedetto, the
heart of the town since the
Middle Ages. At its centre is
a statue of St Benedict (1880).
Facing onto the square is

Palazzo Comunale, of 14th-
century origin but partly
rebuilt after the earthquake in
1859. The portico is original
while the soaring bell tower
dates from the 18th century.

Alongside the palazzo is the
church of **San Benedetto**,
which was founded in the
Middle Ages and extensively
rebuilt in 1389 and at various
later dates. The 14th-century
façade is dominated by a
monumental doorway (1578),
with two statues
representing St
Benedict and Sta
Scolastica on either
side. On the right
side of the church
is a 16th-century
portico, the Portale
delle Misure, which
has a stone step
bearing the
commercial
measures used for the sale of
grain. The interior, which was
reconstructed in the 18th
century, contains a crypt built
on the site where, according
to tradition, St Benedict and
Sta Scolastica were both born.
Traces of the oldest church
and fragments of frescoes
are visible in the crypt.

Lunette from the door of
San Benedetto, detail

The cathedral of **Santa
Maria Argentea**, built in the
16th century and remodelled
in the 18th, also stands on the
piazza but is of little interest.
Much more impressive is the
Castellina, a fortress built for
Pope Julius III in 1554. Its
square layout, centred on a
courtyard with a loggia, was
the work of the prestigious
architect Jacopo Barozzi, also
known as Vignola. The fort

houses the **Museo
Civico Diocesano**,
where the highlights
include two crucifixes
and a five-figured
sculptural group of
the *Deposition* (13th
century). The latter is
perfectly preserved and
provides important
evidence of the popular
art being done at that
time (such groups
would have been
carried in processions).

For a taste of Norcia
of old, follow Via Roma
as far as Porta Ascolana,
or take Via Anicia from the
main square up to the highest
part of the city. The palazzi
here date from the 17th and
18th centuries, when Norcia
was a major trading centre on
the borders with the Adriatic
regions. Here, too, is
Sant'Agostino, with some
fine 16th-century frescoes
by local artists. Also of note
are the Gothic church of
San Francesco on Piazza
Garibaldi, and the 14th-
century **Tempietto** on Via
Umberto, which has some
pretty bas-reliefs.

🏛 **Museo Civico
Diocesano**
Piazza San Benedetto.
Tel *0743 817 030.* ⏱ *Oct–May:
10am–1pm, 3–5:30pm Tue–Sun;
Jun–Sep: 10am–1pm, 4–7pm Tue–
Sun.* 📷 🛍 ♿ 🚻

The courtyard of the Castellina with
its loggia and gallery

A LAND RENOWNED FOR SAINTS

Two of the most important saints in Umbrian history (St Francis apart) were born in this area, just a few kilometres from each other but separated by nearly one thousand years.

St Benedict, founder of the oldest monastic order in the West, was born (with his twin sister Santa Scolastica) in Norcia, in 480. After studying in Rome he settled at Montecassino, where he wrote his famous *Rule*. This became a major influence on medieval monastic life. The patron saint of Norcia (as well as of Europe), St Benedict's saint's day is celebrated on 21 March.

Santa Rita (born Rita Lotti, commemorated on 21 May) was born at Roccaporena, near Cascia, in around 1380, and died in the mid-15th century. The factional struggles between the

Monument to St Benedict by Giuseppe Prinzi, 1880

Guelfs (pro the papacy) and the Ghibellines (pro the German emperors) caused her much suffering. Her parents were part of the so-called "peacemakers of Christ", or mediators between the two factions, and Rita carried on their work, even after the assassination of her husband and the subsequent murder of her two sons, killed while trying to avenge their father.

Rita entered the Augustine convent of Santa Maria Maddalena at Cascia, where she remained for 40 years, until her death in 1457. She developed a sore on her forehead, which was said to have been caused by a thorn falling from a crown of thorns as she knelt in prayer beneath a statue of Christ; it was viewed by fellow nuns as a stigmata. The miraculous story of Rita gave rise to a popular cult that has lasted for centuries. Indeed, it was thanks only to a popular campaign that Rita was eventually made a saint, on 24 May 1900.

View of Roccaporena, with the cliff of Santa Rita behind

Cascia ⑫

Perugia. **Road Map** 5E. 👥 3,300. 🚌 🛈 *Piazza Garibaldi 1, 0743 711 47.* 📅 *Celebrazioni per Santa Rita, 21–22 May.*

Inhabited since late antiquity, because of its strategic position, Cascia has had a turbulent past: Umbrian, then Roman and Byzantine, then part of the Duchy of Spoleto, but independent from the 10th century. In the early Middle Ages, it was a Ghibelline city, locked in bitter struggle with Norcia

and Spoleto, cities owing allegiance to the pope. Taken by Rome in 1517, Cascia immediately acquired great importance because of its position on the border with the Kingdom of Naples. This brought great prosperity.

With the unification of Italy, Cascia lost its political relevance and fell into a long period of decline, halted in the 20th century only thanks to religious tourism, which brought large numbers of pilgrims dedicated to the memory of Santa Rita.

The cult is still a significant feature of life in Cascia today, so the focus is no longer the now-destroyed hilltop fortress, but a modern **Sanctuary** dedicated to the saint. It was built in 1947, replacing a church dating from

1577. To the left of the sanctuary is the convent of Santa Rita, where the saint lived for much of her life.

Other sites to visit in the town include the **Museo Civico** (divided between Palazzo Santi and the church of Sant'Antonio Abate), in particular for the fine wooden sculptures, and the churches of **San Francesco** and Santa Maria. In the outskirts of the town is **Roccaporena**, Rita's birthplace, dominated by a hill known as the "scoglio" (cliff) of Santa Rita. The area's many castles and towers, which formed an effective system of fortification, are evidence of the historical importance of the region.

Not far from Cascia is the Parco Nazionale dei Monti Sibillini (*see pp108–9*).

Fresco in the lunette above the door to the church of San Francesco

Terni ⓭

The only Umbrian provincial capital apart from Perugia, Terni has always been the most developed centre for industry in the region – the result of its position: at the centre of a plain and at the confluence of the River Nera and the Serra and Tescino streams. The availability of water was crucial for the development of heavy industry during the 19th century (the famous Italian steelworks Acciaierie Breda is based here). Terni is also crossed by the Via Flaminia, an extremely important route since Roman times, linking Rome with the north and the Adriatic coast. Terni's industrial importance made it a target for heavy bombardment during World War II and today, despite its Bronze Age origins, it looks decidedly modern compared with most other Umbrian towns. Terni is the unlikely birthplace of St Valentine, the patron of lovers and one of the world's most popular saints.

Madonna and Saints, Benozzo Gozzoli

Exploring Terni

Although it is a fairly large city, Terni – or at least the most important sights – can be visited in a relatively short time and on foot: the historic centre, located on the western side of the River Nera, is reasonably compact.

Visitors should leave their cars near the railway station (to the north of the centre), and then follow Viale della Stazione to Piazza Tacito, from where Corso Cornelio Tacito leads directly to the heart of Terni. This is focused around the squares of Piazza della Repubblica, where the

main public buildings are located, and Piazza Europa. The latter is home to Palazzo Spada, which was designed, according to local tradition, by Antonio da Sangallo the Younger.

🔒 San Francesco
Piazza San Francesco.
⏲ 8am–12:30pm, 3:30–7:30pm daily.
It is worth making a detour to the right halfway along Corso Tacuto to look at this 13th-century church, which was originally designed in typical Franciscan style with a single nave and transept. In the course of the 15th century, the lateral aisles

and the bell tower were added. Inside, the Cappella Paradisi contains a cycle of frescoes (*The Last Judgment*), painted by Bartolomeo di Tommaso, of the Giotto school. The cycle dates from the middle of the 15th century.

🏛 Museum of Modern and Contemporary Art
Viale Campofregoso 98.
Tel 0744 258 946.
⏲ Dec–Oct: 10am–8pm Tue–Sun. 🎫 ♿ ⛔
This former chemical plant houses the Aurelio de Felice collection of modern art, including lithographs by Chagall, Mirò, Picasso and Kandinsky. The museum's broad sweep also encompasses works representative of the medieval Umbrian school, such as by Benozzo Gozzoli (*The Marriage of St Catherine*), Spagna and Nicolò Alunno.

🔒 Sant'Alò
Via Sant'Alò. **Tel** 0744 407 148.
⏲ by appt.
This Romanesque church, just off Via XI Febbraio, dates from the 11th century and is notable for the abundant re-use of Roman statuary on the exterior. It is thought that the church was built on the ruins of an earlier pagan temple.

🔒 Duomo (Santa Maria Assunta)
Piazza Duomo.
⏲ 9am–noon, 3:30–7pm daily.
The Duomo, located south of the city centre, near the public gardens, was built on

A huge ladle in action in a steelworks

INDUSTRIAL TERNI

The industrial importance of Terni goes back to the dawn of the industrial revolution in Italy (beginning of the 19th century), when the Vatican ironworks were based here. During the 19th century the industries multiplied: foundries, saw-mills, wool mills, as well as the hugely successful Acciaierie Breda steelworks. All found an ideal environment on this plain, which is well supplied with water and in a strategic position for trade. Industry has altered both the countryside and the town itself. Today the factories are, for the most part, dismantled or converted for other use, but the industrial archaeology of Terni is still a reason to visit the area. There are other reasons, of course: this "outdoor museum" extends to cover Terni itself, the waterfalls of Marmore and the town of Narni.

Detail of the decoration on the main door of the duomo

the site of earlier religious buildings, the first of which existed at least by the 6th century; numerous churches were later built on the same site. The current basilica is the result of reconstruction in 1653, although there are still some traces of a Romanesque church. Look out for the bird and animal reliefs on the main door as you enter.

🏛 Roman Amphitheatre

Piazza Duomo, Giardini Pubblici. ◯ 10am–1pm, 4–7pm Wed, Fri & Sun.
This amphitheatre (1st century AD), not far from the duomo, is very much a ruin but is still one of the best preserved Roman sites in Terni. Used as a quarry and later covered by buildings, it was discovered in the mid-19th century and was finally excavated in the 1930s.

On the left is Palazzo Vescovile, whose curvilinear rear façade follows the line of the old bastions. There are lovely views from the adjacent public gardens.

🏛 San Salvatore

Via San Salvatore.
◯ 9am–noon, 4–6pm daily.
The town's most interesting church, just off Piazza Europa,

The round church of San Salvatore

was erected on the ruins of Roman buildings, but it has been impossible to establish exactly when. The main body of the church, built on a circular plan, was thought to have been a Roman temple to the sun but is now believed to date from the 11th century; the rectangular avant-corps is more recent, built perhaps in the 12th century.

Inside the church are traces of frescoes; the ones in the Cappella Manassei date from the 14th century.

VISITORS' CHECKLIST

Road Map D6.
🏛 110,000. 🚆 Rome–Ancona line, 892021. 🚌 800 512 141.
🛈 Via Cassian Bon 1, 0744 423 047. 🎭 Feste di San Valentino, 14 Feb; Cantamaggio, May. **www**.regioneumbria.eu

🏛 San Pietro

Piazza San Pietro. ◯ 8am–noon, 3:30–7:30pm daily.
This 14th-century church, not far from Palazzo Comunale, was enlarged and restored several times. It contains many 14th- and 15th-century frescoes representative of the local school.

🏛 Mostra Permanente di Paleontologia

Ex-chiesa di San Tommaso, Largo Liberotti. **Tel** 0744 434 202.
◯ 10am–1pm, 4–7pm Tue, Thu & Sat. ♿&
A vital tool for anyone studying the early history of Umbria, this permanent exhibition has a rich collection of fossils, the remains of several ancient mammals, and a diorama of Umbria when it was covered by the waters of the ancient Tiberine Lake.

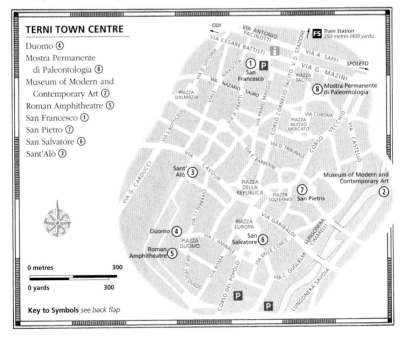

TERNI TOWN CENTRE

ODI
VIA ANTONIO PACINOTTI
VIA CESARE BATTISTI
VIA VITTORIA
VIA RINASCITA
VIA G. MAZINI
VIA A. SAFFI
D. STAZIONE
FS Train Station 350 metres (400 yards)
SPOLETO
① San Francesco
PIAZZA TACITO
⑧ Mostra Permanente di Paleontologia
VIALE NAZARIO SAURO
VIA A. FRATTI
VIA PRIMO MAGGIO
CORSO CORNELIO TACITO
PIAZZA DALMAZIA
VIA CORONA
PIAZZA NUOVO MERCATO
CORSO VECCHIO
VIA S. BOTTICELLI
VIA D. TRIBUNALE
VIA E. BARBERINI
VIA CASTELLO
VIA G. CARDUCCI
Sant' Alò ③
VIA CAVOUR
PIAZZA DELLA REPUBLICA
PIAZZA SOLFERINO
⑦ San Pietro
Museum of Modern and Contemporary Art ②
VIA 1 FEBBRAIO
Duomo ④
PIAZZA DUOMO
PIAZZA EUROPA
VIA L. AMINALE
San Salvatore ⑥
VIA GARIBALDI
VIA DELLE CONCE
LUNGONERA CIMARELLI
Roman Amphitheatre ⑤
VIA DI VESCOVADO
CORSO DEL POPOLO
VIA ROMA
VIA C. GUGLIELMI
LUNGONERA SAVOIA

0 metres 300
0 yards 300

Key to Symbols see back flap

Narni ⑭

Terni. **Road Map** C6. 🚶 20,000.
🚆 *Rome–Ancona line.* 🚌 ℹ️
Piazza dei Priori 3, 0744 715 362. 📷
Corsa dell'Anello, mid-May for two weeks. **www**.comune.narni.tr.it

This fine and unspoilt hill town, located dramatically above a bend in the River Nera, is the geographical centre of Italy. Its origins date back to the Umbri people, who founded *Nequinum*. This settlement was conquered by Rome in 299 BC and was renamed *Narnia*, after the nearby river. Its importance under the Romans derived from the fact that it was the birthplace of Emperor Nerva, in AD 32, and also a major stopping point on the Via Flaminia. Narni grew until it occupied the entire rocky spur above the Nera.

Medieval Narni knew tough years during the wars between the papacy and the empire, but it continued to grow, even after the establishment of papal rule in the mid-14th century. The building of a great fortress, on the orders of Cardinal Albornoz, emphasized papal authority. In the 16th century, Narni was devastated by the Lanzichenecchi on their return north after the Sack of Rome. During the following centuries, the slow rate of growth kept the town centre in the form in which it can still be seen today.

The duomo, facing onto Piazza Garibaldi

Detail of the bas-reliefs to the right of the door of Palazzo del Podestà

Porta Ternana, on the Via Flaminia, is the main point of entry to Narni. From here, Via Roma leads straight to Piazza Garibaldi, at one time known as Piazza del Lago because of a great subterranean cistern, fed by the Roman aqueduct of Formina; this now supplies the water for a 14th-century fountain with a bronze basin.

Most of the sights are close to the main axis of the town, formed by Via Garibaldi and Via Mazzini. At one end is Piazza Garibaldi, home of Narni's **duomo**, an imposing and beautiful building dedicated to San Giovenale, the town's patron saint. It was founded in 1047, but reconstructed in the 12th century. The façade has a portico and a portal decorated with carvings. Inside, two low arcades separate the three aisles. On the right is the mausoleum of the bishops of Narni, which is dominated by a tombstone dating from 558.

From the duomo, it is a short walk up Via Garibaldi to the central Piazza dei Priori, the attractive seat of civic power in Narni. Facing the square are the **Palazzo dei Priori**, with a portico and an impressive loggia designed by Gattapone – responsible also for the Palazzo dei Consoli in Gubbio (*see p60*) – and the **Palazzo del Podestà** (or Palazzo Comunale); both date from the 14th century. In the atrium of the Palazzo del Podestà is a series of Roman

Detail of the fountain in Piazza Garibaldi

and medieval archaeological stones and finds, while inside is a superb *Coronation of the Virgin* by Ghirlandaio, and frescoes by Benozzo Gozzoli and others. **Casa Sacripanti**, also in the square, features three medieval bas-reliefs of gryphons and knights.

Beyond Piazza dei Priori, the main street (now Via Mazzini) continues north. Immediately on the right is the façade of the little Romanesque church of **Santa Maria in Pensole**, built in around 1175. Of particular interest is the exterior, with its attractive portico and three doorways carved with classical motifs. A little further on, where the road widens out into Piazza XIII Giugno, is the church of **San Domenico** (12th century). Now deconsecrated, it houses the Public Library, Historical Archive and the town art gallery. The main reason to go inside is to see some of the most interesting medieval frescoes in Narni: among the often faint fragments, of particular note are those by the Zuccari family, found in the large chapel off the left-hand aisle. San Domenico also has many other works from other churches in the town, among them an *Annunciation* by Benozzo Gozzoli, at the end of the right-hand aisle. In the underground areas of the church, you can visit the Inquisition cells, with graffiti made by the prisoners of the ecclesiastical court.

To return to Piazza dei Priori from San Domenico, make your way along the narrow streets which run parallel to Via Mazzini. This area is home to the church of **San Francesco**, built in the 14th century on the site where it is said that St Francis stayed during his sojourn in Narni in 1213, and where he founded an oratory. The church is Romanesque, but with some Gothic elements. Among these, the most important feature of the exterior is the doorway, with a niche above. Inside, frescoes adorn every inch of wall: of special interest are the frescoes by Mezzastris, in the first chapel, depicting *Scenes from the Life of St Francis* and *Scenes from the Life of St Benedict*, as are those by Alessandro Torresani (16th century), in the sacristy.

On top of the hill that dominates Narni is a vast fortress known as the **Rocca**. It was built in the 1370s by Gattapone, at the behest of Cardinal Albornoz, one of the most important figures in the history of the early Middle Ages in Umbria (*see p41*), and responsible for numerous fortresses which still bear his name. Narni's fortress was abandoned for years, but it has now been restored. There are fine views from the site.

Environs

Heading out of Narni, towards Terni, you reach, after a short detour to the left, a bridge over the River Nera. Though

The Romanesque abbey of San Cassiano, dating from the 12th century

easy to miss among the modern development of industrial Narni Scalo, this is the best possible observation point from which to admire a majestic Roman arch in the middle of the river, the only one surviving from the **Ponte d'Augusto**. At 160 m (525 ft) long and 30 m (98 ft) high, this must have been one of the most impressive bridges in the whole of Umbria when it was built. It is known as the Augustan bridge because it dates from the era of the first emperor (27 BC). This bridge was one of the most popular sights on the Grand Tour.

Continuing along the same road, over the Nera, a climb leads to the **Abbazia di San Cassiano**, perhaps the most important of the many religious buildings that dot the Narni countryside. Set in a panoramic position, the Romanesque, 12th-century complex is enclosed by battlemented walls and

includes a pretty church with a bell tower.

To the southeast, 13 km (8 miles) from Narni, is the **Convento del Sacro Speco**, founded in 1213 by St Francis, who often prayed in a cave nearby. The place is imbued with a mystical atmosphere.

Visciano ⓯

Terni. **Road Map** C7.
🚉 *Narni, 8 km (5 miles), Rome–Ancona line.* 🚌 🛈 *Piazza dei Priori 3, Narni, 0744 715 362.*

Heading south from Narni, a tortuous but scenic road leads up to the hilltop hamlet of Visciano. The reason for coming here is to visit the small and simple church of **Santa Pudenziana** (it is advisable to ring the curator first on 0744 735 541 to book a visit). This is a typical example of Umbrian Romanesque, built in the 12th and 13th centuries, and making abundant use of Roman materials. It has a tall stone campanile and a sober façade with a small portico. The interior is divided into three aisles, with an inlaid floor of precious marble and fragments of Roman mosaics.

The church is famous for its frescoes. Behind the façade are *Christ, San Vittore* and *San Medico*, and other saints, as well as the *Madonna and Child*, all contemporary with the construction. The other figures, such as *Santa Pudenziana*, date from the 14th and 15th centuries.

The Rocca, one of many fortresses built by Cardinal Albornoz

Parco Fluviale del Nera ⑯

Known as the "water park", this natural park extends
along the course of the River Nera from Terni to
Ferentillo, leading to the heart of the National Park of
the Monti Sibillini *(see pp108–9)*, and thereby forming
what is virtually a single protected reserve of huge
interest. Within the park is one of the most famous and
much-loved sights in Italy, the Cascata delle Marmore,
the highest waterfalls in the country, where the waters
from the River Velino spill over from the upland of the
Marmore down into the River Nera. Visitors should
note that the water for the waterfall is switched on only
for brief periods, which vary from month to month, so
you should call ahead if you don't want to miss the
spectacle. The park has much else of interest, however,
and offers excellent opportunities for water sports.

Sweet violets, found in the
pasture areas in the park

The Observatory along the
upper road, in the village of
Marmore, is one of many
points from which to admire
the falls in all their glory. It
dates from 1781.

Cascata delle Marmore

*The tremendous spectacle
of the falls, a popular
destination with travellers
throughout the ages, is
created by the River Velino,
which reaches this point
via an artificial channel.
Water then cascades down
in three stages, over a total
height of 165 m (541 ft), to
reach the River Nera below.
The falls can be seen from
both the lower road
(SS209) and the
upper road (S79).*

0 kilometres   1

0 miles   1

TERNI ←

S209

Nera

Nera

Velino

Marmore

CONSTRUCTING A WATERFALL

In antiquity, the River Velino did not spill into the
River Nera as it does today, but stagnated in the
marshes of the Rieti plain. In 271 BC the Romans
decided to link the two by digging a channel, the
Cavo Curiano, which feeds today's main waterfall.
Since then, the Cascata delle Marmore has been
at the centre of the entire river system of central
Italy, provoking bitter debate between those who
wanted to close it down and others who wanted
to extend it. The latter option was chosen in the
15th and 16th centuries, with the work entrusted
by the popes to the great architects of the day
(Antonio da Sangallo, Giovanni Fontana and
Carlo Maderno), who were to transform the
falls. The latest alterations, to adapt the falls for
hydroelectric power, took place in the 1920s.

**The hydroelectric plant at the Marmore falls, one
of Italy's main sources of energy**

Montefranco

This small village, perched in a splendid panoramic position, is a centre for mountain sports. There are numerous rock climbing schools and manageable cliff faces.

VISITORS' CHECKLIST

Terni. **Road Map** D6. ⏻ Terni, Rome–Ancona line. 🚌 ℹ️ Via Pacinotti 34, Terni, 0744 423 047. **Park Tel** 0744 629 82 ◯ Jan: 11am–5pm Sat; Feb, Nov & Dec: 11am–5pm daily (Feb: to 6pm Sat & Sun); Mar: 10am–6pm daily (to 10pm Sat & Sun); Apr & May: 10am–7pm Mon–Fri, 9am–10pm Sat & Sun; Jun–Sep: 10am–10pm daily (from 9am Sat & Sun); Oct: 10am–6pm Mon–Fri, 10am–8pm Sat & Sun. **www**.marmore.it

Monterivoso

S209

Nera

Montefranco

Ferentillo

Guarded from above by twin 14th-century citadels, Ferentillo is a major climbing centre. It owes its fame also to the church of Santo Stefano, whose crypt contains several mummified bodies.

S209

Arrone

Casteldilago

Forca dell'Arrone

KEY

⣿⣿⣿	Park road
▨▨▨	Scenic road
☀️	Viewpoint
🅰️	Campsite

🅰️

Lago di Piediluco

↓ RIETI

Piediluco is popular because of its pretty setting on the shores of Lake Piediluco, the second largest lake in Umbria after Trasimeno, and just outside the park. The church of San Francesco is worth a visit, and boat rides on the lake are recommended.

Rafting

Water is the crucial element in the park and various water sports can be practised here, including rafting, canoeing and kayaking.

The 17th-century Porta Romana, inserted into the ancient walls

Amelia ⓱

Terni. **Road Map** C6. 🏛 11,000.
FS Narni, 11km (7 miles),
Rome–Ancona line. 🚌 ℹ Via
Orvieto 1, 0744 981 453.

Perched on a hill between the Tiber and Nera valleys, Amelia is a city of ancient origin. In fact, it was in antiquity that the town knew its greatest importance, when it was located on the Via Amerina, one of several Roman roads linking southern Etruria with Umbria.

Still standing today are parts of the impressive **Mura Poligonali** (Polygonal Walls), built by the Umbri and among the oldest walls in Italy. Their age is not certain, but they date from no later than the 5th century BC. Some 8 m (26 ft) high, and 3 m (10 ft) wide, the bastions are, for the most part, made up of vast polygonal stone blocks, fitted together without mortar. The size of the walls can best be seen at **Porta Romana**, framed by a Classical-style 17th-century arch.

This same gate is also the main entrance to the historic centre. Close by, in Palazzo Boccarini, is the **Museo Archeologico**, home to all manner of Roman finds from tablets to sarcophagi. Of huge interest is a magnificent statue of the Roman general Germanicus; discovered locally, it was for years kept in Perugia; Amelia has won it back, for the time being at least.

A short way up Via della Repubblica is the 13th-century church of **Santi Filippo e Giacomo**. It contains seven tombs of the Geraldini family, one of the most important dynasties in Amelia. Cardinal Alessandro Geraldini is famous for helping to persuade the Spanish monarchy to authorize the first voyage of Christopher Columbus to the Indies. The church's funerary monuments include the 15th-century tombs of Elisabetta and Matteo Geraldini, the work of Agostino di Duccio.

Palazzo Farattini, just off Via della Repubblica, is Amelia's most impressive private building. It was designed by Antonio da Sangallo the Younger in the 16th century for the Farattini, the other family to feature large in the history of Amelia. Via della Repubblica climbs further up Piazza Marconi, the town's lovely main square, and then continues up Via Duomo to the highest point of the city and the **duomo**.

The cathedral's appearance today is the result of almost total reconstruction in the 17th century, which replaced the original Romanesque church, though the fine 11th-century bell tower remains. Inside are several works of importance including a panel with a *Madonna and Child* attributed to Antoniazzo Romano, and two paintings by Nicolò Pomarancio in the Oratorio del Sacramento.

Returning to the lowest part of the town along Via Geraldini, you reach Piazza Matteotti, whose architectural highlight is the charming **Palazzo Comunale**.

Beyond Porta Romana, you can visit the country church of **Santa Maria delle Cinque Fonti**, built on the site where St Francis is said to have given a sermon in 1213. The church is named after a fountain with five spouts that stands nearby.

Detail from the tomb of Matteo and Elisabetta Geraldini

🏛 **Museo Archeologico**
Piazza Augusto Vera.
Tel 0744 978 120. ⏰ Apr–Jun &
Sep: 10:30am–1pm, 4–7pm
Tue–Sun; Jul & Aug: 10:30am–1pm,
4:30–7:30pm Tue–Sun; Oct–Mar:
10:30am–1pm, 3:30–6pm Fri–Sun.
⏰ 1 Jan, 25 Dec. 🖾 🗋

View of Amelia, showing how the village expanded down the hillside

◁ **The impressive Cascata delle Marmore, with the second level in the foreground**

Environs

The area around Amelia is dotted with abbeys and sanctuaries that are easy to reach and a delight to visit. About 4km (2 miles) southwest of Amelia, on the road to Attigliano, is the 13th-century **Monastery of the Santissima Annunziata**, which belongs to the Friars Minor. There is a *Last Supper* on the wall of the refectory. Heading eastwards, past the village of Capitone – which was the castle of nearby Narni in the Middle Ages – you reach the village of La Cerqua and the **Sanctuary of the Madonna della Quercia**. This was built in the 16th century to hold an image of the Virgin Mary, now on the apse altar.

The Roman **Via Amerina** is a historical object in itself, and has maintained its role as a communication route.

Interior of Santa Maria Assunta, in Lugnano

Lugnano in Teverina ⑱

Terni. **Road Map** C6. 🏯 *1,600.* Ⓕ *Attigliano, 11km (7 miles), Milan–Rome line.* 🚌 🛈 *Pro Loco, Piazza S Maria 1, 0744 900 072.* 🎄 *Christmas concerts and Living Nativity, 24 Dec–6 Jan.*

Following the main road S205 from Amelia towards Lago di Alviano, after around 10 km (6 miles) you come to the small town of Lugnano in Teverina. Set in a panoramic position along a ridge and enclosed by medieval walls,

Lago di Alviano, along the border with neighbouring Lazio

Lugnano began life as the feudal village of a Provençal count, in around 1000.

Although some way from the usual tourist trails, Lugnano is well worth visiting simply to see one of the most interesting Romanesque churches in Umbria, the church of **Santa Maria Assunta**. The building dates from the 12th century, although it has undergone much restoration, especially in the 15th century. In common with various other Umbrian churches of the same era, such as the cathedral of Spoleto, the façade features a beautifully decorated portico, some of which is the work of the famous Roman marble workers, the Cosmati. There is more Cosmati work inside, both in the nave (which has a Cosmatesque pavement) and in the crypt, which also has a finely sculpted screen. Other works of art include a triptych of the *Annunciation* by Niccolò Alunno, in the apse, and a *Crucifixion* of the Giotto school.

Capital in Santa Maria Assunta

Environs

A short distance southwest of the town centre are traces of the Assisi saint in the church of **San Francesco**. It was erected in 1229 on the spot where a miracle occurred, as shown in the fresco above the right-hand altar.

After passing ancient Roman ruins, the road descends towards the Tiber and the hamlet of **Attigliano**.

Proceeding north on the Via Amerina, along the banks of the Tiber, after about 8 km (5 miles) you come to the **Lago di Alviano** (open Sundays and public holidays). This is part of an artificial basin created to generate hydroelectricity and today is an oasis run by the World Wide Fund for Nature and part of the Parco Fluviale del Tevere *(see p133)*. From the nearby medieval town of Alviano, birthplace of condottiere Bartolomeo di Alviano, steps lead to **Santa Illuminata**, a pilgrimage site linked to an order of hermits called the Camaldolese.

A lovely 10-km (6-mile) stretch of the Via Amerina runs to **Montecchio**, with an interesting necropolis (6th–4th centuries BC) nearby.

One of the chambers in the necropolis near Montecchio

Gate at the entrance to the medieval town of San Gemini

San Gemini ⑲

Terni. **Road Map** D6. 👥 *4,300.*
🚂 *Rome–Ancona line, Terni,
11 km (7 miles); FCU Perugia–Terni
line.* 🚌 🛈 *Piazza San Francesco 4,
0744 630 130.*

The medieval town of San
Gemini was built over the
ruins of an ancient Roman
settlement, alongside the Via
Flaminia. The only traces of
the Roman town are a tomb,
the so-called Grotta degli
Zingari and a ruined villa.

The heart of San Gemini
is Piazza di Palazzo Vecchio,
home to the medieval
Palazzo Pubblico, whose
tower was much altered in
the 1700s. Under an exterior
arcade is an image of St
George, patron saint of
the town. The 13th-century
Oratorio di San Carlo, nearby,
has striking frescoes.

On the edge of town are the
churches of **San Francesco**,
with a fine Gothic doorway,
and **San Giovanni Battista**,
with a 13th-century façade
and a lovely Romanesque
door decorated with mosaics.
One of the façade inscriptions
bears the date of its founding,
1199, with the names of the
architects and sculptors
Nicola, Simone and Bernardo.

Just outside San Gemini's
old gateway is the privately
owned church of San Nicolò.
The beautifully sculpted
Romanesque portal is a copy,
since the original is in the

Metropolitan Museum in New
York. There is more fine (and
original) sculpture inside.

Environs
Just to the north, on flatter
ground, is the modern spa
town of San Gemini Fonte,
with facilities for spa water
treatments. The famous
mineral waters of Sangemini
and Fabia are bottled here.
Sangemini water, known in
antiquity and exploited since
the late 19th century, is rich
in calcium but low in chlorine
and sodium, so is particularly
recommended for children.
Fabia water has average levels
of minerals and is today
promoted as a light table
water good for the digestion.

**The ancient spring at the Terme di
San Gemini**

Carsulae ⑳

Terni. **Road Map** D6. 🚂 *Rome–
Ancona line, Terni, 14 km (9 miles);
FCU Perugia–Terni line.* 🚌 🛈 *Soprin-
tendenza Archeologica dell' Umbria,
0744 630 420; Sito Archeologico di
Carsulae, 0744 334 133.* 🕐 *8:30am–
7:30pm daily (to 5:30pm Oct–Mar).*

From San Gemini Fonte a
detour of 3 km (2 miles)

along part of the old Via
Flaminia brings you to the
ruined Roman town of
Carsulae, founded in the
3rd century BC on the slopes
of the mound bearing the
pretty name of Chiccirichì.

At first merely a staging
and garrison post, then a
village, Carsulae eventually
became a town in Augustus'
Region VI. It experienced its
greatest period of splendour
between 30 and 10 BC, when
work was being done on
the Via Flaminia. The town
was abandoned following
the decline in importance
of the road. Carsulae was
attacked and raided by
barbarians and marauders
on a number of occasions,
and was also badly damaged
by earthquakes.

From the 16th century
onwards, the aristocratic
families of the region, in
particular the Cesi family of
Acquasparta, began to carry
out excavations in search of
objects of interest for their
own private collections.
The modern archaeological
excavations date back to the
1950s, when a number of
sites were uncovered, including a basilica, the old forum,
and temples. The great value
of Carsulae as an archaeological site lies in the fact that the
original layout has remained
complete for the most part,
despite the encroachment
of the modern Via Flaminia,
which crosses the site.

The small church of **San
Damiano** was built in the
11th century, using the
remains of a Roman temple.
From here, you can follow a

The little church of San Damiano, inside Carsulae's archaeological area

The ruins of the Roman theatre at Carsulae, showing clearly the supports for the stalls

stretch of the original Via Flaminia to the **Forum**, with an adjacent basilica with three aisles and an apse. In front of the forum is a public square where numerous low walls – the ruins of religious and secular buildings – can be seen: among them are the bases of the **Tempietti Gemelli** (twin temples) and the remains of baths.

Continuing up the old Via Flaminia, visitors arrive at the **Arco di San Damiano**, a monumental gate which once had three arches: only the central one survives. A burial site is also nearby. Behind the basilica, beyond the modern Via Flaminia, is the **Amphitheatre**, used for circus games, and the **Theatre**; sadly only the foundations of the stage and the supports for the stalls (orchestra seats) remain of this building.

Acquasparta ㉑

Terni. **Road Map** D6. 🏛 *4,500.* 🚉 *Rome–Ancona line, Terni, 20 km (12 miles); FCU Perugia–Terni line.* 🚌 🛈 *Via Tiberina 43, 0744 943 286.* 🎭 *Arte estate, Jul–Aug.*

The first records of Acquasparta date from the 10th century. The name derives from the local spa waters, which were known to the Romans and, it is said, taken by St Francis. Acquasparta's appearance today recalls the influence of the Cesi family, who changed the face of the town during the 15th and 16th centuries. Among the features dating from this era are a palace named after the noble family, walls and towers.

Palazzo Cesi, commissioned by the Cesi family from the architect Giovanni Domenico Bianchi, was completed in 1565. The interior of this aristocratic residence is richly decorated: Giovan Battista Lombardelli produced the first paintings, while an artist from the north was responsible for the remainder. The rooms have splendid coffered wooden ceilings; the one in the Sala di Ercole (Room of Hercules) is particularly fine. Palazzo Cesi belongs to the University of Perugia and is used for seminars and

Palazzo Cesi, now part of the University of Perugia

conferences as well as a summer art exhibition.

Along Corso Umberto I, the main street, are the church of **Santa Cecilia** and the **Oratorio del Sacramento**, where a mosaic floor from the ruins of Roman Carsulae has been put into new use.

The 200,000-year-old fossil forest at Dunarobba

Environs

A detour 15 km (9 miles) west of Acquasparta, skirts Casteltodino and leads to the fossil forest of **Dunarobba**, close to the village of Avigliano Umbro. This ancient forest, which dates from the Pliocene age, is made up of around 40 petrified trunks of large trees similar to today's sequoia. The trees were preserved for centuries under a blanket of clay on the shores of Lago Tiberino (which once filled the Tiber Valley).

A few kilometres north is the medieval castle and village of **Casigliano**. Within is Palazzo Atti, a project of Antonio da Sangallo the Younger which was based on Roman designs. It was the inspiration for Palazzo Cesi.

Todi ❷

St Peter,
in the duomo

The city of Todi occupies a stunning spot, on a hilltop halfway between Perugia and Terni. First built on land occupied by the Umbri, Todi was later appropriated by the Etruscans (its name derives from the Etruscan word *tutere*, meaning "border") and then, in 89 BC, by the Romans. Under the Romans, Todi's two hilltops were levelled out to make Piazza del Popolo and new walls were built around the Etruscan ones. Todi today would not have looked very different during the Middle Ages, a time of great splendour, when the town expanded southwards and was divided into four districts, surrounded by a third circle of walls. The city became a papal possession, along with all the other towns of Umbria, and there was only minor subsequent modification during the Renaissance.

Exploring Todi

The centre of the city is, as it was in Roman times, Piazza del Popolo. This truly magnificent square contains the duomo, as well as three fine monuments to temporal power:

The eagle of Todi,
Palazzo dei Priori

Palazzo del Popolo, Palazzo del Capitano and Palazzo dei Priori. Following years of research, this largely medieval square was chosen as the starting point for excavations which have provided the information necessary to reconstruct the layout of the ancient city.

🏛 Palazzo dei Priori

Piazza del Popolo. **Tel** *075 894 4148.* ⬤ *to the public.*
This palace, situated on the southern side of Piazza del Popolo, is the least attractive of the three palazzi. It was

built between 1293 and 1385. At the top left of the façade is an eagle in bronze, the symbol of the city and the work of Giovanni di Gigliaccio in 1339. (According to tradition, the original Umbrian town was built where an eagle had dropped a tablecloth taken from a local family.) Over the centuries the palazzo has housed the city's various and varied rulers, including the leaders of the medieval commune and the papal governors.

🏛 Palazzo del Popolo

Piazza del Popolo. **Tel** *075 894 41 48.* ◯ *see Palazzo del Capitano.*
This is one of the oldest buildings of its type in Italy: construction began in 1213, though the palace has been

considerably restored. Built in Lombard-Gothic form, the palace's left-hand side faces Piazza del Popolo, while the front can be admired from nearby Piazza Garibaldi. In particular, look out for the swallowtail crenellations (a Guelf motif) and the external staircase, which gave access to the hall on the first floor, above the porticoed space of the ground floor. Public assemblies were held here.

The palace shares an entrance with Palazzo del Capitano and houses part of the Museo Pinacoteca.

Three-mullioned window, Palazzo del Capitano

🏛 Palazzo del Capitano

Piazza del Popolo. **Museo Pinacoteca Tel** *075 894 4148.* ◯ *10am–1pm, 3–6pm (Nov–Mar: to 5pm) Tue–Sun.* ⬤ *Mon (except hols), 25 Dec.* ♿ 🎫 📷
This palace dates from the late 13th century and faces the eastern side of the square. The façade has mullioned Gothic windows and a monumental arched staircase which serves both the Palazzo

Piazza del Popolo, an excellent example of a well-preserved medieval square

For hotels and restaurants in this region see pp148–51 and pp161–7

del Capitano and the adjacent Palazzo del Popolo. In particular, it gives access to the Sala del Capitano, with remains of frescoes, medieval coats of arms and a 14th-century *Crucifixion*.

Sculptural detail from the door of the duomo

The **Museo** Pinacoteca, which spans the adjacent palazzi, includes a decent archeological collection, the **Museo Etrusco-Romano**, as well as paintings, of which the most significant is a *Coronation of the Virgin* (1507–11) by Giovanni di Pietro, known as Spagna. The palazzo also houses the Museo della Città (Civic Museum).

🏛 Duomo

Piazza del Popolo. *Tel* 075 894 30 41. ☐ summer: 8:30am–12:30pm, 2:30–6:30pm; winter: 8:30am–4:30pm Mon–Sat, 8:30am–12:30pm, 2:30–6:30pm Sun.

Dedicated to Maria Santissima Annunziata, the duomo was founded in the 12th century, probably on the site of a Roman temple, but wasn't completed for another 200 years, with further additions being made after that. The simple façade, which is divided horizontally by cornices, is lovely. An 18th-century flight of steps leads up to a carved 16th-century door set into a decorative framework, above which, as befits the façade's Romanesque simplicity, is a beautiful rose window (1515). Pilaster strips, small loggias and mullioned windows decorate the right-hand side and the tall apse.

Inside, the church has a decorative beamed roof and splendid Gothic capitals, as well as a superb 16th-century choir. The entire central space as well as the chapels contain various works of art, the most interesting of which are near the altar: two paintings by Spagna, to the sides, and, above, a painted wooden Crucifix dating from the 13th and 14th centuries. There is

also a crypt, which contains three figures originally on the façade, as well as a handful of Roman remains.

The magnificent rose window on the façade of the cathedral

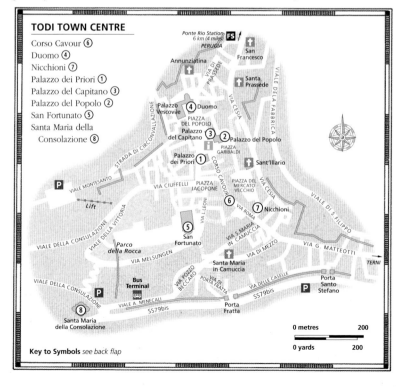

TODI TOWN CENTRE

Corso Cavour ⑥
Duomo ④
Nicchioni ⑦
Palazzo dei Priori ①
Palazzo del Capitano ③
Palazzo del Popolo ②
San Fortunato ⑤
Santa Maria della Consolazione ⑧

Key to Symbols *see back flap*

| 0 metres | 200 |
| 0 yards | 200 |

Detail from the main door of the church of San Fortunato

🏠 San Fortunato

Piazza Umberto I. ◯ *Nov–Mar: 10:30am–1pm, 2:30–5pm Tue–Sun; Apr–Oct: 10:30am–1pm, 3–6:30pm Tue–Sun.* ● *25 Dec.*

Heading south along Via Mazzini, which skirts around the medieval heart of Todi, is the enormous hilltop church of San Fortunato, a sight which is not to be missed.

This is a Franciscan church, but with many anomalies: the dedication, for example, is not to the Assisi saint but to Fortunato, patron of Todi. (The reason for this was that the church replaced a building used by Benedictine monks.) The construction took place in two phases: the first from 1292–1328, the second in the 1400s. It was commissioned by the bishop of Todi, Matteo d'Acquasparta.

The unfinished façade, a mixture of Romanesque and Gothic styles, stands out at the top of an imposing flight of steps. Through the fine Gothic central doorway lies a wonderfully airy Gothic interior, which does not follow the traditional Franciscan model. It is a rare example in Italy of a Gothic hall church; that is, in which the two side aisles are as high as (though much narrower than) the nave. Note the lovely and unusual ribbed cross vaults, the fine late 16th-century choir stalls, the raised chapels along the sides, and the Gothic baptismal font.

Frescoes decorate many of the chapels and include, in the fifth chapel on the left, some scenes from the *Life of St John the Baptist* by the Giotto school, and, in the fourth chapel on the right, a *Madonna and Child* (1432) by Masolino di Panicale.

The church is also famous for the tomb of Jacopone da Todi, in the crypt beneath the altar. Jacopone was a rich merchant who, following the death of his devout wife, Vanna, became a mystic and a poet. His devotion was reputedly so extreme that he was rejected even by the Franciscans. He was accused of heresy on a number of occasions and is mainly remembered for his *Laudi*, one of the fundamental texts in the birth of Italian literature (*see p30*). The great man, a native of Todi, died in 1306 and gradually became the symbol of the medieval city. He is still the best-known figure in the cultural history of Todi.

Extending westwards from San Fortunato is a large public park, where a fortress commissioned by Cardinal Albornoz stood until 1503.

🚊 Corso Cavour

Descending the steps of Via San Fortunato brings you to the steep Corso Cavour, the "Rua degli Speziali" (spice sellers' street) of medieval Todi. Halfway along is a fountain known as the **Fonte Rua** (1606), or Fonte Cesia (after the bishop who had it built), and, at the end, **Porta Marzia**, a medieval arch made out of material salvaged from other buildings.

The 17th-century Fonte Rua, in Corso Cavour

🚊 Nicchioni

Piazza del Mercato Vecchio.

Walk through Porta Marzia, and turn left into Via Mercato Vecchio, which leads to Piazza Garibaldi (a car park). The level part of this street, the old medieval market square, is dominated by four Roman arches, the so-called Nicchioni (niches). These most probably date from the Augustan era, and either supported a raised street, or formed part of the wall of a Roman basilica.

🏠 Santa Maria della Consolazione

Viale della Consolazione.

◯ *9:30am–12:30pm, 2:30am– 6:30pm (winter: 2–5pm) Tue–Sun.*

This church, located outside the city walls, is one of the masterpieces of the Umbrian Renaissance. Begun in 1508

The unfinished façade of the church of San Fortunato

The church of Santa Maria della Consolazione, outside Todi

and finished in 1607, it has been attributed by some to Bramante, one of the architects of St Peter's in Rome. In fact, there is no documentary evidence of any such project by the great architect, though it is just possible that Cola di Caprarola, who started the project, may have used drawings by Bramante.

The distinctive silhouette of the church – familiar from the covers of dozens of publications devoted to Todi – is built on a square plan and rises to a great dome. Encircling the main structure are four apses, of which one, to the north, is semicircular and three are polygonal; they have two orders of pilasters, with a mixture of capitals, and are pierced by elegant windows. The drum which supports the great dome is narrower than the main body of the church, leaving space for a raised terrace, guarded by four eagles sculpted by Antonio Rosignoli in the 17th century. There are great views from here. The Baroque doorways date from the 18th and 19th centuries.

The airy and light interior, in the form of a Greek cross, is also Baroque and contains statues of the apostles. In the apse is the venerated fresco of the *Madonna della Consolazione* (15th century). The church was built to protect the fresco.

Eagle on the terrace, Santa Maria della Consolazione

Parco Fluviale del Tevere ㉓

Terni. **Road Map** C5. ⏹ *Orvieto, Milan–Rome line; Todi, FCU Perugia–Terni line.* 🚌 🛈 *Ente Parco, Civitella del Lago, Baschi, 0744 950 732.* **www.**parks.it

This river park extends for some 295 ha (18,025 acres) from the bridge of Montemolino, at the gates of Todi, south as far as Lago di Alviano, and has great wildlife and lovely scenery. It includes around 50 km (31 miles) of land along the banks of the Tiber, the largest river in central Italy, and two artificial lakes (Alviano and Corbara). The main access to the park is at the medieval hill town of Baschi, about 24 km (15 miles) from Todi, close to the junction of road S448 and the motorway.

The Tiber river, one moment placid and the next turbulent, is home to a variety of birds, among them blue heron and kingfishers, as well as freshwater fish. Poplars, alders and willows, typical riverside vegetation, cloak the sides.

Steep valleys sweep away from the river and extend as far as the Apennines: the wildest is the **Gole del Forello**, considered one of the most interesting biotopes in the region. On the northern banks of Lago di Corbara, not far from the fortified village of Prodo, winds the **Gole di Prodo**, a deep gorge best suited to hikers or experienced and well-equipped mountain climbers. Diverse birds of prey, including buzzards, sparrowhawks and kites, can be seen in these inaccessible areas, where the vegetation consists mainly of trees such as holm oaks and hornbeams and shrubs such as broom and heather. The marshes in the Lago di Alviano basin *(see p127)*, with its own particular birdlife and plants, are also of great interest.

Besides the natural beauty and the opportunities for outdoor sports, the park also incorporates sites of historical and archaeological interest. Digs are under way in various spots, including in the Vallone di San Lorenzo (site of several necropolises) and in the area of the ancient river port of **Pagliano**, at the confluence of the Paglia and Tiber rivers; the port's existence confirms the importance of the Tiber as a communication route of the central Italic peoples.

The wild Gole del Forello, a fascinating wildlife habitat

Orvieto ㉔

A sheer tufa outcrop, the remains of ancient volcanoes fractured by millennia of ice, sun and rain, rises abruptly from the plain and supports the spectacular medieval city of Orvieto. In the Etruscan era a city called Velzna stood here and became rich through commerce with traders from the Tyrrhenian Sea (part of the Mediterranean) and the north. The Romans took over in 264 BC and virtually destroyed the town. Revival came only in the Middle Ages, when Orvieto developed into a free and powerful commune, albeit one troubled by civic strife. The Black Death of 1348 was devastating, however, and Orvieto eventually came under papal control. The old city, with its superb duomo (which is reached by bus from the train station or by funicular and shuttle bus), has changed little in the last 500 years, and attracts thousands of tourists every year.

The imposing tufa platform supporting Orvieto

🏛 Duomo
See pp136–7.

🏛 Museo Archeologico Nazionale
Piazza del Duomo. **Tel** 0763 341 039. ◯ 8:30am–7:30pm daily. ◉ 1 Jan, 1 May, 25 Dec. 🎫 &

On the scenic Piazza del Duomo, next to the imposing mass of the cathedral, stands the **Palazzo Papale**, which includes three 14th-century buildings, commissioned by Popes Urban IV, Gregory X and Martin IV and later combined into one complex.

The **Museo Archeologico Nazionale**, housed in the Palazzo del Martino IV, has a particularly fine Etruscan collection, including bronzes and mirrors. Several tombs and funerary objects are among the exhibits, including frescoes from 2nd-century-BC tombs and two painted 4th-century tombs from Settecamini.

🏛 Museo dell'Opera del Duomo
Piazza del Duomo. **Tel** 0763 343 592. ◯ 9:30am–1pm, 3–5pm Wed–Mon (Apr–Oct: 9:30am–7pm daily).

The Palazzo Papale also houses a museum dedicated to the cathedral. Exhibits include

ORVIETO TOWN CENTRE

Duomo pp136–7 ①
Museo Archeologico Nazionale ②
Museo dell'Opera del Duomo ③
Palazzo del Popolo ⑨
Palazzo Faina ⑤
Palazzo Soliano ④
Pozzo di San Patrizio ⑪
Rocca dell'Albornoz ⑫
San Domenico ⑩
San Francesco ⑥
Sant'Andrea ⑧
Torre del Moro ⑦

0 metres 250
0 yards 250

Key to Symbols see back flap

UNDERGROUND ORVIETO

⋂ Parco della Grotte
Società Speleotecnica.
Tel 0763 344 891, 339 733 2764.
⬚ *tours depart from Piazza del Duomo; call ahead to book.* 🅿
www.orvietounderground.it

⋂ Pozzo di Via della Cava
Trattoria Sciarra, Via della Cava 28.
Tel 0763 342 373. ⬚ *9am–8pm Tue–Sun.* ⬤ *Sun after Epiphany– 2 Feb.* 🅿 www.pozzodellacava.it

The people of Orvieto are used to living with cellars: every house or shop has its own cave, and every family has its own story to tell of the unde͏̈ no, for example, an antiques ͏̈ found the remains of the ͏̈ the world by digging in ͏̈ collection of 15th-century

A group of enthusiasts d͏̈ some of Orvieto's caves to ͏̈ Speleotecnica is one of the g͏̈ underneath the embankment t͏̈ from the walls of the cliff are ex͏̈ Orvieto: caves which were re-use͏̈ workshops, and storerooms for ce͏̈ addition to the intriguing Pozzo di ͏̈ it is well worth visiting the Pozzo di ͏̈ Etruscan well. Used in the 16th centur͏̈ up, the well now forms part of the base͏̈

Passages below the to͏̈

VISITORS' CHECKLIST

Perugia. **Road Map** B5.
🚆 22,000. 🚇 *Milan–Rome line, 892021.* 🚌 🛈 *Piazza del Duomo 24, 0763 341 772.*
🎭 *Corpus Domini procession; Palombella Pentecoste, 30 May.*

⊞ Palazzo Faina (Museo Civico and Museo Claudio Faina)
Piazza del Duomo 29. *Tel 0763 341 511.* ⬚ *Apr–Sep: 9:30am–6pm daily; Oct–Mar: 10am–5pm Tue–Sun.*
🅿 ♿ www.museofaina.it

This 19th-century palazzo opposite the duomo houses two museums. The Museo Civico, on the ground floor, is of much less interest than the Museo Claudio Faina, an extraordinarily rich private ͏̈ollection gathered by the ͏̈na counts in the 19th ͏̈ury. Among the exhibits ͏̈eautiful Etruscan vases, ͏̈ jewellery from the 5th ͏̈ BC onwards, and a ͏̈exquisite Attic vases. ͏̈ wonderful view of ͏̈uomo from the top ͏̈loor.

paintings, statues and other works of art that once filled the cathedral, dating from the Middle Ages up to the 18th century. Among them are paintings by Simone Martini, a series of large statues formerly in the cathedral and also a collection of church ornaments.

Detail from an Etruscan fresco, Museo dell'Opera del Duomo

⊞ Palazzo ͏̈ano and Museo Emilio Greco
Piazza del Duomo.
Tel 0763 344 605. ⬚ *Apr–Sep: 10:30am–1pm, 2–6:30pm Mon– Fri, 10:30am–1pm, 2–7pm Sat, Sun & day before public hols; Oct–Mar: 10:30am–1pm, 2–5:30pm daily.*
🅿 ♿

Commissioned in 1297 by Pope Boniface VIII, this austere building was not completed until 1359. In the early days, it was used as a storehouse by the Fabbrica del Duomo (cathedral works). Later, from the mid-16th century onwards, the hall on the ground floor was used by Orvieto's stone-masons. The structure is very simple, consisting of two large rooms one on top of the other. The lower room has a line of pilasters and arches and opens out into a grand, monumental staircase.

Palazzo Soliano houses a substantial collection of 20th-century sculptures, drawings and lithographs given to the city by Emilio Greco, a contemporary Sicilian artist.

Cinerary urn kept in the Museo Civico, Palazzo Faina

⛪ San Francesco
Piazza dei Febei.

The Romanesque church of San Francesco was founded in 1240, but it has been much altered over the centuries.

The large church has a tufa façade with three arched door-ways and mullioned windows. Inside, the vault is supported by wooden trusses of huge dimensions given the era in which they were made.

Look out for the 14th-century wooden *Crucifixion*, attributed to Maitani (a key person involved in the construction of the duomo) or his school.

Orvieto: Duomo

Lunette on the door with the Madonna and Child

Orvieto's magnificent Duomo, which dominates the skyline, was founded by Pope Nicholas IV in 1290. Things got off to a bad start and, in 1308, the Sienese architect and sculptor, Lorenzo Maitani, was brought in to save the building. It wasn't finished for another 300 years.

Maitani himself was largely responsible for the 52-m (170-ft) façade, with his own magnificently detailed bas-reliefs of scenes from the Old and New Testaments, a superb rose window, 16th-century statues and multi-coloured mosaics (not original). The striped design outside is carried through into the Romanesque nave, which has alabaster windows and is divided by columns with elaborate capitals. Inside, the master-piece is the chapel of the Madonna di San Brizio, with frescoes by Fra Angelico and Luca Signorelli and portraits of famous poets such as Dante.

Stained Glass
Among the stained glass in the apse is this Nativity *by Giovanni Bonino di Assisi.*

Sanctuary
The sanctuary walls feature 14th-century frescoes by Ugolino di Prete Ilario, a local artist. Above is a detail from the Adoration of the Magi.

The Reliquario del Corporale, the design of which copies the duomo's façade, contains the altar cloth associated with the Miracle of Bolsena.

The exterior is characterized by horizontal bands of white travertine and blue-grey basalt.

Cappella del Corporale
This chapel contains the superb 14th-century Madonna dei Raccomandati *(left) by the Sienese artist Lippo Memmi, and frescoes (1357–64) of the* Miracle of Bolsena *and* Miracles of the Sacrament *by Ugolino di Prete Ilario.*

STAR FEATURES

★ Cappella della Madonna di San Brizio

★ Façade

FRESCOES BY LUCA SIGNORELLI

A fascinating cycle of frescoes narrating events related to the Apocalypse unfolds on the walls of the Cappella della Madonna di San Brizio. Signorelli tackles the themes of the Last Judgment – *The Day of Judgment*, *The Preaching of the Antichrist*, *The Resurrection of the Dead*, *The Damned Consigned to Hell*, *The Blessed Entering Heaven*, and *Angels Guide the Elect to Paradise* – blending spatial harmony and dynamism in a synthesis of the art of central Italy of the time. The three-dimensionality and energy emanating from the figures heighten the drama and anticipate the painting of Michelangelo in the Sistine Chapel.

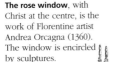

Detail from the fresco of Day of Judgment by Signorelli

VISITORS' CHECKLIST

Piazza Duomo. **Tel** *0763 341 167, 0763 343 592 (tickets)*. **Duomo and Chapel** ☐ *Apr–Jun: 9:30am–7:30pm daily (1–5:30pm Sun); Jul–Sep: 9:30am–7:30pm daily (1–6pm Sun); Oct: 9am–7:30pm daily (1–5:30pm Sun); Nov–Mar: 9am–1pm, 2:30–5pm daily (to 5:30pm Sun).* 📷 ♿

★ Cappella della Madonna di San Brizio
The fresco cycle in this Gothic chapel, begun by Fra Angelico (1447) with the assistance of Benozzo Gozzoli, and later completed by Luca Signorelli (1499–1504), is one of the finest of the Renaissance.

The rose window, with Christ at the centre, is the work of Florentine artist Andrea Orcagna (1360). The window is encircled by sculptures.

★ Façade
Bas-reliefs and statues (the originals of some are in the Museo dell'Opera), mosaics, pilasters and arches characterize this perfect synthesis between architecture and the decorative arts. It is a stunning example of Italian Gothic.

Main Door
The decorated bronze panels of the main door were the work of Emilio Greco in the 1960s.

🏯 Torre del Moro

Corso Cavour 87. **Tel** 0763 344 567. ☐ Mar, Apr, Sep, Oct: 10am–7pm; May–Aug: 10am–8pm; Nov–Feb: 10:30am–1pm, 2:30–5pm daily. 🎫

The 12th-century "Tower of the Moor" towers 42 m (137 ft) above Corso Cavour, Orvieto's main street, where it meets Via del Duomo. It owes its name to the figure on the coat of arms of the Pucci, a local family. Its 14th-century bell is still in working order.

Alongside the tower is the **Palazzo dei Sette** (1300), built as the seat of the seven (*sette*) magistrates in charge of the commune, and later the seat of the papal governor.

The Torre del Moro rising above the roofs of old Orvieto

🏛 Sant'Andrea

Piazza della Repubblica.

This church is one of the oldest buildings in Orvieto. Founded in the 7th century, Sant'Andrea was built upon walls of probable Etruscan origin, over which a Roman temple was later built. It was then rebuilt in stages during the 12th–14th centuries.

Sant'Andrea was once the most important church

in Orvieto. It was here that Pope Innocent III proclaimed the Fourth Crusade in 1201 and that Martin IV was crowned pope in 1281, in the presence of Charles of Anjou.

Important elements include the Gothic door, by Marco da Siena, designed by Maestro Vetrino (1487), and the imposing 12-sided bell tower, with three orders of two-mullioned windows and a series of coats of arms, placed here when restoration was undertaken in 1920–30. The interior is supported by great granite columns, probably Roman, and is decorated with fragments of frescoes and a 10th-century pulpit.

🏯 Palazzo del Popolo

Piazza del Popolo. 🚫 to the public.

The heart of the city in ancient times, Piazza del Popolo is home to the Palazzo del Popolo, first described in the town records at the end of the 13th century. Built from the local tufa stone and topped by a bell tower, it is an important example of Orvieto civic architecture from the late 13th century. Ornamentations include an external staircase, an open loggia, crenellations, and mullioned windows linked by a cornice. It is now a conference centre.

Detail from the Palazzo del Popolo

The façade of San Domenico with the original striped pilasters

🏛 San Domenico

Piazza XXIX Marzo.

It was here that the unusual striped stonework, in dark-coloured basalt and pale travertine, appeared for the first time in Orvieto, in the late 13th century. The style was then extensively used in the duomo and became a signature motif for the city. Despite substantial restoration in the Baroque era, the façade maintains its simple Romanesque-Gothic austerity, with a beautiful doorway, a tall two-mullioned window and a rose window which repeats the two-coloured motif.

Half the church was taken down in the 20th century to make room for the nearby barracks; the interior space today consists merely of the original transept and the tribune. The main work of art is the splendid tomb of Cardinal Guglielmo de Braye by Arnolfo di Cambio (1282), but there are also frescoes and other examples of sculpture.

🏯 Pozzo di San Patrizio

Viale Sangallo. **Tel** 0763 343 768. ☐ daily. Mar, Apr, Sep & Oct: 9am–7pm; May–Aug: 9am–8pm; Nov–Feb: 10am–5pm. 🎫

Located at the eastern end of Corso Cavour is one of Orvieto's best-known monuments. Commissioned in 1527 by Pope Clement VII and designed by Antonio da Sangallo the Younger, the

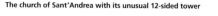

The church of Sant'Andrea with its unusual 12-sided tower

The impressive depths forming the Pozzo di San Patrizio

62-m (203-ft) well is a superb piece of engineering. Crucial to the design are two 248-step spiral staircases: one was used for the descent and one for the ascent, so that donkeys carrying pitchers of water would not meet on the way. The stairways are lit by 72 windows.

Looking over the plain from the bastions of the Rocca

Rocca dell'Albornoz
Viale Sangallo. ☐ always open.
Dominating the eastern end of Orvieto, near the terminus of the funicular that connects the old city with the railway station down on the plain, is the **Rocca**, built by Cardinal Albornoz in 1364 to bolster the power of the papacy. The locals destroyed it soon afterwards, and not much remains today.

The Rocca is an excellent vantage point from which to enjoy superb views over the city and the plain, as well as being a tranquil spot, surrounded as it is by several pretty gardens.

Environs
Around 1.5 km (1 mile) north of Orvieto, at the foot of the tufa cliff, is the **Necropoli del Crocifisso del Tufo**. This Etruscan cemetery complex dates from the 6th–3rd centuries BC and consists of small chambered tombs built of tufa blocks and containing a stone bench for laying out the corpse. On the lintel over the entrance to each tomb is the name of the person or family buried there. The site seems to have an essentially "urban" layout, following what would be defined today as a town plan.

The site was discovered only in the 19th century, by foreign archaeologists who passed on some of the finds to the Louvre and the British Museum. It wasn't until 1880 that the site was first explored in a scientific, non-intrusive way and finally began to arouse the interest of the Italian authorities. Over 100 tombs have now been found. The majority of the important funerary objects

discovered in the tombs are now distributed among Orvieto's museums.

On the south side of the cliff is the **Necropoli della Cannicella**, another burial site used by the Etruscans from the 7th–3rd centuries BC. It follows a similar layout to the necropolis at Crocifisso del Tufo.

Around 3 km (2 miles) south of Orvieto, just off SS71, is the **Abbazia di Santi Severo e Martino**, a great medieval monastery complex. Now partly converted into a hotel (La Badia, see p150), the monastery belonged to the Benedictines until 1221 and then the Premonstratensians (a French Order founded in 1120 by St Norbert).

Apart from the rooms used by the hotel, several areas of the monastery can still be visited. There is much that dates from the original construction (12th–13th-centuries). The splendid 12-sided Romanesque tower dates from the 12th century. The church, reached through a great 13th-century arch, features a single nave with a ribbed vault, an inlaid marble floor in the Cosmatesque style and several fragments of medieval frescoes. The barrel-vaulted Oratorio del Crocifisso, once the monks' refectory, is adorned with a 13th-century fresco depicting the *Crucifixion with Saints*. Also of interest is the 13th-century Abbot's House.

Necropoli del Crocifisso del Tufo
Tel 0763 343 611. ☐ 8:30am–7pm (winter: 5pm) daily.

Etruscan necropolis of the Crocifisso del Tufo, 6th century BC

TRAVELLERS' NEEDS

WHERE TO STAY

The range of accommodation in Umbria is impressively varied and caters to all tastes and pockets. While the traditional hotel is still an option in the main tourist centres, a large number of *agriturismo*, or working-farm, establishments have sprung up out of town, as have more luxurious country-house hotels, some with spas or wellness centres.

Logo of the consortium of Umbria hoteliers

Bed-and-breakfast accommodation has also become more popular, and there is now a substantial network of B&Bs, both in the countryside and in the region's towns. More basic accommodation is offered by religious institutions to groups and individuals alike, while camping is another popular option in this region, often referred to as the green heart of Italy.

GRADING AND PRICES

Hotels in Umbria are classified according to the standards followed in the rest of Italy. The categories run from one to five stars, plus a top luxury hotel category (L). Services offered are generally good. Prices vary according to the season and are higher during festivals and major cultural events. In general, the three-star category offers the best value for money.

Most hotels accept credit cards, except perhaps some in the lower-starred categories. If in doubt, it is best to check beforehand.

BOOKING

Umbria does not really have much of a low season, although visitor numbers drop between November and February. Booking ahead is strongly advised; a fax or an email to confirm the booking is often requested.

HOTELS

Many of the hotels in Umbria's major towns are grouped into local consortiums – this is done in order to promote standards and to protect the interest of both the hotel and the guests. Lists with prices and other information are published annually by the Perugia tourist office (APT).

HISTORIC RESIDENCES

A strong sense of the past is palpable in Umbria. For an unforgettable holiday, you might want to stay in a place that is steeped in history. The region features a wealth of centuries-old buildings, a number of which have been adapted to accommodate visitors. Standards are strictly regulated, so that the carefully refurbished interiors lose none of their character and charm; period furniture and artistic treasures abound in these establishments.

A luxury hotel complex created out of 17th-century farm buildings

For a night or two in the peaceful environment of a monastery try the tranquil La Badia *(see p150)*, just outside Orvieto, or the equally lovely Eremo delle Grazie *(see p151)*, near Spoleto.

Those with aspirations of grandeur, could opt for an actual castle. Try the opulent Castello dell'Oscano *(see p147)*, near Perugia, or, near Gubbio, the Castello di Petroia *(see p145)*, where a great Renaissance ruler, Duke Federico da Montefeltro, was born.

AGRITURISMO AND COUNTRY HOUSES

Holidaying at a working farm, or *agriturismo*, has become a tremendously popular option throughout Umbria. As well as accommodation – either in rooms on B&B terms, or in independent self-catering apartments – many places offer a wide variety of facilities, including swimming pools and bikes. Horse-riding and other activities, such as cookery, pottery or yoga classes, are sometimes

The welcoming reception area at Le Silve hotel in Assisi

◁ **Market traders in the Piazza del Mercato in Spoleto**

available, and guests are often encouraged to take an active part in farm life. Meals prepared with traditional local ingredients, some of which must be produced by the farm itself, are usually served to external diners as well as guests. The self-catering option generally requires a longer stay, paid for in advance, especially in high season.

Country-house hotels are a more upmarket option to stay in rural surroundings. A country house is usually more luxurious than an *agriturismo*, often with more sports and wellness facilities and a more refined restaurant, without the home-grown produce aspect.

Local tourist offices can provide visitors with full listings containing information on costs and facilities.

CAMPSITES

There are campsites all over the region: all the historic Umbrian towns have at least one, and the area around Lake Trasimeno has a range of sites suited to tents, camper vans or caravans.

All Umbrian campsites are registered with the authorities and listed in regional tourist guides issued by the Perugia and Terni tourist offices.

Sites are usually clean and well run, and often located in attractive settings. Overnight stops by camper vans are strictly regulated; overnight stays are prohibited in historic centres, while in the modern or less touristy centres there are often designated parking places.

A rustic, cosy room with antique furniture at Agriturismo Cigliano

Hilltop hamlet converted into *agriturismo* accommodation

BED & BREAKFAST

Bed-and-breakfast establishments can be found throughout Umbria, both in the region's towns and in the countryside. Expect to find homely, simple accommodation and a friendly welcome. Rooms are usually limited, so if you wish to stay at a particular place, it is wise to book well in advance.

SELF-CATERING APARTMENTS

Falconry, practised at some *agriturismo* farms

One option for a longer stay in the area is to rent an apartment. Whether you want to be based in the countryside, by a lake, in the mountains or in a town, you'll find there's a good choice of properties available for short-term lets. Many of them are attached to an *agriturismo* or grouped together in a holiday village, with the benefit of shared facilities.

RELIGIOUS INSTITUTIONS

Many religious institutions offer simple accommodation to visitors. This may be in the form of a no-frills hotel, but some convents or monasteries provide special lodgings for pilgrims. There is a wide choice in Assisi, a major pilgrimage destination, but it is also worth looking in much smaller places, such as Bevagna or Spello. Meals are not normally provided, with the exception of the

busy hostels in Assisi. The accommodation lists supplied by the tourist office are the best source of information.

YOUTH HOSTELS AND STUDENT ACCOMMODATION

Perugia, a university town, has youth hostels and student accommodation of various types; for sources of information, *see p175*.

DIRECTORY

Agriturist Umbria
www.agrituristumbria.com
Perugia
Via Savanarola 38.
Tel 075 32028.

Perugia IAT
Piazza Matteotti 18.
Tel 075 573 64 58.
http://turismo.comune.perugia.it

Terni IAT
Via Cassian Bon 1.
Tel 0744 423 047.
www.marmore.it

Umbria Bed and Breakfast
www.bed-and-breakfast-in-umbria.it

Umbria Information
Umbrian region tourist information.
www.regioneumbria.eu
www.bellaumbria.net
www.lamiaumbria.it

Choosing a Hotel

The following hotels have been selected across a wide price range for their good value, facilities and location. They are divided into two sections, corresponding to the sightseeing chapters in this guide. Within each area, establishments are listed in alphabetical order by town or village, and in ascending price order.

PRICE CATEGORIES
The following price ranges are for a double room per night, in high season, including breakfast, tax and service.

€ Under €85
€€ €85–€150
€€€ €150–€250
€€€€ €250–€350
€€€€€ Over €350

NORTHERN UMBRIA

ASSISI Hotel Berti　　　　　　　　　　　　　€
Piazza San Pietro, 06081 **Tel** *075 81 34 66* **Fax** *075 81 68 70* **Rooms** *10*　　　**Road map** *D4*

The best thing about this hotel is the convenient central location at the bottom of a hill in old Assisi, not far from the bus stop linking the town with the railway station. The decor is cosy and old-fashioned with antique furniture, parquet floors and a sunny terrace restaurant. Bedrooms are a good size and smartly decorated. **www.hotelberti.it**

ASSISI Tre Esse Country House　　　　　　　　€
Via di Valecchie 41, 06081 **Tel** *075 81 63 63* **Fax** *075 81 61 55* **Rooms** *20*　　**Road map** *D4*

This country house, less than a kilometre from central Assisi, was built in the 1920s over a medieval structure – the ancient watchtower still stands. It boasts lovely gardens and wonderful views; the antique furnishings make the interior even more special. This is an ideal place for winding down. **www.countryhousetreesse.com**

ASSISI Fontebella　　　　　　　　　　　　　€€
Via Fontebella 25, 06081 **Tel** *075 81 28 83* **Fax** *075 81 29 41* **Rooms** *46*　　**Road map** *D4*

Inside an old oil mill, this ivy-covered stone house spread over seven floors has tranquil gardens. The large bedrooms are painted yellow and have modern bathrooms. Some also have a private balcony with views. Spend the evening in the tasteful sitting room, which features a lovely fireplace and frescoed ceilings. **www.fontebella.com**

ASSISI Hotel Alexander　　　　　　　　　　€€
Piazza Chiesa Nuova 6, 06081 **Tel** *&* **Fax** *075 81 61 90* **Rooms** *8*　　**Road map** *D4*

This small hotel right in the centre of old Assisi is perfect for those on a budget. Its decorative features include wooden beams, antique furniture and high ceilings. The bedrooms are large and can accommodate extra beds, making it an ideal option for families. There is also a roof terrace with a lovely view. **www.assisi-hotel.com**

ASSISI Hotel Giotto　　　　　　　　　　　€€
Via Fontebella 41, 06081 **Tel** *075 81 22 09* **Fax** *075 81 64 79* **Rooms** *83*　　**Road map** *D4*

Set in a terrific position in the highest part of Assisi, this family-run hotel has some breathtaking views, which you can enjoy from the panoramic terraces and from some of the elegantly but comfortably furnished rooms. The service is pleasant and polite. **www.hotelgiottoassisi.it**

ASSISI Hotel Il Palazzo　　　　　　　　　　€€
Via San Francesco 8, 06081 **Tel** *075 81 68 42* **Fax** *075 81 23 70* **Rooms** *12*　　**Road map** *D4*

The decor is pleasantly light and bright in this traditional hotel located in the 16th-century Palazzo Bartocci Fontana, halfway between St Francis Basilica and Assisi's main square. The hotel has a cosy reading room, a traditional, brick-vaulted restaurant and splendid views over the surrounding hills. **www.hotelilpalazzo.it**

ASSISI Hotel Umbra　　　　　　　　　　　€€
Via degli Archi 6 (Piazza del Comune), 06081 **Tel** *075 81 22 40* **Fax** *075 81 36 53* **Rooms** *24*　　**Road map** *D4*

Tucked away on a small street, not far from the town hall, this is a very popular little hotel and restaurant, with a courtyard garden offering alfresco dining in the summer months. Quiet and family-run, the Umbra has tiled floors and antiques throughout. Bedrooms are airy and elegantly decorated. **www.hotelumbra.it**

ASSISI Il Maniero　　　　　　　　　　　　€€
Via San Pietro Campagna, Via Biagiano 11, 06081 **Tel** *075 81 63 79* **Fax** *075 81 51 47* **Rooms** *17*　**Road map** *D4*

The original stone walls of this medieval castle, built around a pretty inner courtyard, give the place a feeling of timelessness. There are some fantastic views over the Umbrian hills from the tastefully decorated, comfortable rooms, and the attractive garden is a great place to sit and relax. **www.ilmaniero.com**

ASSISI Hotel Le Silve　　　　　　　　　　€€€
Località Armenzano 82, 06081 **Tel** *075 801 90 00* **Fax** *075 801 90 05* **Rooms** *15*　　**Road map** *D4*

This charming 10th-century farmhouse is a tranquil hideaway in the Subasio national park, 10 km (6 miles) from Assisi. It offers sun terraces, a pool and horse-riding facilities, as well as independent apartments. Bedrooms have lovely views, stone walls, terracotta floors, wooden beams, fireplaces and antiques. Closed Dec–Mar. **www.lesilve.it**

Key to Symbols *see back cover flap*

BETTONA Relais La Corte di Bettona

€€€ · Road map C4

Via Santa Caterina 2, 06084 **Tel** *075 98 71 14* **Fax** *075 986 91 30* **Rooms** *39*

This pretty hotel in a 14th-century building in the attractive medieval centre of Bettona offers good fitness facilities, as well as a sauna and swimming pool and a terrific restaurant specializing in local cuisine. There is also a wide choice of bedrooms featuring various levels of comfort. **www.relaisbettona.com**

CALZOLARO La Preghiera

€€€ · Road map B2

Via del Refari, 06018 **Tel** *075 930 24 28 or +44 (0)20 7060 0393* **Rooms** *11*

With beautifully furnished rooms, a lovely garden and pool and a private chapel, this wonderfully secluded, yet easily accessible, 12th-century monastery is the ideal location for a relaxing break. Yoga retreats and cookery courses are organized here, and there are also good opportunities for walking. **www.lapreghiera.com**

CIGLIANO Agriturismo Cigliano

€ · Road map D2

Frazione Colpalombo 22, 06020 **Tel & Fax** *075 925 33 33* **Rooms** *8*

At this attractive grey-stone house in a rural setting, bedrooms are lit by candlelight only, which adds to the sense of getting away from it all. This is a great place for stargazing: the young owner is a keen astronomer and happy to share his knowledge with guests. Table tennis and archery facilities are also available. **www.agriturismo-cigliano.it**

CITTÀ DELLA PIEVE Hotel Piccolo Eden

€ · Road map A4

Via Santa Lucia 53, 06062 **Tel** *0578 29 70 65* **Fax** *0578 29 70 66* **Rooms** *36*

Just a short walk to the city walls, Piccolo Eden is a friendly and relaxing hotel, with a swimming pool and sunbathing area as well as a terrace where food is served, weather permitting. It's also a good base for visits to Lake Trasimeno, Arezzo, Siena and Castiglione del Lago. **www.hotelpiccoloeden.it**

CITTÀ DELLA PIEVE Hotel Vannucci

€€€ · Road map A4

Via Vanni 1, 06062 **Tel** *0578 29 80 63* **Fax** *0578 29 79 54* **Rooms** *30*

This pretty American-run villa in a historic palazzo is charmingly decorated, combining stunning antique furniture with modern artworks. Located in the heart of the old town, the Vannucci offers friendly service and lovely gardens. Highly recommended. **www.hotel-vannucci.com**

CITTÀ DI CASTELLO Hotel Garden

€€ · Road map B2

Via Aldo Bologni, 06012 **Tel** *075 855 05 87* **Fax** *075 852 13 67* **Rooms** *59*

This hotel is about a 15-minute walk from the centre of Città di Castello, in the beautiful Tiber river valley. If the walk sounds too strenuous, there is also a regular bus service. The hotel's decor and furnishings are fairly simple and basic, but there's a great swimming pool and a spa. **www.hotelgarden.com**

CITTÀ DI CASTELLO Hotel Tiferno

€€€ · Road map B2

Piazza R Sanzio 13, 06012 **Tel** *075 855 03 31* **Fax** *075 852 11 96* **Rooms** *47*

Located in a former 11th-century convent on a small square in the *centro storico*, this is one of Umbria's oldest hotels, in business since 1895. The public areas are elegant, with fireplaces and vaults and a collection of Alberto Burri's paintings. The rooms are modern and comfortable. **www.hoteltiferno.it**

CORCIANO La Contea B&B

€ · Road map C3

Via Cattaneo 25, San Mariano di Corciano, 06073 **Tel** *333 127 25 47* **Rooms** *3*

The lovely 17th-century stone building housing this B&B was used for a time as a monastery. The bedrooms are simply but pleasantly furnished, and breakfast is served in the tower room. The hotel is set in its own extensive grounds and borders a golf course. **www.bblacontea.it**

DERUTA Antica Fattoria del Colle

€ · Road map C4

Strada Colle delle Forche 6, 06053 **Tel** *075 97 22 01 or 329 989 72 72* **Rooms** *7*

Owned by a charming couple from Rome, this *agriturismo* is just outside Deruta, in woodland on a hill surrounded by olive groves and vineyards. It consists of two brick and stone farmhouses with antiques, terracotta floors, wooden beams and sunny terraces. Excellent home cooking and delicious wines are on offer. **www.anticafattoriadelcolle.it**

DERUTA Relais il Canalicchio

€€€ · Road map C4

Via della Piazza 13, Collazzone, 06053 **Tel** *075 870 73 25* **Fax** *075 870 72 96* **Rooms** *49*

The Canalicchio's fabulous 11th-century walled structure remains intact, enhancing the almost tangible feeling of history here. Great care is taken over details, and the furniture and furnishings fit in well. There's also plenty to do, with tennis courts, a gym and a swimming pool. **www.relaisilcanalicchio.it**

GUBBIO Grotta dell'Angelo

€ · Road map D2

Via Gioia 47, 06024 **Tel** *075 927 17 47* **Fax** *075 927 34 38* **Rooms** *18*

In the heart of old Gubbio, this quietly located family hotel offers clean, simple accommodation in a small medieval house with whitewashed stone walls, and a log fire in winter. Bedrooms are very clean and cheerful, all en suite. The Grotta dell'Angelo has a garden and a delightful restaurant under a pergola in summer. **www.grottadellangelo.it**

GUBBIO Castello di Petroia

€€ · Road map D2

Località Petroia, Scritto di Gubbio, 06020 **Tel** *075 92 02 87* **Fax** *075 92 01 08* **Rooms** *11*

The sense of history is strong at this castle where Duke Federico da Montefeltro was born nearly 600 years ago, and the antique furnishings and open fires add to the charm. Each room has something special about it – one room is in the castle tower. There is also a fantastic outside area with lovely views over the hills. **www.castellodipetroia.com**

GUBBIO La Rocca

Località Monte Ingino 15, 06024 **Tel & Fax** *075 922 12 22* **Rooms** *12*   **Road map** *D2*

Built against the rock-face, parts of which are even visible in some rooms, this hotel is situated near the Sant'Ubaldo basilica. Its location makes for some wonderful views over the town of Gubbio below. You can travel between the hotel and the city centre by the curious birdcage cable-car, or by road. Closed Jan–Mar. **www.laroccahotel.net**

GUBBIO Villa Montegranelli

Località Monteluiano, 06024 **Tel** *075 922 01 85* **Fax** *075 927 33 72* **Rooms** *21*   **Road map** *D2*

This 18th-century building (erected on the site of a medieval structure) lies 4 km (2.5 miles) from Gubbio. Located at the end of an avenue of cypresses, the villa is filled with stuccoes, frescoes and antiques. Bedrooms are luxurious, with lovely views over the valley. Good restaurant. **www.villamontegranellihotel.it**

GUBBIO Park Hotel ai Cappuccini

Via Tifernate, 06024 **Tel** *075 92 34* **Fax** *075 922 03 23* **Rooms** *95*   **Road map** *D2*

This large hotel in a beautifully restored 17th-century monastery is set in lovely secluded grounds, just a stroll from the town centre. The hotel features an excellent range of sports and wellness facilities, including a 25 m indoor swimming pool. The highly regarded hotel restaurant serves typical Umbrian fare. **www.parkhotelaicappuccini.it**

GUBBIO Relais Ducale

Via Galeotti 19, 06024 **Tel** *075 922 01 57* **Fax** *075 922 01 59* **Rooms** *30*   **Road map** *D2*

This stately building is situated just off Gubbio's main square, the Piazza della Signoria. Rooms vary in size and decor, but all are elegant, some with balconies and views over the city and surrounding hillsides. Rooms and public areas are furnished with handsome antiques. Breakfast is served on a lovely terrace. **www.mencarelligroup.com**

LAKE TRASIMENO – CASTIGLIONE DEL LAGO La Bandita

For info: Via del Melograno 34, 53044 Chiusi Scalo (SI) **Tel & Fax** *057 82 14 59* **Rooms** *11*   **Road map** *B3*

Accommodation is in variously sized apartments, all attractively restored and furnished with antiques. All have independent entrances, as well as their own garden, with outside tables, chairs and barbecues. There are wonderful views over Lake Trasimeno and Castiglione del Lago. **www.casedelmelograno.it**

LAKE TRASIMENO – CASTIGLIONE DEL LAGO Locanda Poggio Leone

Via Indipendenza 116b, Pozzuolo, 06061 **Tel** *075 95 95 19* **Fax** *075 95 96 09* **Rooms** *12*   **Road map** *B3*

There's plenty to do at this peaceful spot near the Tuscan border. As well as the swimming pool, facilities include table tennis, table football and mountain-bike riding. The decor is smart and rustic at the same time, with beamed ceilings and terracotta floors. Oil, wine and jam are produced in-house. **www.locandapoggioleone.it**

LAKE TRASIMENO – CASTIGLIONE DEL LAGO Miralago

Piazza Mazzini 6, Castiglione del Lago, 06061 **Tel** *075 95 11 57* **Fax** *075 95 19 24* **Rooms** *19*   **Road map** *B3*

In a central position in the town of Castiglione del Lago, this charming red building has comfortable, old-fashioned rooms, each decorated individually. Views of either the lake or the square can be enjoyed from each room. The hotel garden faces Lake Trasimeno and offers alfresco dining in the summer months. **www.hotelmiralago.com**

LAKE TRASIMENO – ISOLA MAGGIORE Da Sauro

Via Guglielmini 1, Isola Maggiore, 06069 **Tel** *075 82 61 68* **Fax** *075 82 67 27* **Rooms** *12*   **Road map** *B3*

Da Sauro is located at the northern end of the little fishing village on Isola Maggiore, on Lake Trasimeno. This lovely family-run hotel in an old stone building has an excellent fish restaurant and a charming verandah with lake views. Bedrooms are comfortable and en suite. B&B or half- and full-board options are available. **www.dasauro.it**

LAKE TRASIMENO – PASSIGNANO Hotel Kursaal

Via Europa 24, Passignano sul Trasimeno, 06065 **Tel** *075 82 80 85* **Fax** *075 82 71 82* **Rooms** *16*   **Road map** *B3*

A family-owned villa with a large garden on the shores of Lake Trasimeno, close to the town centre. In summer, delicious breakfasts are served on the sun terrace beside the pool. The seafood restaurant is popular all year round. Bedrooms are comfortable, with private balconies that are perfect for watching the sunset. **www.kursaalhotel.net**

MIGLIANO DI MARSCIANO Il Casale di Buccole Country House

Vocabolo Buccole 25, 06050 **Tel** *075 870 81 26* **Fax** *06 594 36 08* **Rooms** *8*   **Road map** *C4*

This 19th-century farmhouse has been converted into an elegant country-house hotel without losing any of its charm. Refined yet comfortable, the rooms are all individually decorated and furnished, some with four-poster beds. The restaurant is renowned for its excellent home cooking. **www.countrybuccole.com**

PANICALE Romantik Hotel – Villa di Monte Solare

Via Montali 7, Colle San Paolo, 06068 **Tel** *075 83 23 76* **Fax** *075 835 54 62* **Rooms** *28*   **Road map** *C4*

This charming place has a historic feel and extensive grounds that contain olive groves, vineyards and woodland, as well as a formal garden, an orangerie and a chapel. The interior, furnished with antiques, is warm and welcoming, and the restaurant, the renowned Villa di Monte Solare, is recommended *(see p159)*. **www.villamontesolare.it**

PERUGIA Hotel Rosalba

Via del Circo 7, 06121 **Tel** *075 572 82 85* **Fax** *075 572 06 26* **Rooms** *11*   **Road map** *C3*

The Rosalba is located in a simple but elegant 18th-century townhouse with a pleasant façade. The hotel is conveniently located in the lower part of central Perugia. The furnishings in the bedrooms are fairly basic, but the views of the city from the terrace are wonderful. **www.hotelrosalba.com**

Key to Price Guide *see p144* **Key to Symbols** *see back cover flap*

PERUGIA Hotel Sant'Ercolano

Via del Bovaro 9, 06122 **Tel** & **Fax** *075 572 46 50* **Rooms** *15* **Road map** *C3*

Near the church of Sant'Ercolano, in the *centro storico*, this budget hotel is housed within a 17th-century building. Two minutes from the bus station, it is a convenient base for exploring the surrounding region. The rooms are simple but comfortable, all en suite and with cooling fans in summer. Breakfast is extra. **www.santercolano.com**

PERUGIA Albergo Lo Spedalicchio

Piazza Bruno Buozzi 3, Ospedalicchio, 06080 **Tel** & **Fax** *075 801 03 23* **Rooms** *25* **Road map** *C3*

This medieval fortress is located in a tiny hamlet halfway between Assisi and Perugia, just off the main road. A latter-day inn used by travellers and pilgrims, it is a quiet enclave. Bedrooms are spacious and en suite, with wooden beams and antique furniture. Breakfast is extra. The restaurant serves fine regional fare. **www.lospedalicchio.it**

PERUGIA Etruscan Chocohotel

Via Campo di Marte 134, 06124 **Tel** & **Fax** *075 583 73 14* **Rooms** *94* **Road map** *C3*

Fitting in with Perugia's reputation as the Italian chocolate capital, this is the ideal accommodation for chocoholics! The hotel aims to immerse guests in all things chocolate as much as possible. The three floors are dedicated to different varieties, and the restaurant even offers a menu completely based on the cocoa bean. **www.chocohotel.it**

PERUGIA Hotel La Fortuna

Via Luigi Bonazzi 19, 06123 **Tel** *075 572 28 45* **Fax** *075 573 50 40* **Rooms** *34* **Road map** *C3*

A restored palazzo with a lovely rooftop terrace, modern facilities and friendly, professional staff. There are frescoes in the restaurant and in some of the pricier rooms, many of which also have sitting rooms and terraces. Economy rooms are basic, without air conditioning; standard rooms are larger, with air conditioning. **www.umbriahotels.com**

PERUGIA Relais San Clemente

Località Bosco **Tel** & **Fax** *075 591 51 00* **Fax** *075 591 50 01* **Rooms** *64* **Road map** *C3*

Housed in a converted 13th-century convent just east of Perugia, this elegant and comfortable hotel boasts large and imaginatively furnished rooms. Tennis courts, a swimming pool and other sports facilities are available in the substantial and well-kept grounds. **www.relais.it**

PERUGIA Alla Posta dei Donini

Via Deruta 43, San Martino in Campo, 06029 **Tel** & **Fax** *075 60 91 32* **Rooms** *48* **Road map** *C3*

Accommodation is in two lovely villas dating from the 17th century and linked by a covered walkway. Prestigious works of art adorn the walls, and the rest of the decor is equally sumptuous. The extensive grounds are perfectly maintained and feature some fine collections of trees and plants. **www.postadonini.it**

PERUGIA Castello dell'Oscano

Strada Forcella 37, Cenerente, 06070 **Tel** *075 58 43 71* **Fax** *075 69 06 66* **Rooms** *11* **Road map** *C3*

A stay at this grand old manor house situated in its own extensive grounds makes for a truly memorable experience. In the autumn you can take part in the olive harvest and watch olive oil being made. Excellent service and beautifully decorated rooms complete the pleasant picture. **www.oscano.com**

PERUGIA Albergo Brufani Palace

Piazza Italia 12, 06100 **Tel** *075 573 25 41* **Fax** *075 572 02 10* **Rooms** *94* **Road map** *C3*

This four-storey luxury hotel on a hill in central Perugia offers lovely views over the valleys below. High, frescoed ceilings, parquet floors, stone fireplaces, chandeliers and antiques abound; bedrooms are particularly sumptuous. The swimming pool has a glass floor above Etruscan ruins. Fine restaurant. **www.brufanipalace.com**

PETRIGNANO La Torretta

Via del Ponte 1, 06086 **Tel** *075 803 87 78* **Fax** *075 803 94 74* **Rooms** *31* **Road map** *D3*

In a lovely farmland location, this is a great place to enjoy the delights of the Umbrian countryside. A river runs along one side of the grounds, and there are great views over the surrounding hills. In summer, breakfast is served alfresco on the extensive patio. **www.assisionline.com/latorretta**

PETRIGNANO Locanda ai Cavalieri

Via Matteotti 47, 06086 **Tel** *075 803 00 11* **Fax** *075 803 97 98* **Rooms** *24* **Road map** *D3*

Set in well-kept extensive gardens, with a particularly beautiful rose walk, the Locanda offers a wonderfully relaxing stay. The interior has been carefully restored and decorated, in keeping with the style of the house, and each bedroom is individually furnished. The hotel restaurant is also extremely good *(see p161)*. **www.aicavalieri.it**

PIEGARO Ca' de' Principi

Via Roma 43, 06066 **Tel** *075 835 80 40* **Fax** *075 835 80 15* **Rooms** *18* **Road map** *B4*

Luxuriously plush, this former home of princes has been made into a fabulous hotel. There are panoramic views over the Umbrian countryside from the swimming pool and Jacuzzi – stylish relaxation is guaranteed. Inside, the walls are adorned with some fantastic, carefully restored frescoes and trompe l'oeils. **www.dimorastorica.it**

TORGIANO Le Tre Vaselle

Via Garibaldi 48, 06089 **Tel** *075 988 04 47* **Fax** *075 988 02 14* **Rooms** *60* **Road map** *C4*

This enchanting 17th-century villa set amid vines offers extensive terraces and gardens, a spa centre and two pools. The rooms are elegant, with hand-woven fabrics and terracotta floors; suites have fireplaces. There are also apartments for rent on the grounds. A shuttle service is available to Perugia and Assisi. **www.3vaselle.it**

SOUTHERN UMBRIA

ACQUASPARTA Castello di Casigliano
Piazza Corsini 1, 05021 **Tel** *0744 94 34 28* **Fax** *0744 94 40 56* **Rooms** *7 apartments*   **Road map** *D6*

With its location at the centre of the region, this fabulous medieval hamlet makes an ideal base for visiting south Umbria. The 16th-century cottages have been restored into comfortable, cosy holiday apartments. There's a private panoramic garden and a great restaurant, Il Re Beve *(see p161)*. **www.castellodicasigliano.com**

BASCHI La Penisola Villa Bellago
SS 448, Todi-Baschi, Lago di Corbara, 05023 **Tel** *0744 95 05 21* **Fax** *0744 95 05 24* **Rooms** *19*   **Road map** *B6*

In a leafy setting on the banks of Lake Corbara, this centuries-old hotel building was once a farmhouse. Tennis and five-a-side football are available, as is an open-air swimming pool. The hotel restaurant specializes in local cuisine, including freshwater-fish dishes. **www.albergolapenisola.it**

BEVAGNA L'Orto degli Angeli
Via Dante Alighieri 1, 06031 **Tel** *0742 36 01 30* **Fax** *0742 36 17 56* **Rooms** *14*   **Road map** *D4*

Two historic buildings, linked by a terrace garden, make up this elegant hotel. Each room is furnished individually with a combination of handsome antique pieces and more modern designs created by local craftsmen. Redibis, the hotel restaurant *(see p162)*, has been labelled as one of the country's best. **www.ortoangeli.it**

BRUFA DI TORGIANO Borgo Brufa
Via del Colle 38, 06089 **Tel** *075 98 52 67* **Fax** *075 48 01 06* **Rooms** *15*   **Road map** *C4*

Set on a hilltop with fantastic panoramic views, and surrounded by vineyards and olive trees, Borgo Brufa is the perfect place to be pampered in a relaxing environment. The wellness centre provides a gym and swimming pool, as well as various treatments and massages. **www.borgobrufa.it**

CALVI DELL'UMBRIA Casale San Martino Agriturismo
Colle San Martino 10, 05032 **Tel & Fax** *0744 71 06 44* **Rooms** *4 apartments*   **Road map** *D6*

From its hilltop position, the Casale enjoys a fantastic panorama, with views over the lush rolling hills of Umbria. Four apartments are available, all individually furnished with antique furniture. Facilities include barbecues, a swimming pool and a large children's playground. **www.casalesanmartino.com**

CAMPELLO SUL CLITUNNO Il Vecchio Molino
Via del Tempio 34, Località Pissignano, 06042 **Tel** *0743 52 11 22* **Fax** *0743 27 50 97* **Rooms** *13*   **Road map** *D5*

B&B accommodation is available at this 15th-century mill, which produced flour and olive oil. Powered by the waters of the Fonti del Clitunno, the mill stopped working only recently, but the lovely location beside the tumbling river remains. Rooms are simple, rustic and comfortable. Closed Nov–Mar. **www.perugiaonline.com/vecchiomolino**

CASCIA Casale Sant'Antonio Agriturismo
Casale Sant'Antonio 59, 06043 **Tel** *074 37 68 19* **Rooms** *6*   **Road map** *E5*

Located 850 m (2,800 ft) above sea level, on the slopes of Monte Meraviglia, this working farm is great for a relaxed holiday. The farm follows organic principles, producing various grains and pulses, and rearing cattle. The area features good footpaths and opportunities for exploring the Umbrian countryside. **www.casalesantantonio.it**

FIANO D'ABETO Nonna Rosa B&B
Località Fiano d'Abeto **Tel** *0743 93 80 24* **Rooms** *5*   **Road map** *F5*

Named after the elderly but sprightly lady owner, Rosa, this rustic house in the countryside, just a five-minute drive from Norcia, is a very attractive proposition. Each room has been tastefully decorated and is named after a colour. Excursions, including rafting, can be arranged at the front desk. **www.nonna-rosa.it**

FOLIGNO Casa Mancia
Via Trinci 44, 06034 **Tel** *074 22 22 65* **Fax** *074 22 07 95* **Rooms** *14*   **Road map** *D4*

A clever combination of ancient and modern characterizes this well-run resort hotel. The bedrooms and two self-contained apartments have been carefully restored with atmospheric ceiling beams and wooden floors. Guests can use the bicycles provided to explore the surrounding area. Restaurant closed Sunday. **www.casamancia.com**

FOLIGNO Le Mura
Via Bolletta 29, 06034 **Tel** *0742 35 73 44* **Fax** *0742 35 33 27* **Rooms** *38*   **Road map** *D4*

Overlooking the river – some rooms have a view – and located right beside the medieval town walls, near the church of San Giacomo, this is a peaceful, traditional family hotel offering a good standard of service. The hotel restaurant *(see p163)* serves good Umbrian cuisine. **www.lemura.net**

MONTEFALCO Albergo Ristorante Ringhiera Umbra
Corso Mameli 20, 06036 **Tel & Fax** *0742 37 91 66* **Rooms** *13*   **Road map** *D4*

This charming family *locanda*, offering accommodation and good food in the heart of Montefalco, has been run by the same family since it opened in 1938. Bedrooms are single, double or triple (only triple rooms have en-suite bathrooms). Rooms are simple but cosily furnished. The restaurant is very popular. **www.ringhieraumbra.com**

Key to Price Guide *see p144* **Key to Symbols** *see back cover flap*

MONTEFALCO Villa Pambuffetti

Viale della Vittoria 20, 06036 **Tel** *0742 37 94 17* **Fax** *0742 37 92 45* **Rooms** *15* **Road map** *D4*

The charismatic poet Gabriele d'Annunzio used to stay regularly at this lovely villa set inside a private park. Rooms all face the landscaped gardens and many top-floor rooms have panoramic views as far as Monte Subasio and Assisi. Antiques abound, and there is a good restaurant serving regional fare. **www.villapambuffetti.com**

NARNI Colle Abramo delle Vigne Agriturismo

Strada di Colle Abramo 34, Vigne, 05035 **Tel** *0744 79 64 28* **Fax** *178 603 19 41* **Rooms** *8* **Road map** *C6*

A group of rustic stone-walled farm buildings has been turned into an *agriturismo* with a selection of cosy rooms and apartments. Facilities are good, and the owners are keen to satisfy guests' requirements. The farm grows various crops and produces its own wine and olive oil. **www.colleabramo.com**

NARNI Terra Umbra

Via Rosciano 61, Narni Scalo, 05035 **Tel** *0744 75 03 04* **Fax** *0744 75 10 14* **Rooms** *27* **Road map** *C6*

A smart hotel that keeps up to date with the latest technology and is often used for corporate meetings. A sauna is available to guests, as are a gym and a Jacuzzi. The restaurant chef is also keen to stay in line with the latest culinary trends, offering superior fare. **www.terraumbra.it**

NORCIA Grotta Azzurra

Corso Sertorio 24, 06046 **Tel** *0743 81 65 13* **Fax** *0743 81 73 42* **Rooms** *45* **Road map** *F5*

Close to the main square, this is one of several hotels owned by a local family. An inn dating from 1850, it has a lovely restaurant and a wide choice of rooms. The most basic are small and street-facing, with little balconies; deluxe rooms are larger and grander, with whirlpool bathtubs (two have impressively frescoed walls). **www.bianconi.com**

NORCIA Il Casale nel Parco

Località Fontevena 8, 06046 **Tel** & **Fax** *0743 81 64 81* **Rooms** *12* **Road map** *F5*

A delightful *agriturismo* just outside Norcia, at the foot of the Monte Sibillini mountains. Located inside a converted stone farmhouse and outer-buildings, the rooms are cosy and charming, with wooden beams, wrought-iron beds and attractive garden views. Excellent picnics and dinners are available on request. **www.casalenelparco.com**

ORVIETO Agriturismo Titignano

Località Titignano, 05010 **Tel** *0763 30 80 00* **Fax** *0763 30 80 02* **Rooms** *6* **Road map** *B5*

Set within a large park in a medieval hamlet, this *agriturismo* rises on a hill between Orvieto and Todi, overlooking enchanting Lake Corbara. It is a peaceful environment, if a little isolated – a car is essential. Rooms are simple, and some have cooking areas. Excellent food is served in a grand dining room with a fireplace. **www.titignano.com**

ORVIETO L'Elmo Agriturismo

Via San Faustino 18, 05018 **Tel** *0763 21 52 19* **Fax** *1782 71 17 55* **Rooms** *8, plus 7 apartments* **Road map** *B5*

Situated on a hill facing Orvieto, this *agriturismo* has a selection of attractive stone-walled buildings, with simple but cosy rustic-style rooms. The main feature at L'Elmo is the excellent horse-riding stables. Lessons and rides through the countryside are organized for all levels of ability. **www.lelmo.it**

ORVIETO Filippeschi

Via Filippeschi 19, 05018 **Tel** & **Fax** *0763 34 32 75* **Rooms** *14* **Road map** *B5*

With its location just off Piazza della Repubblica, the Filippeschi makes a great accommodation choice in central Orvieto. The hotel is well kept, with a bright but pleasantly homely style of decor in the bedrooms, which feature wooden floorboards and floral wallpaper. Service is both professional and friendly. **www.albergofilippeschi.it**

ORVIETO Hotel Duomo

Vicolo di Maurizio 7, 05018 **Tel** *0763 34 18 87* **Fax** *0763 39 49 73* **Rooms** *18* **Road map** *B5*

Centrally located on a small road near the cathedral, the Hotel Duomo offers very clean, modern rooms with large bathrooms. Staff are friendly and helpful, and some of the rooms have balconies overlooking the cathedral. With a small garden, this hotel is very popular and perfect for a short stay. **www.orvietohotelduomo.com**

ORVIETO Hotel Maitani

Via Lorenzo Maitani 5, 05018 **Tel** *0763 34 20 11* **Fax** *0763 34 20 12* **Rooms** *30* **Road map** *B5*

Traditional and smart, this hotel is housed in a 13th-century palazzo in a wonderful location, just a stone's throw from beautiful Piazza Duomo. Some of the bedrooms have fantastic views of the cathedral, and so does the summer terrace, where breakfast is served when weather permits. **www.hotelmaitani.com**

ORVIETO Locanda Rosati

Località Buonviaggio 22, 05018 **Tel** *0763 21 73 14* **Rooms** *7* **Road map** *B5*

Set in a lovely part of the Umbrian countryside, this farmhouse is truly idyllic. Bedrooms are decorated by a well-known local wood sculptor, while the cosy dining room and lounge, with its log fire and selection of English books, are satisfyingly rustic. Hot water and heating are fuelled by hazelnut shells. **www.locandarosati.it**

ORVIETO Villa Ciconia

Via dei Tigli 69, Orvieto Scalo, 05018 **Tel** *0763 30 55 82* **Fax** *0763 30 20 77* **Rooms** *12* **Road map** *B5*

Despite having been surrounded by the suburbs, this lovely 16th-century villa in the lower part of Orvieto has its own extensive grounds and retains its countryside character. Original frescoes are still present in some rooms, and the furnishings include wrought-iron four-poster beds. **www.hotelvillaciconia.com**

ORVIETO La Badia

Località Badia 8, 05019 **Tel** *0763 30 19 59* **Fax** *0763 30 53 96* **Rooms** *18, plus 9 suites*   **Road map** *B5*

There is a magical atmosphere about this place, located at the foot of Orvieto's rocky perch and with fantastic views up to the city. The former abbey building dates back to the 6th century, although the curiously shaped tower was added later by Matilde di Canossa. The hotel restaurant *(see p165)* specializes in local cuisine. **www.labadiahotel.it**

ORVIETO Palazzo Piccolomini

Piazza Ranieri 36, 05018 **Tel** *0763 34 17 43* **Fax** *0763 39 10 46* **Rooms** *33*   **Road map** *B5*

Orvieto's grandest hotel is housed in a converted 16th-century palazzo situated in a quiet part of town, near the lift down to the public car park. Public areas and bedrooms are elegant, with vaulted ceilings, whitewashed walls and wrought-iron candelabra. Rooms on the upper floors have panoramic views. **www.hotelpiccolomini.it**

PARRANO Il Poggiolo di Parrano

Contrada Bagno 43, 05010 **Tel** *0763 83 84 71* **Fax** *0763 83 87 76* **Rooms** *1, plus 4 apartments*   **Road map** *B5*

This organic farm, which produces top-quality olive oil, wine and honey, as well as a variety of fruit and vegetables, provides spacious accommodation in carefully restored, picturesque stone-walled buildings. Open fires, wooden beams and terracotta floors add to the cosy, rustic feel of the place. **www.ilpoggiolo.com**

PRECI Hotel agli Scacchi

Quartiere Scacchi 12, 06047 **Tel** *074 39 92 21* **Fax** *0743 93 72 49* **Rooms** *26*   **Road map** *E5*

The hotel building, in the hilltown of Preci, was the home of the prestigious Scacchi family in the 16th and 17th centuries. The bedrooms are simply furnished, spacious and most have lovely views over the peaceful hills of the surrounding Monti Sibillini National Park. **www.hotelagliscacchi.com**

SAN GEMINI Hotel Duomo

Piazza Duomo 4, 05029 **Tel** *0744 63 00 15* **Fax** *0744 63 03 36* **Rooms** *17*   **Road map** *D6*

Right in the centre of the medieval town of San Gemini, the Hotel Duomo is located in an 18th-century building that was once home to the Santa Croce princes. Many aspects from that time remain, including some beautiful frescoes. Some rooms are set in the building's atmospheric towers. **www.gruppobacus.com/hotelduomo**

SPELLO Hotel del Teatro

Via Giulia 24, 06038 **Tel** *0742 30 11 40* **Fax** *0742 30 16 12* **Rooms** *11*   **Road map** *D4*

This elegant family-run hotel is situated near the Arch of Augustus, in Spello's picturesque old town. The building, as it stands, dates from the 18th century, but parts of the previous medieval structure are also incorporated. Rooms are comfortable and attractively furnished. **www.hoteldelteatro.it**

SPELLO La Bastiglia

Piazza Vallegloria 7, 06038 **Tel** *0742 65 12 77* **Fax** *0742 30 11 59* **Rooms** *33*   **Road map** *D4*

On the slopes of Monte Subasio, in an old mill surrounded by cypress and olive trees, is this hotel featuring a Michelin-starred restaurant. Junior suites have private terraces and whirlpool baths; deluxe rooms have private gardens; while standard rooms make do with splendid views. There is also a heated pool. **www.labastiglia.com**

SPELLO Terme Francescane

Via delle Acque, 06038 **Tel** *0742 30 11 86* **Fax** *0742 65 14 43* **Rooms** *14*   **Road map** *D4*

This spa resort makes excellent use of its sulphur springs to offer guests all sorts of health and beauty treatments. The decor and atmosphere of the hotel rooms, as well as the spa centre, are smart and refined. Facilities include a lovely garden and tennis courts. **www.termefrancescane.com**

SPELLO Palazzo Bocci

Via Cavour 17, 06038 **Tel** *0742 30 10 21* **Fax** *0742 30 14 64* **Rooms** *23*   **Road map** *D4*

This beautifully restored hotel is housed within a 17th-century palazzo in Spello's historical district. It consists of a warren of rooms and public areas, with terracotta floors, frescoes, fireplaces and wooden beams. Outside there's a fountain, hanging garden, palm trees and sunny terraces. Excellent restaurant. **www.palazzobocci.com**

SPOLETO Hotel Aurora

Via Apollinaire 3, 06049 **Tel** *0743 22 03 15* **Fax** *0743 22 18 85* **Rooms** *23*   **Road map** *D5*

A small, family-run hotel in a very central position, near the stop for the bus that connects old Spoleto with the train station. Set back from the road, the bedrooms are quiet, clean and comfortable, with views over the city rooftops. Guests can dine at special rates at the restaurant next door, the Apollinaire. **www.hotelauroraspoleto.it**

SPOLETO Clitunno

Piazza Sordini 6, 06049 **Tel** *0743 22 33 40* **Fax** *0743 22 26 63* **Rooms** *38*   **Road map** *D5*

The rooms in this family-run hotel have been furnished with care. The ceilings feature attractive wooden beams, and the floors are paved in terracotta tiles. San Lorenzo, the hotel restaurant *(see p166)*, serves tasty Umbrian fare. Excellent central location near the cathedral. **www.hotelclitunno.com**

SPOLETO Palazzo Dragoni

Via del Duomo 13, 06049 **Tel** *0743 22 22 20* **Fax** *0743 22 22 25* **Rooms** *15*   **Road map** *D5*

Next to the cathedral, this 14th-century building has spacious bedrooms, tiled floors, wrought-iron beds, vaulted ceilings and antiques. Some rooms have French windows opening on to views of the rooftops and the valley; others have four-poster beds. There is also an elegant dining room and small garden. **www.palazzodragoni.it**

Key to Price Guide *see p144* **Key to Symbols** *see back cover flap*

SPOLETO Eremo delle Grazie

🏢 P W   €€€

Strada per Monteluco 13, Monteluco, 06049 **Tel** *074 34 96 24* **Fax** *074 34 96 50* **Rooms** *10*   **Road map** *D5*

Thanks to a fantastic conversion, this secluded 5th-century monastery building, not far from Spoleto, has become an extremely atmospheric and luxurious hotel. The library contains some rare and ancient volumes, and much of the furniture is antique. The ancient church is another appealing feature. **www.eremodellegrazie.it**

SPOLETO Hotel Gattapone

🚹 🍽 P   €€€

Via del Ponte 6, 06049 **Tel** *0743 22 34 47* **Fax** *0743 22 34 48* **Rooms** *15*   **Road map** *D5*

In a romantic position beneath the Rocca Albornoziana, opposite the famous Ponte delle Torri, is this hotel named after that bridge's architect. The old villa has mainly standard rooms, while a modern annexe has en-suite accommodation. There is also a garden and a terrace with views of the valley. **www.hotelgattapone.it**

SPOLETO Hotel San Luca

    €€€

Via Interna delle Mura 21, 06049 **Tel** *0743 22 33 99* **Fax** *0743 22 38 00* **Rooms** *35*   **Road map** *D5*

A charming, family-run hotel in a converted tannery dating from the 18th-century, the San Luca features gardens and a sunny courtyard where breakfast is served in summer. Bedrooms are large and soundproofed, with gorgeous bathrooms, some with whirlpool tubs. A few have frescoed walls or a private balcony. **www.hotelsanluca.com**

SPOLETO Palazzo Leti

🚹 🍽   €€€

Via degli Eremiti 8–10, 06049 **Tel** *0743 22 49 30* **Fax** *0743 20 26 23* **Rooms** *12*   **Road map** *D5*

Situated in the centre of Spoleto, this historical residence, which for centuries was the family home of the noble Leti family, has been restored with care and made into an attractive hotel. All rooms look out over the Monteluca mountain, and some of the city's monuments can also be seen. **www.palazzoleti.com**

TERNI Locanda di Colle dell'Oro

🍽 🏢 🍽 P   €€

Strada di Palmetta 31, 05100 **Tel** *0744 43 23 79* **Fax** *0744 43 78 26* **Rooms** *10*   **Road map** *D6*

This award-winning hotel set in a group of restored 19th-century buildings on the Colle dell'Oro hill, overlooking Terni, prides itself on its decor. Imaginatively decorated rooms, wooden floorboards and hand-decorated furniture evoke the rustic style of the past, but without forsaking any of today's comforts. **www.colledelloro.it**

TODI San Lorenzo Tre

€€

Via San Lorenzo 3, 06059 **Tel & Fax** *075 894 45 55* **Rooms** *6*   **Road map** *C5*

Staying in this little inn is like stepping back in time. Steeped in an atmosphere from another era, this family home offers few modern conveniences – instead, you will find antiques, paintings and a library. All the bedrooms have lovely views over the rooftops and hills north of Todi; three have en-suite bathrooms. **www.sanlorenzo3.it**

TODI Fontecesia

    €€€

Via Lorenzo Leonj 3, 06059 **Tel** *075 894 37 37* **Fax** *075 894 46 77* **Rooms** *35*   **Road map** *C5*

In the centre of Todi, this renovated 17th-century palazzo beside the former church of San Benedetto has large and comfortable standard rooms, while the four suites are truly sumptuous, each one individually decorated. Some bedrooms have views over the old town, others over the Umbrian countryside. **www.fontecesia.it**

TODI Hotel Bramante

    €€€

Via Orvietana 48, 06059 **Tel** *075 894 83 81* **Fax** *075 894 80 74* **Rooms** *54*   **Road map** *C5*

Located beyond the city walls, near Bramante's church of Santa Maria della Consolazione, this hotel was a convent dating from the 1200s and has lovely views over the surrounding countryside. The rooms are large, with parquet floors and painted in elegant warm colours. **www.hotelbramante.it**

TODI Relais Todini

    €€€

Vocabolo Cervara 24, Collevalenza, 06059 **Tel** *075 88 75 21* **Fax** *075 88 71 82* **Rooms** *12*   **Road map** *C5*

This warm and welcoming quality hotel set in a 14th-century building is attractive both inside and out. The decor is enriched with tapestries and open fires, as well as antique paintings and furniture. Horse riding and tennis are available in the extensive grounds, which also feature lakes. **www.relaistodini.com**

TODI Tenuta di Canonica

    €€€

Località Canonica 75–76, 06059 **Tel** *0758 94 75 45* **Fax** *0758 94 75 81* **Rooms** *11*   **Road map** *C5*

The warm tones of the decor add to the cosy atmosphere at this small country hotel surrounded by woodland, olive groves and fruit trees, just 5 km (3 miles) from Todi. The location is idyllic, while the stone-walled hotel building itself incorporates a medieval lookout tower. **www.tenutadicanonica.com**

TREVI Antica Dimora alla Rocca

   €€

Piazza della Rocca 1, 06039 **Tel** *074 23 85 41* **Fax** *074 78 925* **Rooms** *34*   **Road map** *D5*

Two 17th-century buildings in the heart of historic Trevi house this delightful and well-kept hotel. Many of the rooms have original frescoes, and all are carefully furnished in keeping with the style of the place. The hotel restaurant serves interesting dishes made with fresh local ingredients. **www.hotelallarocca.it**

TREVI Casa Giulia

🏢 🍽 P W   €€

Via Corciano 1, Bovara, 06039 **Tel** *0742 782 57* **Fax** *0742 38 16 32* **Rooms** *9*   **Road map** *D5*

Near the Clitunno springs, this 17th-century home has been in the same family for generations. The rooms are furnished with antiques and have wooden beams, white walls and wrought-iron beds. A few have original frescoes depicting the countryside around the house. The pool is set among fragrant oleanders. **www.casagiulia.com**

WHERE TO EAT

One of the main reasons to visit Umbria is the excellent food. A land of robust flavours, ancient culinary traditions and fabulous fresh produce, Umbria is brimming with cosy, family-run *trattorias* and traditional restaurants where you can try the local cuisine, often in atmospheric, historical surroundings.

The region's many food-based festivals and fairs, known as *sagre*, offer an ideal opportunity to find out more

Ciaramicola, a traditional Easter cake

about and taste some authentic local produce. These lively events are often devoted to a particular crop, such as mushrooms, chestnuts, truffles or olives. Most *agriturismo* structures (farm lodgings) provide meals for their guests, and some are open to external diners, too, offering splendid home-grown food cooked to traditional recipes and served in a friendly environment, the hosts often eating together with the guests.

OPENING HOURS AND PRICES

Restaurant and trattoria opening hours in Umbria are similar to those found all over central Italy. Generally, lunch is served from noon to 2:30pm, and evening meals from 7pm onwards – this is to cater for tourists used to eating earlier than the locals, who tend to go out later. Closing times depend on the season and on the type of place: earlier for small trattorias and in winter; later in summer and during the holiday season, and in busy historic centres.

Prices vary enormously depending on the type of establishment. In some of the most famous restaurants, the bill can easily exceed 50 euros per person, excluding wine, while in a village trattoria you can usually eat for 15–17 euros per person. Most establishments charge a *coperto* (cover charge), which is usually 1–3 euros per customer; some places also add a 10 per cent service charge to the bill.

The dining room at Le Mura restaurant in the historic centre of Foligno

THE PRODUCE OF UMBRIA

Umbrian cuisine consists of dishes deriving from an ancient tradition, sometimes re-interpreted by enterprising chefs. The region yields excellent produce of all kinds, and crops cultivated using organic methods are becoming increasingly widespread.

Umbria produces high quality red and white wine, which are highly respected all over the country; the region also produces some of Italy's best olive oil. Mushrooms are

another delicacy, and some of the finest black and white truffles in the world are found here. Cured meats are another speciality, particularly in Norcia, while good freshwater fish can be found in Lake Trasimeno and other lakes around the region. The tiny village of Castelluccio, in the Monti Sibillini, gives its name to a renowned and tasty variety of lentil.

TOP RESTAURANTS

In response to the growing interest in the region's gastronomic traditions, some prestigious restaurants have been established in Umbria. Such places alone can make a trip to the region worthwhile.

One of the most famous is the restaurant of chef Gianfranco Vissani (*see p162*), in Baschi, on the shores of Lago di Corbara, but there are other restaurants worthy of note, including Il Postale (*see p161*) of Marco Bistarelli, in Perugia. Tables at these and other top-class restaurants are in high demand, so booking ahead as far as possible is a necessity.

TRATTORIAS

A traditional trattoria is a good choice for an authentic taste of the local specialities. Often family-run, and

Specialities of the Lake Trasimeno area, including local wine and oil

Relaxing outside the San Francesco restaurant in Assisi

sometimes incorporating an all-day bar or general store, down-to-earth trattorias can be found in every town and village around Umbria. Unpretentious and affordable, they are often the first choice among the locals when eating out with family or friends, so they make an ideal spot for people-watching, too.

AGRITURISMO

Agriturismo farms are obliged to use locally grown ingredients, some of which are usually produced on the farm itself. The sometimes limited choice of dishes is made up for by the genuine farmhouse flavours and the welcoming atmosphere. Furthermore these properties often have lots of space, as well as play areas – perfect for small children.

COOKERY COURSES

Umbria has numerous cookery schools, where both professionals and amateurs can learn the secrets of the region's traditional cuisine. There are also plenty of *agriturismo* farms that run cookery courses.

BARS AND CAFÉS

Bars are an important part of everyday life all over Italy, and no less so in Umbria. Although the locals will often just pop in for a quick espresso or an aperitif standing at the bar, many places also have plenty of seating – both inside and out– for you to linger and take in the view. Table service

generally costs a little extra. Hot and cold snacks are usually available, and if it's a *bar-pasticceria*, the cakes will be made on the premises.

A baker's stall at the Mercato delle Gaite festival, Bevagna

LOCAL FESTIVALS

The traditional fairs and festivals held all over Umbria attract visitors and locals alike, and they provide a great opportunity to try local food and wine specialities at reasonable prices. People

flock to Norcia (in February) and Città di Castello (in November) to taste the precious truffle, while wine is the attraction at Todi and Torgiano, and particularly at the Sagrantino festival in Montefalco, held in September. Olives are the draw at Spello, and *caciucco* (a soup made with lake fish) is the speciality of Lake Trasimeno.

One event of great interest is the Mercato delle Gaite, held in June in Bevagna *(see p104)*. The town adopts the dress and ways of the 14th and 15th centuries, and local restaurants offer tasty menus that feature ancient dishes and unusual flavours.

A more modern event of international importance is Perugia's Eurochocolate festival, held in October.

DISABLED PEOPLE

More and more places in Umbria are upgrading their buildings in order to facilitate access for the disabled. Even so, the streets can be steep in Umbria's medieval hill towns, and steps are common.

SMOKING

All restaurants and bars throughout Italy are obliged to adhere to a strict no-smoking policy. Some places do have a properly ventilated room for smokers, and the no-smoking restrictions do not apply at outside tables.

The Festa di San Benedetto in Norcia, held in March

The Flavours of Umbria

Umbria has an earthy cuisine based on what ingredients are in season. Like their Etruscan ancestors, Umbrians have an affinity with the land and enjoy hunting for edible bounty from their beautiful countryside. In spring there is wild asparagus, and in summer there are fruit and herbs to be picked and preserved. Autumn and winter have their fair share of culinary delights; as the weather turns colder, market stalls and restaurants display the hunters' catch – hare, pheasant, pigeon, woodcock and quail, as well as chestnuts, porcini mushrooms and truffles sniffed out by the hunters' dogs. Winter vegetables like *cavolo nero* are also popular.

Black truffles

Local olives mixed with tiny chillies on a market stall

NORTHERN UMBRIA

Landlocked Umbria has always depended on its rivers and lakes for fish, including Lake Trasimeno. In waterside villages, the daily catch of carp, trout, perch, pike, tench and eel are made into soups and stews, or baked with herbs. Eel is simmered with fresh tomatoes, while trout is cooked with wild fennel.

The largest carp are roasted whole in a the same way as a suckling pig *(regina in porchetta)*. There is fine lamb from the hillside herds of prime beef-cattle. The regional capital, Perugia, is noted for its Chianina beef, as well as for its chocolate.

A wide variety of vegetables and cereals, like barley and spelt, are cultivated on the fertile land. Olive trees are everywhere: their oil is some of Italy's finest – light but scented, and full of flavour. Special sweets and pastries are made to mark historical and religious celebrations. Perugia's patron saint, San Costanzo, is honoured with the *torcolo*, a ring-shaped cake studded with aniseed, pine nuts and dried fruit. From Assisi, *ossa di morta* are bone-shaped marzipan sweets prepared for All Souls' day in November.

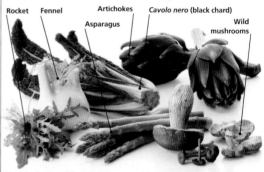

Rocket   Fennel   Artichokes   *Cavolo nero* (black chard)

Asparagus   Wild mushrooms

Typical selection of fresh Umbrian vegetables

UMBRIAN DISHES AND SPECIALITIES

Cured meats, salami and black olives marinated with orange peel, are typical *antipasti*. Asparagus is used in tomato or cheese sauces with pasta, or fried with beaten eggs to make a *frittata*. Pastas include *cariole* (like tagliatelle), often served with fried onions and garlic. *Porchetta* is a whole young pig, stuffed with offal and herbs, and roasted on a spit until the skin is deliciously crisp; it is sometimes served sliced, in bread rolls. Game is roasted or cooked with wine to make rich stews such as *piccione in salmi* (pigeon). *Torta al testo* is a flattish bread made with olive oil and stuffed with herbs, sausage or ham. *Pan pepato* is sweetened with sugar, candied fruit and nuts. Coffee may be accompanied by Baci (meaning "kisses") from Perugia *(see p171)*.

Baci chocolates

Teggacmaccio *is a stew from Lake Trasimeno, made with perch, trout, tench and eel, in a tomato and wine broth.*

Chefs prearing to serve freshly roasted *porchetta*

SOUTHERN UMBRIA

The south of the region has prime agricultural areas, like the Castelluccio plains, where tiny, distinctively flavoured lentils are grown and used in many local dishes, such as rustic hearty soups made with seasonal vegetables. Among these are cardoons *(cardone)*, which look like giant celery and have a rather bitter taste.

Traditionally, meat is often grilled or spit-roasted with herbs, especially sage and rosemary. Norcia is an important gastronomic centre, famous for black truffles and as the home of marvellous hams *(prosciutti)*, salami and sausages. Throughout Italy, *norcino* means pork butchery. Dozens of recipes hail from the town, including *mazzafegati* (pig's liver sausages with raisins, pine nuts and orange peel) and *beccacce alla norcina* (woodcock stuffed with sausage, herbs and truffles). Orvieto is wine country, as reflected in *gallina umbriaca* ("drunken chicken", cooked

Black grapes, ripe and ready to be pressed to make wine

in wine). Oriveto is also known for quails *(quaglie)* baked in bread, while Todi's speciality is ox tongue *(lingua di bue)* in a sweet-and-sour *(agrodolce)* sauce.

UMBRIAN TRUFFLES

Truffles are part of Umbrian life and are used liberally in its cuisine, elevating even basic salads or scrambled eggs to gourmet fare. They appear in classic recipes, grated over risottos or sliced thinly onto *crostini* (bread fried in olive oil). Black truffles are added to cheese *(pecorino tartufato)* and can be frozen or preserved. Rarer white truffles are always eaten fresh.

REGIONAL WINES

Orvieto Famous for crisp, dry white wines, but there are also some lesser-known reds and dessert wines.

Torgiano Rosso Riserva Possibly Umbria's finest red, it is made from Sangiovese grapes and ages well.

Sagrantino di Montefalco This full, rich red wine has been produced for centuries in vineyards around Montefalco.

Colli Perugini Red and white wines from a number of grape varieties, including Pinot Grigio, Grechetto and Montepulicano.

Vin Santo A lusciously sweet wine, pressed from semi-dried Grechetto or Malvasia grapes.

Cinghiale alla cacciatore *is wild boar cooked with red wine, herbs and vegetables until tender.*

Lenticche di Castelluccio *(lentils) are often served as an accompaniment to fennel-flavoured pork sausages.*

Strangozzi *pasta with sugar, walnuts, cinnamon, cocoa and lemon is a Christmas Eve treat in Umbria.*

Choosing a Restaurant

The following restaurants have been selected across a wide range of price categories for the quality of the food, good value and enjoyable atmosphere. They are divided into two sections, Northern and Southern Umbria, and are then listed alphabetically by town and in ascending price order.

PRICE CATEGORIES
The following price ranges are for a three course meal for one, including a half bottle of house wine, cover charge, tax and services.
€ Under €25
€€ €25–€35
€€€ €35–€45
€€€€ €45–€55
€€€€€ Over €55

NORTHERN UMBRIA

ASSISI La Fortezza

€

Vicolo della Fortezza/Piazza del Comune, 06081 **Tel** *075 81 29 93*   **Road map** D4

Family-run for more than 45 years, this restaurant is located halfway up a staircase-cum-street off the main piazza. Creative regional cooking at this level of quality normally costs twice as much. Try the *cannelloni all'assisiana* (pasta sheets wrapped around a ragout of veal and baked under tomatoes and Parmesan cheese).

ASSISI Castel San Gregorio

€€

Via San Gregorio 16, 06081 **Tel** *075 803 80 09*   **Road map** D4

This hotel restaurant has a fantastic setting in a 13th-century castle, in the countryside near Assisi. The menu offers typical Umbrian dishes, with house specialities including lamb, wild boar and game. Delicious local truffles are often used to season the dishes, and the house wine is actually made on the premises.

ASSISI Da Erminio

€€

Via Montecavallo 19, 06081 **Tel** *075 81 25 06*   **Road map** D4

Located in the highest part of Assisi's medieval centre, this is one of the town's most traditional trattorias. Founded in 1954, it is now run by the third generation of Erminio's family. Specialities include charcoal-grilled meat, which you can watch being prepared, and the *strangozzi alla boscaiola*, a pasta dish with mushrooms, rocket and walnuts.

ASSISI Medioevo
€€

Via Arco dei Priori 4b, 06081 **Tel** *075 81 30 68*   **Road map** D4

An elegant restaurant set under the medieval stone vaults of an ancient palazzo in the centre of Assisi. Try the home-made pastas (featuring black truffles in season), or the meats, such as the *agnello al tartufo* (lamb with truffles), which is cooked to a traditional recipe. They also work wonders with steak. Great home-made desserts.

ASSISI Trattoria Pallotta
€€

Vicolo della Volta Pinta 3/Via San Rufino 4, 06081 **Tel** *075 81 26 49*   **Road map** D4

This humble, homely place is one of the least expensive trattorias in the centre of town. The mixed antipasto platter is massive, then you can dine on local specialities such as *torta al testo* (flatbread stuffed with a variety of vegetable or meat fillings) and *strangozzi* (hand-rolled spaghetti in an olive-and-mushroom pesto).

ASSISI Armentum
€€€

Località Armenzano, 06081 **Tel** *075 801 90 00*   **Road map** D4

This atmospheric restaurant in the Hotel Le Silve (*see p144*) is about more than just the eating experience. As well as an excellent wine and spirit list, there is a selection of different olive oils, served according to the dish and to the diner's preference. It is a good idea to book ahead, since the restaurant is fairly small and very popular.

ASSISI Buca di San Francesco

€€€

Via Eugenio Brizi 1, 06081 **Tel** *075 81 22 04*   **Road map** D4

Located in the medieval cellars of an historic building in the centre of Assisi, this popular restaurant also features a pleasant summer terrace. The menu contains mainly traditional Umbrian dishes, but there are usually some interesting specials too, according to the season. The filet steak flavoured with truffle is worth trying. Closed Mon.

ASSISI Il Frantoio

€€€

Vicolo Illuminati 10, 06081 **Tel** *075 81 29 77*   **Road map** D4

A 17th-century former olive press is the setting of this refined Umbrian restaurant, part of the Fontebella hotel (*see p144*). There is a renowned wine steward who is head of the Italian sommelier association. Sample the delicious *stringozzi paesani* (thick ropes of hand-rolled spaghetti tossed with onions, artichokes and hot chilli flakes).

ASSISI La Locanda del Cardinale

€€€

Piazza del Vescovado 8, 06081 **Tel** *075 81 52 45*   **Road map** D4

Part of an attractive hotel, this is a refined elegant restaurant, often chosen for formal celebrations or ceremonies. Indeed, the restaurant is listed among the most prestigious historical bars and restaurants in the whole of Italy. The building itself is ancient, dating back as far as the Roman era.

Key to Symbols *see back cover flap*

ASSISI San Francesco

Via San Francesco 52, 06081 **Tel** *075 81 23 29* **Road map** *D4*

Overlooking Assisi's famed basilica, this fine restaurant has slightly inflated prices as a result of the touristy location. Be assured, however, that the food on the seasonal menu is worth the extra cost: *carpaccio* of porcini mushrooms (served raw and thinly sliced), home-made pâtés, and steak with truffles are all highlights.

ASSISI Brilli Bistrot

Via Los Angeles 83, 06081 **Tel** *075 804 34 33* **Road map** *D4*

A modern, refined restaurant about 5 km (3 miles) out of central Assisi. The menu features a wide range of dishes based on the extensive international experience of the owner/chef. There are plenty of fish options on offer, and a good combination of innovative and traditional flavours. A large selection of spirits and liqueurs is also available.

BETTONA Osteria dell'Oca

Corso Marconi 3, 06084 **Tel** *075 988 50 19* **Road map** *C4*

The atmosphere here is cosy and friendly, and the decor is rustic yet refined with an attractive brick ceiling. The menu changes daily but always uses the freshest local ingredients to create tasty Umbrian dishes, including the local pasta speciality, *strangozzi*. The wine list is particularly good and very varied, including some international wines.

BETTONA Il Poggio degli Olivi

Località Montebalacca, Passaggio di Bettona, 06084 **Tel** *075 986 90 23* **Road map** *C4*

This *agriturismo* is set in a group of converted 16th-century farm buildings and has a swimming pool, a park and a restaurant. The cooking is traditional Umbrian, and the local ingredients include beans, lentils, truffles and honey, as well as the olive oil, which is made on the premises. There are always vegetarian options and children's choices.

CITTÀ DELLA PIEVE Trattoria Bruno Coppetta

Via Vannucci 90, 06062 **Tel** *0578 29 81 08* **Road map** *A4*

The rather uninspiring decor of this restaurant is richly compensated by the wonderful food: all the dishes are home-made using seasonal produce. Located in the centre of Città della Pieve, near the church of Santa Maria dei Bianchi, this trattoria offers a friendly environment and excellent prices given the quality of the food. Closed Mon.

CITTÀ DI CASTELLO Amici Miei

Via del Monte 2, 06012 **Tel** *075 85 59 904* **Road map** *B2*

Set in the brick-vaulted storerooms of a 16th-century palazzo in the historic centre, this restaurant offers a menu based firmly on regional cuisine. Sample the *strangozzi con baccalà* (hand-rolled spaghetti with salt cod) and the *cinghiale in umido con fagioli* (a stew of wild boar served with beans).

CITTÀ DI CASTELLO Il Bersaglio

Via Vittorio Emanuele Orlando 14, 06012 **Tel** *075 85 55 534* **Road map** *B2*

At this traditional Umbrian restaurant, specialities vary according to the seasons. The chef is fond of using mushrooms and truffles, as well as game. Sample the *gnocchetti* (little potato dumplings) with truffles, or the *menù degustazione* (tasting menu) of several different preparations of porcini.

CITTÀ DI CASTELLO La Miniera di Galparino

Vocabolo Galparino 34, Sansecondo, 06010 **Tel** *075 854 07 84* **Road map** *B2*

The restaurant at this attractive *agriturismo* comes highly recommended. At long wooden tables in the converted stables, you can enjoy some delicious dishes made with fresh local ingredients, including game, mushrooms and truffles, both black and white. La Miniera di Galparino produces its own tasty jams, honey, olive oil and vin santo.

DERUTA Osteria Il Borghetto

Via Garibaldi 102, 06053 **Tel** *075 972 42 64* **Road map** *C4*

Come to this small informal trattoria, open in the evenings only, to enjoy good home cooking. Choose from a selection of tasty dishes based on the best Umbrian culinary traditions, or go for the cold meats and the tangy sheep's cheeses, which are made at the restaurant owner's farm. The service is pleasant and relaxed.

DERUTA Ristor'Arte La Fontanina

Via Solitaria 14, 06053 **Tel** *075 972 41 12* **Road map** *C4*

Located in the old town centre, this lively restaurant is housed in an atmospheric building dating from the 13th century, and aspects of the original structure are still visible. The dishes are mainly traditional, but with some innovative ideas, and there is a particularly good wine cellar. The panoramic garden is enclosed in winter.

DERUTA L'Antico Forziere

Via della Rocca 2, Casalina, 06053 **Tel** *075 972 43 14* **Road map** *C4*

Set in a rustic country house at Casalina, near the ceramic-producing town of Deruta, L'Antico Forziere boasts a traditional atmosphere and elegant decor, with a certain Renaissance style. The menu includes some delicious grilled meats and tasty fish dishes, as well as a selection of tempting home-made desserts. Reservations advised.

GUBBIO Alcatraz

Località Santa Cristina 53, 06020 **Tel** *075 92 29 938* **Road map** *D2*

This *agriturismo* 25 km (15 miles) southwest of Gubbio is an Italian version of an eco-resort. The ingredients are 99 per cent organic, and the menu features traditional recipes in addition to the chef's flights of fancy. The food is served as a fixed-price buffet with communal seating. Reservations are recommended.

GUBBIO Taverna del Lupo €

Via Ansidei 21, 06024 **Tel** *075 92 74 368*   **Road map** *D2*

Half the hotels and restaurants in Gubbio are run by the Mencarelli family, including this excellent, romantic set of medieval dining rooms in the city centre. Plump for one of the exquisitely prepared tasting menus featuring a procession of traditional regional dishes.

GUBBIO Grotta dell'Angelo €€

Via Gioia 47, 06024 **Tel** *075 927 17 47*   **Road map** *D2*

Prices are reasonable, and the dishes are hearty and tasty at this traditional local trattoria in a hotel *(see p145)* in central Gubbio. The atmosphere inside the 13th-century rooms is warm and welcoming, but in summer the tables in the walled garden can be even more appealing. Typical local pasta and meat dishes are the mainstays. Closed Tue.

GUBBIO Locanda del Cantiniere €€

Via Dante 30, 06024 **Tel** *075 927 59 99*   **Road map** *D2*

Exposed brick and original wooden beams add to the rustic charms of this central Gubbio eatery. Ingredients for the classic Umbrian cuisine are sourced locally (including all the meats) and freshly prepared in the restaurant. The bread is baked in their own oven, and pasta is handmade each morning. Great value. Closed Tue.

GUBBIO Villa Montegranelli €€€

Località Monteluiano, 06024 **Tel** *075 92 20 185*   **Road map** *D2*

Set in an 18th-century villa with an elegantly rural atmosphere, this restaurant produces exquisitely made dishes. Specialities cover regional, national and international recipes and include *crostini* (toasts); *strangozzi* pasta with sausage, porcini and pecorino cheese; and chestnut-flour pancakes with melted cheese and ricotta.

GUBBIO Bosone Garden €€€€

Via Galeotti 18, 06024 **Tel** *075 922 12 46*   **Road map** *D2*

Set in Palazzo Raffaelli, the beautiful former home of a local noble family, this restaurant has a lovely garden where you can eat in the summer. The atmosphere inside is warm but refined, with antique furnishings and an open fire. The menu features plenty of traditional dishes with an inventive twist. Many include the delicious local truffle.

GUBBIO La Fornace di Mastro Giorgio €€€€€

Via Mastro Giorgio 2, 06024 **Tel** *075 922 18 36*   **Road map** *D2*

This elegant restaurant in central Gubbio is located in a beautiful medieval building that housed the workshop of world-famous ceramic artist Mastro Giorgio Andreoli during the 16th century. Great attention is paid to details, both in the kitchen and in the decor. Specialities include the *tagliata di chianina* – filet steak and tagliatelle with truffle.

LAKE TRASIMENO – CASTIGLIONE DEL LAGO La Cantina €

Via Vittorio Emanuele 89, 06061 **Tel** *075 965 24 63*   **Road map** *B3*

As well as delicious fish dishes traditional to the Lake Trasimeno area, this friendly and welcoming restaurant serves all sorts of Umbrian specialities, including some magnificent grilled meats. The menu includes options that are suitable for children, and pizzas are also served. The outside tables are particularly pleasant on summer evenings.

LAKE TRASIMENO – CASTIGLIONE DEL LAGO L'Acquario €€€

Via Vittorio Emanuele 69, 06061 **Tel** *075 965 24 32*   **Road map** *B3*

This small, welcoming restaurant in the centre of the old part of town is Castiglione del Lago's oldest. Close attention is paid to all the details, including the decor, service, presentation and the quality of the dishes. Fish from Lake Trasimeno feature highly on the menu, as do locally grown vegetables and herbs. There is also a good choice of wines.

LAKE TRASIMENO – CASTIGLIONE DEL LAGO La Fontana €€€

Piazza Mazzini 8, 06061 **Tel** *075 95 11 57*   **Road map** *B3*

Set in the lower part of the Hotel Miralago *(see p146)*, but with an independent entrance, this restaurant serves a range of dishes based on a variety of ingredients, not just the produce of the lake. From the terrace garden diners can enjoy fabulous views over the water. La Fontana is a great place to relax on a summer's evening.

LAKE TRASIMENO – CASTIGLIONE DEL LAGO L'Essenza €€€€

Località I Giorgi, Petrignano del Lago, 06061 **Tel** *075 968 90 08*   **Road map** *B3*

This small, meticulously kept restaurant is part of a holiday complex located in a converted medieval structure near the border with Tuscany. Indeed, the menu includes a number of Tuscan specialities, as well as purely Umbrian fare, and the wines on offer are mainly from the same two regions. Tables are set on the terrace in the summer.

LAKE TRASIMENO – ISOLA MAGGIORE Da Sauro €€

Via Guglielmi 1, 06060 **Tel** *075 82 61 68*   **Road map** *B3*

Take the boat from Tuoro sul Trasimeno to reach Isola Maggiore – Da Sauro is at the northern tip. A small hotel *(see p146)* and restaurant, it is set in an attractive rustic stone building. The menu contains traditional dishes from the Lake Trasimeno area, including fantastically fresh fish caught from around the island. You can get a water taxi back afterwards.

LAKE TRASIMENO – PASSIGNANO Trattoria del Pescatore €

Via San Bernardino 5, 06065 **Tel** *075 829 60 63*   **Road map** *B3*

Delicious local cuisine and excellent value for money can be found at this old-fashioned family trattoria in the heart of old Passignano. Among the specialities is a variety of lake fish, including grilled perch, eel cooked in a rich tomato and bean soup or carp wrapped in *porchetta* (crunchy pork) with herbs. The atmosphere is also very friendly.

LAKE TRASIMENO – PASSIGNANO Cacciatori da Luciano €€€

Via Lungolago 3, 06065 **Tel** *075 82 72 10* **Road map** *B3*

The menu is based on both fresh- and salt-water fish – the restaurant is on the lake, and the chef makes the trip from landlocked Umbria to a seaside seafood market three times a week. The menu includes a mixed-fish *carpaccio* (raw, thinly sliced fish), a risotto studded with different types of prawn, shrimp and grilled sole.

LAKE TRASIMENO – PASSIGNANO Il Fischio del Merlo €€€

Località Calcinaio 17a, 06065 **Tel** *075 82 92 83* **Road map** *B3*

Comfortable and welcoming, with a definite homely feel, this charming restaurant overlooking Lake Trasimeno serves some excellent dishes. Much of the menu centres on fish, including freshwater fish from the nearby lake, but there is also a good choice of hearty meat dishes, such as filet steak. There is an excellent wine list, too.

MAGIONE La Fattoria di Montemelino €

Via dei Montemelini 22, Località Montemelino, 06063 **Tel** *075 84 36 06* **Road map** *B3*

The dining rooms at this simple, reliable *agriturismo* restaurant are decorated with ancient farming implements, and the fare on offer is traditionally Umbrian. The grilled steaks come from the farm's own herd of Chianina cattle. When the mushrooms are in season, try the delicious ravioli of porcini mushrooms.

MAGIONE Al Coccio €€

Via del Quadrifoglio 12a/b, 06063 **Tel** *075 84 18 29* **Road map** *B3*

This pleasant trattoria opened in 1994 and quickly became a popular place to eat. The name refers to the terracotta cooking vessels used to serve the hearty soups and other dishes. Pasta and desserts are all home-made, and the wine list includes a good variety of local labels. The house speciality is *maialino* – oven-cooked suckling pig with herbs.

MAGIONE Rosso di Sera €€

Via Fratelli Papini 81, 06063 **Tel** *075 847 62 77* **Road map** *B3*

The terrace outside this cosy hostelry is a fantastic place to sit and enjoy the views over Lake Trasimeno. The decor is cheery and rustic, and the atmosphere is informal and friendly. The menu changes according to the season and the best ingredients available; it always features tasty local dishes, though, including many fish-based specialities.

MONTELEONE DI SPOLETO Da Pietro €

Statale 471, Km 12,800, Ruscio, 06045 **Tel** *074 37 01 11* **Road map** *E6*

At this traditional old-style trattoria in the tiny village of Monteleone, the service is cordial and the atmosphere relaxed. Genuine home-cooking is offered here: the pasta served, for example, is all home-made. The menu centres on typical Umbrian flavours, and the house specialities include the fragrant *agnello alla cacciatora* lamb.

MONTONE Taverna del Verziere €€

Via Ospedale 19, 06014 **Tel** *075 930 65 12* **Road map** *C2*

This traditional tavern specializes in characteristic Umbrian dishes. Hearty soups, substantial pasta dishes, succulent meat and good local red wine make for a satisfying meal. The setting in Montone, not far from Umbertide, means that there are fantastic views over the rolling hills and valleys of Northern Umbria from the panoramic terrace.

NOCERA UMBRA La Costa €

Località Costa 3, 06025 **Tel** *0742 81 00 42* **Road map** *D3*

An attractive medieval farmhouse immersed in the countryside is the setting for this restaurant. The menu is made up of traditional dishes, and the home-made pasta is particularly worth trying. *Strangozzi al tartufo* is the local pasta, served with deliciously fragrant truffle. The tempting desserts are also home-made.

PACIANO La Loggetta €€

Largo Santa Maria 3/Via Marconi 35, 06060 **Tel** *075 83 01 44* **Road map** *B4*

The atmosphere is courteous but relaxed at this attractive restaurant with wood-beamed ceilings and terracotta floors. The cooking is excellent and features particularly flavourful dishes made with freshwater fish from nearby Lake Trasimeno. A good one to try is *gnocchi con gamberoni di lago* (potato dumplings with crayfish).

PANICALE Le Grotte di Boldrino €€€

Via Virgilio Ceppari 30, 06064 **Tel** *075 83 71 61* **Road map** *B4*

In a delightful setting next to the medieval town walls, with a garden for summer dining, this restaurant is attractive and welcoming. The menu includes many traditional Umbrian dishes, including charcoal-grilled meats, handmade tagliatelle and truffles and porcini mushrooms. The wine list includes some of Umbria and Tuscany's best bottles.

PANICALE Lillo Tatini €€€€

Piazza Umberto I 13, 06064 **Tel** *075 83 77 71* **Road map** *B4*

It's a good idea to book a table at this small, popular place overlooking the main square of the delightful medieval hilltown of Panicale. The atmosphere is warm and welcoming, and great attention is paid to detail. There is a particularly good wine list and a choice of tasty, creative dishes based on the best Umbrian traditions.

PANICALE Villa di Monte Solare €€€€

Vocabolo Colle San Paolo 7, 06064 **Tel** *075 83 23 76* **Road map** *B4*

This restaurant is part of the splendid Villa di Monte Solare complex, which includes the lovely Hotel Romantik *(see p146)*. The grounds are magnificent and the restaurant itself, set in an 18th-century villa with its own formal garden, has very high standards. The menu features traditional and innovative versions of typical Umbrian dishes.

PERUGIA Dal Mi'Cocco

Corso Garibaldi 12, 06123 **Tel** *075 573 25 11*   **Road map** *C3*

Renowned for serving hearty meals at extremely low prices, this trattoria gets very busy, so be prepared to wait. The four-course set menu is based on traditional genuine Umbrian fare, including local pasta dishes and grilled meats. The decor is jovial, with checked tablecloths and menus written in the local dialect.

PERUGIA Il Falchetto

Via Bartolo 20, 06100 **Tel** *075 573 17 75*   **Road map** *C3*

Brilliantly prepared Perugino cooking is on offer at this 14th-century palazzo a few steps off the main square, with tables out on the piazza for al fresco dining in summer. Whatever else you order, start with the *falchetti verdi* (a casserole of rich spinach-and-ricotta gnocchi baked in tomato sauce and cheese), followed by veal or lamb.

PERUGIA Altromondo

Via Cesare Caporali 11, 06123 **Tel** *075 572 32 21*   **Road map** *C3*

This is one of a number of lively informal places to eat in central Perugia. The welcoming interior has an attractive brick-vaulted ceiling. The food served is well prepared, using local ingredients cooked to traditional recipes of the region. Among the house specialities, the succulent fried lamb is a good one to try.

PERUGIA Da Cesarino

Piazza IV Novembre 4–5, 06123 **Tel** *075 572 89 74*   **Road map** *C3*

This popular eating place is right in the centre of Perugia, opposite the Fontana Maggiore. The tables set outside in summer are ideal for enjoying a meal while watching the world go by. The menu changes with the seasons, but genuine local flavours, such as aromatic truffle-based dishes and succulent grilled meats, are a constant feature.

PERUGIA Giò Arte e Vini

Via Ruggero d'Andreotto 19, 06124 **Tel** *075 573 11 00*   **Road map** *C3*

This modern hotel and restaurant on the outskirts of town is renowned for its spectacular selection of wines (some 1,200 choices), modern art on the walls and well-chosen regional dishes prepared with special touches. The pumpkin ravioli and the *treccia di agnello* (lamb) are particularly good.

PERUGIA La Bocca Mia

Via Ulisse Rocchi 36, 06123 **Tel** *075 572 38 73*   **Road map** *C3*

There is a fantastically romantic atmosphere at this restaurant. The decor is light and bright, and great attention is paid to details such as the tablecloths and flowers. Traditional Umbrian fare is served, with a wide range of well-prepared dishes made using local ingredients, such as mushrooms. There's also a good selection of fish dishes.

PERUGIA La Lanterna

Via U Rocchi 6, 06122 **Tel** *075 572 63 97*   **Road map** *C3*

Brick-vaulted rooms under a medieval palazzo provide the backdrop for creative Umbrian cuisine that might include *ravioli all'arancia e petali di rosa* (cheese ravioli in a cream sauce with mandarin oranges and rose petals) and *arrosto misto* (mix of roast lamb, guinea fowl, rabbit and other meats).

PERUGIA La Taverna

Via delle Streghe 8, 06123 **Tel** *075 572 41 28*   **Road map** *C3*

The place in Perugia to go for an impressive candlelit dinner with romantic music. First courses are classic Umbrian – tagliatelle in a duck ragout, ravioli, fava-bean soup – while the chef gets more inventive with the main courses. Try the *baccalà* (salt cod) with prunes, pine nuts and raisins. Leave a little room for the excellent desserts.

PERUGIA Ristorante del Sole

Via Guglielmo Oberdan 28, 06121 **Tel** *075 573 50 31*   **Road map** *C3*

It is worth coming to eat at this place for the views alone. The fabulous location in the old town centre means that the view from the terrace tables, and even from inside the restaurant itself, is unique. There is a wide selection of traditional Umbrian fare on the menu and some good local wines.

PERUGIA Caffè di Perugia

Via Mazzini 10, 06122 **Tel** *075 573 18 63*   **Road map** *C3*

There's a choice of eating and drinking establishments all under one roof at the lively stylish Caffè di Perugia. The elegant Malacucina restaurant, specializing in grilled meats and other traditional Umbrian fare, is on the top floor. Below that is a pizzeria. Then there's a smart café on the ground floor and a wine bar downstairs.

PERUGIA Antica Trattoria San Lorenzo

Piazza Danti 20, 06122 **Tel** *075 572 19 56*   **Road map** *C3*

With a great location right in the centre of Perugia, by the cathedral and the Fontana Maggiore, this restaurant serves some delicious dishes. It's a popular place, so be sure to book ahead of your visit. A great combination of tradition and creativity goes into the cooking. Fish is served, as well as all kinds of other mouthwatering delights.

PERUGIA Osteria del Gambero

Via Baldeschi 17, 06123 **Tel** *075 573 54 61*   **Road map** *C3*

Advanced booking is recommended at this highly regarded restaurant that spins innovative touches on traditional Umbrian dishes. For example, try the *pappardelle di crusca con lardo di Colonnata* (wide pasta ribbons with salt-cured lard, chickpeas, cantaloupe melon and mint).

Key to Price Guide *see p156* **Key to Symbols** *see back cover flap*

PERUGIA Il Postale

Strada Monteville 3, Residenza d'Epoca Castello di Monterone, 06126 **Tel** *075 852 13 56* **Road map** *C3*

This restaurant is the best in town, and the ideal place to come for a memorable meal. The cooking is fantastically creative, with a menu that includes traditional Umbrian meat-based recipes, re-interpreted by the imaginative chef, and a number of simple but tasty fish dishes. There is a good choice of fragrant breads and olive oils.

PETRIGNANO Locanda ai Cavalieri

Via Matteotti 47, 06086 **Tel** *075 803 00 11* **Road map** *D3*

This elegant restaurant is part of the fabulous Hotel Locanda ai Cavalieri *(see p147)*, which is set in its own extensive gardens. The food served uses typical local ingredients, and recipes are traditionally Umbrian. The pasta, bread and desserts, as well as the butter, are all home-made. A well-stocked wine bar serves a range of lighter meals.

TORGIANO Il Toscanino

Località Signoria, 06089 **Tel** *075 98 24 47* **Road map** *C4*

After years working in one of Florence's most prestigious restaurants, Alessandro Fanini returned home to open Il Toscanino. The restaurant serves tasty Umbrian food, including the local speciality pasta, *strangozzi*, and game, but there's also a good choice of typically Tuscan dishes such as the famous *fiorentina* steak. The wine list is very good.

TORGIANO Osteria I Birbi

Località Le Casacce, Miralduolo, 06089 **Tel** *075 988 90 41* **Road map** *C4*

Just a ten-minute drive from central Perugia, this lively restaurant is located in an old farmhouse in the luscious Umbrian countryside, not far from the border with Tuscany. In the summer you can eat outside and enjoy the spectacular views. The menu consists mainly of Tuscan dishes, including succulent steaks and home-made pasta.

TORGIANO Le Melograne

Via Giuseppe Garibaldi 48, 06089 **Tel** *075 988 04 47* **Road map** *C4*

This refined restaurant in the Tre Vaselle Hotel *(see p147)* is located in its own delightful garden amid beautiful countryside. The main claim to fame is the wine, since the place is owned by the prestigious Lungarotti wine producers, but the food served is top quality, too. The menu features traditional Umbrian dishes, including fish.

UMBERTIDE Locanda di Nonna Gelsa

Via Caduti di Pentola 30, Niccone, 06019 **Tel** *075 941 06 99* **Road map** *C2*

This typical local trattoria is set in a picturesque location in the countryside just outside Umbertide. There's a homely atmosphere and plenty of traditional Umbrian flavours to try. The local meat dishes are the main house specialities – try the mixed grill or the rabbit. The choice of wine is also local, featuring mainly Umbrian and Tuscan labels.

UMBERTIDE L'Abbazia di Montecorona €€€

Vocabolo Montecorona, 06019 **Tel** *075 941 35 01* **Road map** *C2*

This restaurant's stunning location, in a former abbey, makes it a particularly special place to enjoy a meal. The decor of the brick-lined interior is no less attractive than the exterior – it is indeed very atmospheric. The menu contains a good selection of dishes, including a good choice of fish dishes, and the wine cellar is terrific.

UMBERTIDE Poggiomanente €€€

SS 219, E45 exit Umbertide/Gubbio, 06019 **Tel** *075 941 30 85* **Road map** *C2*

The specialities here are hearty and traditionally Umbrian. There are plenty of truffle- and mushroom-based dishes, but also some delicious meat dishes, including the aromatic duck or *anatra in porchetta* (duck with bacon) and roast lamb. The restaurant is both rustic and refined, making the most of its lovely location in the cellars of an old inn.

SOUTHERN UMBRIA

ACQUASPARTA Locanda Il Re Beve

Piazza Corsini 11, 05021 **Tel** *0744 94 34 28* **Road map** *D6*

The setting of this restaurant is an impressive medieval castle in the countryside outside the village of Acquasparta. The restaurant interior is well maintained and elegant, but at the same time welcoming and rustic. There is a staggering choice of wines, and the menu covers a wide range of Umbrian dishes, many with a creative twist. Closed Wed.

AMELIA Anita

Via Roma 31, 05022 **Tel** *0744 98 21 46* **Road map** *C6*

This simple restaurant and hotel just outside the city centre has been run by the Pernazza family since 1938. They offer no-frills Umbrian fare, such as *crostini* (toasted bread with various toppings), roasted meats, pasta with porcini mushrooms and wild boar. The delectable desserts are made in-house.

ARRONE Il Grottino del Nera

SS Valnerina, Vocabolo Colleporto 21, 05031 **Tel** *0744 38 91 04* **Road map** *D6*

Dating from 1860, this is the oldest restaurant in the area around the famous Cascata delle Marmore waterfall. It's an informal and welcoming family-run place serving authentic and tasty Umbrian dishes. Try the wild boar or other types of game, the grilled trout or the tagliatelle cooked with truffle. The terrace tables are ideal in the summer.

ARRONE Rossi

Vocabolo Isola 7, 05031 **Tel** *0744 38 83 72*   **Road map** *D6*

In the heart of the Valnerina, just a few kilometres from the spectacular Cascata delle Marmore waterfall, is this traditional Umbrian restaurant. Along with its adjoining hotel, it has been run by the Rossi family since the late 1920s. The food offered ranges from charcoal grilled local meats, to truffle-flavoured pasta and fresh river fish.

BASCHI Vissani

Strada Statale 448, km 606, Todi-Baschi, 05020 **Tel** *0744 95 02 06*   **Road map** *B6*

Gianfranco Vissani is famous throughout Italy for his balanced flavours and haute cuisine of game and meat, served in impeccably elegant surroundings. The recipes are inventive and original, and based around regional ingredients. For dessert, you move to a separate room, just as you would in an old-fashioned household.

BEVAGNA Osteria Il Podestà
Corso Giacomo Matteotti 67, 06031 **Tel** *0742 36 18 32*   **Road map** *D4*

This welcoming, well-run restaurant is located in the former town-hall building, in the centre of the lovely medieval village of Bevagna. The menu changes according to what's in season but is generally based on traditional local dishes. Try the delicious *taglierini al Sagrantino* – the sauce is made with the eponymous prestigious local red wine.

BEVAGNA Il Poggio dei Pettirossi
Via del Poggio 1, 06031 **Tel** *0742 36 17 40*   **Road map** *D4*

This restaurant is part of a complex that includes a hotel located in attractively converted buildings in the Umbrian countryside, a few kilometres from Bevagna. The room is dominated by an attractive stone fireplace and a fantastic panoramic view. The food on offer is traditionally Umbrian, and there are good wines from nearby Montefalco.

BEVAGNA Locanda Piazza Onofri
Piazza Onofri 1, 06031 **Tel** *0742 36 19 26*   **Road map** *D4*

This trattoria and wine bar is located in a traditional 12th-century building, complete with vaulted ceilings and an open fire. There are around 500 wines to choose from, the atmosphere is lively and the food is terrific too. Pasta is home-made, and there is a wide choice of cold meats and cheeses, including some from France.

BEVAGNA Redibis

Via dell'Anfiteatro, 06031 **Tel** *0742 36 01 30*   **Road map** *D4*

With a spectacular location in part of a Roman theatre in the medieval village of Bevagna, this is a restaurant to remember. Exceptional traditional Umbrian dishes are served alongside some refined and imaginative creations. Specialities include stuffed roast wood pigeon and *crescionda*, a dessert that originates from Spoleto.

CAMPELLO SUL CLITUNNO Fonti del Clitunno
Località Fonti Clitunno, 06042 **Tel** *0743 27 50 57*   **Road map** *D5*

Set in the lovely Fonti del Clitunno park, known since ancient times for its springs, this restaurant is a great place to relax and enjoy great food. The menu consists of old favourites, while the wine list covers all parts of Italy and even includes some wines from further afield. There are plenty of vegetarian choices and lighter snacks too.

CAMPELLO SUL CLITUNNO Trattoria Pettino
Frazione Pettino 31, 06042 **Tel** *0743 27 60 21*   **Road map** *D5*

Occupying an old restored house in the middle of the mountains, Trattoria Pettino offers delicious *bruschetta* (toasted bread with various toppings) and, in season, a plethora of dishes made with truffles. Try the *stringozzi al tartufo* (thick, hand-rolled ropes of pasta dressed in black truffles) and the *agnello al tartufo* (lamb with truffles).

CAMPELLO SUL CLITUNNO Camesena
Via del Castello 3, Lizori, Pissignano Alto **Tel** *0743 52 03 40*   **Road map** *D5*

Set in the tiny village of Lizori, in the Umbrian hills not far from the famous springs of Clitunno, Camesena is an unusual place to eat. In this restaurant art and gastronomy are united by a life-loving philosophy, turning a meal here into a real experience. The menu includes some especially good fish options. It is wise to book ahead.

CANNARA Perbacco
Via Umberto I 16, 06033 **Tel** *0742 72 04 92*   **Road map** *D4*

This delightful restaurant, decorated with antique mirrors and an open fire, is located in the centre of Cannara. The village and surrounding area are famous for their particular variety of red onion, which you can try here cooked in a variety of ways. There is also a good selection of wines, spirits and liqueurs.

CIVITELLA DEL LAGO Trippini
Via Italia 14, 05023 **Tel** *0744 95 04 55*   **Road map** *B5*

This tiny restaurant has a romantic atmosphere – both inside and outside on the panoramic terrace. The menu changes according to what's in season but is always based on local ingredients, featuring old recipes that are cooked with flair and imagination. A tempting selection of cheeses and a good wine list complete the picture.

FABRO La Bettola del Buttero
Via dei Pini 2, 05015 **Tel** *0763 83 20 63*   **Road map** *B5*

This picturesque countryside hotel and restaurant is close to the A1 motorway – perfect for an idyllic break on a long journey. There's a fireplace in the middle of the restaurant, used for grilling meat, and a wood-burning oven where cakes are made and onions and potatoes are baked. In summer, tables are set outside in the delightful garden.

Key to Price Guide *see p156* **Key to Symbols** *see back cover flap*

FERENTILLO Il Cantico

Via Macenano 4, 06034 **Tel** *0744 78 00 05*   €€€   **Road map** *D3*

This compact restaurant, part of a charming hotel, is set in a converted former Benedictine abbey building. The menu consists of a range of local dishes that change according to what's in season. The pasta is a particular speciality – it's made by hand on the premises – and there are plenty of dishes flavoured with the local truffles.

FERENTILLO Piermarini

Via Fosso Ancaiano 230, 05034 **Tel** *0744 78 07 14*   €€€   **Road map** *D6*

Set among the beautiful Umbrian countryside, this restaurant is decorated in a simple fashion. The food served, on the other hand, is fantastic. Traditional Umbrian recipes are used and sometimes adapted according to the freshest ingredients available. Truffles feature highly on the menu, and there are numerous other tempting flavours to try.

FOLIGNO Basilikò

Via Bagni 6, 06034 **Tel** *0742 35 96 90*   €   **Road map** *D4*

This charming restaurant is located in a 13th-century building that has been decorated with a combination of rustic elements and contemporary pieces, creating a refined but welcoming environment. The menu contains a range of typical Umbrian dishes, but with some innovative variations that add a touch of southern-style cooking.

FOLIGNO Il Bacco Felice

Via Garibaldi 73 / 75, 06034 **Tel** *0742 62 14 38*   €€   **Road map** *D4*

Great attention is paid to the quality of the food here and, in fact, the vegetables served are grown in the restaurant's own organic field. The cold meats are top quality – the Norcia ham is particularly good – and the grilled meats and soups made with local pulses are very well prepared. There is also a full vegetarian menu.

FOLIGNO Le Mura

Via Bolletta 27, 06034 **Tel** *0742 35 46 48*   €€   **Road map** *D4*

This restaurant is part of the Hotel Mura *(see p148)*, set in Foligno's historic centre. The atmosphere is welcoming and homely, and hearty meals are served. Watch as the chunky steaks and other meats are charcoal-grilled. Other specialities include a varied range of vegetable dishes, some very tasty soups and traditional pasta dishes.

FOLIGNO Villa Roncalli

Via Roma 25, 06034 **Tel** *0742 39 10 91*   €€€   **Road map** *D4*

This charming 17th-century country inn is set in its own garden about 1 km (half a mile) from Foligno. Regional specialities are well prepared using fresh ingredients. Try the ravioli or fettucine with truffles, braised lamb, wild asparagus or the châteaubriand with field herbs.

FOLIGNO Exedra et Cenatio

Via delle Industrie 17, San Eraclio **Tel** *0742 67 73 76*   €€€€   **Road map** *D4*

This restaurant is located in Foligno's industrial district, but the attractively converted 19th-century farmhouse setting and the quality of the food make it worth seeking out. The menu features a wide range of dishes, with a good fish section – try the sole lasagne – and plenty of choice for vegetarians. There is a great selection of Italian wines.

LUGNANO IN TEVERINA Frateria dell'Abate Loniano

Località San Francesco 6, 05020 **Tel** *0744 90 21 80*   €€   **Road map** *C6*

The restaurant is in a charming 13th-century converted monastery building, not far from Amelia. There are beautiful views from here, and it is lovely to sit outside to eat on a summer's day. The interior is also atmospheric – the dining room is in the former refectory. The food is made with fresh local ingredients cooked to traditional recipes.

MONTEFALCO Coccorone

Vicolo Fabbri 7, 06036 **Tel** *0742 37 95 35*   €€   **Road map** *D4*

This attractive, rustic but elegant restaurant in the historic centre is proud of the traditional tastes it offers to diners. Indeed, care has been taken to restore ancient countryside recipes that otherwise may have been forgotten. The menu includes some delicious home-made pasta dishes, charcoal-grilled meats and other Umbrian specialities.

MONTEFALCO Villa Pambuffetti

Via della Vittoria 20, 06036 **Tel** *0742 37 94 17*   €€€   **Road map** *D4*

The service is impeccable and the food is delicious at this special hotel restaurant, set in an elegant 19th-century villa *(see p149)*. It is a popular spot for wedding celebrations, including those of the rich and famous. The menu features mainly simple but tasty traditional Umbrian dishes, and there is a good choice of excellent wines.

NARNI Cavallino

Via Flaminia Romana 220, Località Testaccio, 05035 **Tel** *0744 76 10 20*   €   **Road map** *C6*

A cordial atmosphere underscores the solid home cooking offered here. Food is firmly in the Umbrian tradition, including interesting pastas such as *manfricoli* and *ciriole* (both of which are eggless) served with tomato sauce, wild boar or porcini. They also do nice *scaloppine al limone* (veal escalope in lemon sauce), grilled meats and pigeon.

NARNI Il Gattamelata

Via Pozzo della Comunità 4, 05035 **Tel** *0744 71 72 45*   €€   **Road map** *C6*

The decor is that of a typically cosy local trattoria, while the food served features a particularly good range of Umbrian specialities. Alongside the traditional menu, it is possible to choose from one of two full medieval menus and a list of vegetarian choices. This is a good place to try the traditional wood pigeon *alla ghiotta*.

NARNI Il Feudo
€€€

Via del Forno 10, Montoro, 05035 **Tel** *0744 73 51 68*   **Road map** *C6*

Located in the centre of Montoro, about 7 km (4.25 miles) from the ancient hilltown of Narni, Il Feudo is a refined restaurant with well-maintained traditionally rustic decor. It consists of three rooms, which run over two floors. The menu contains a variety of old-fashioned specialities, including some tasty pasta dishes; pizza is also served.

NORCIA Dal Francese
€

Via Riguardati 16, 06046 **Tel** *0743 81 62 90*   **Road map** *F5*

In season, this country-style trattoria in the centre of town offers a truffle-based *menù degustazione* (tasting menu). The list also includes specialities such as *pappardelle alla norcina* (wide pasta ribbons in a cream sauce with sausage) and *agnello scottadito* (lamb so succulent, the name says that you'll "burn your fingers" in your haste to eat it).

NORCIA La Cucina del Casale
€€

Vocabolo Fontevena 8, 06046 **Tel** *0743 81 64 81*   **Road map** *F5*

This *agriturismo* near Norcia uses organic techniques to cultivate its farmland, and all the vegetables and pulses that go into the tasty meals are farmed on site. Much of the meat is also from the farm itself, and most of the other various ingredients, including the famous Norcia truffles, as well as the cheeses and salami, are locally produced.

NORCIA Taverna de' Massari
€€

Via Roma 13, 06046 **Tel** *0743 81 62 18*   **Road map** *F5*

Located in the old town centre of Norcia, Italy's cured-meat capital, this relaxed informal eaterie is a good place to come to enjoy some of the delicious local produce. This includes the black truffle of Norcia and the area's cheeses, as well as the famous meat products. Try the delicious sausage cooked with lentils.

NORCIA Beccofino
€€€

Piazza San Benedetto 12, 06046 **Tel** *0743 81 60 86*   **Road map** *F5*

Beccofino is well known for serving excellent meals without charging over the odds. The menu is made up of a variety of traditional and innovative Umbrian dishes. Norcia's fragrant black truffles feature highly in many recipes, and there is plenty of choice of local sausages and salamis worth trying, such as the wild-boar ham.

NORCIA Il Granaro del Monte
€€€

Via Alfieri 10, 06046 **Tel** *0743 81 75 51*   **Road map** *F5*

This restaurant within the Hotel Grotta Azzurra *(see p149)* has been run by the Bianconi family for over 200 years. The 16th-century building is very atmospheric, and there is a period fireplace. The menu consists of a variety of Umbrian specialities, with truffle flavours featuring highly. There are some terrific desserts and an extensive wine list.

ORVIETO Cantina Foresi
 €

Piazza Duomo 2, 05018 **Tel** *0763 34 16 11*   **Road map** *B5*

A fabulous wine bar in a unique location in Orvieto's Piazza Duomo. Sit outside for a breathtaking view of the cathedral, or in the cosy interior at one of the chunky tree-trunk tables. The wine list is terrific, and there's a good choice of locally produced meats and cheeses to eat, as well as other hearty snacks. Open 9:30am–7:30pm.

ORVIETO La Volpe e l'Uva
€

Via Ripa Corsica 1, 05018 **Tel** *0763 34 16 12*   **Road map** *B5*

This popular and friendly trattoria in the centre of Orvieto offers a variety of regional dishes at reasonable prices. Dishes change with the season, and the meat and game recipes are joined by a good selection of lake fish, as well as lots of egg-based dishes. The owners make an effort to cater to vegetarians too.

ORVIETO Al Pozzo Etrusco d'Aronne
€€

Piazza Ranieri 1a, 05018 **Tel** *0763 34 44 56*   **Road map** *B5*

This charming trattoria is located right opposite the escalators from the car park below the medieval town centre. The outside terrace is particularly attractive, the service professional but friendly, and the quality of the food excellent. Try the local speciality *ombrichelli* pasta or the delicious sweet-and-sour wild boar.

ORVIETO Le Grotte del Funaro
€€

Via Ripa Serancia 41, 05018 **Tel** *0763 34 32 76*   **Road map** *B5*

An atmospheric series of cave-rooms carved from the tufa at the cliff's edge, once the workshop of a *funaro* (rope-maker) in the 12th century, is the setting for this restaurant. The *ombrechelli del Funaro* is handmade spaghetti with tomatoes, sausage, artichokes and mushrooms. The mixed platter of grilled meats is also very tasty.

ORVIETO Duca di Orvieto
€€€

Via della Pace 5, 05018 **Tel** *0763 34 46 63*   **Road map** *B5*

The traditional Medieval and Renaissance dishes on the menu at this unusual restaurant in central Orvieto have all been carefully researched, and a good one to try is the Renaissance-style chicken cooked with lemon and honey. The tangy home-made chutneys served with a selection of local cheeses are also delightful.

ORVIETO I Sette Consoli
€€€

Piazza Sant'Angelo 1a, 05018 **Tel** *0763 34 39 11*   **Road map** *B5*

A comfortable, friendly restaurant installed in the sacristy of an old church, with a garden for summer dining. Try the *baccalà* (salt cod) marinated in apple vinegar with potato salad, the stuffed rabbit, the *ravioli di anatra* (duck-filled ravioli) and the *zuppa di fave con finocchio* (bean soup with fennel) – all are exceptionally flavourful.

ORVIETO Dell'Ancora

 €€€€

Via di Piazza del Popolo 7–9, 05018 **Tel** *0763 34 27 66*   **Road map** *B5*

Located in the heart of Orvieto, this welcoming restaurant has been run by the same family since the 19th century, when it was frequented by the local bourgeoisie who held political and cultural meetings here. The food served is based on traditional recipes, the pasta is handmade and there is an interesting choice of deep-fried dishes.

ORVIETO La Badia

€€€€

Località Badia 8, 05018 **Tel** *0763 30 19 59*   **Road map** *B5*

This restaurant is located within the Hotel La Badia *(see p150)*, in a restored abbey complex at the foot of the town. The romantic dining room is extremely atmospheric, and the standards of both service and food are high. The menu covers a range of Umbrian specialities, with plenty of charcoal-grilled meats and other traditional local flavours.

ORVIETO Il Giglio d'Oro

€€€€€

Piazza Duomo 8, 05018 **Tel** *0763 34 19 03*   **Road map** *B5*

This elegant restaurant is positioned right next to Orvieto's magnificent cathedral, and tables are set outside on the square in summertime. There is a good selection of wines and a varied menu, which features some interesting and innovative dishes alongside more traditional Umbrian cuisine. One speciality is the roast goose with fennel.

PORANO Il Boccone del Prete

 €€

Via Eugenio Bellini 12, 05010 **Tel** *0763 37 47 72*   **Road map** *B5*

This restaurant is located in the village of Porano, in the area famous for Etruscan tombs, among the hills just south of Orvieto. The service is slick, and the standard of food excellent. The menu contains a selection of traditional Umbrian specialities, and the atmospheric wine cellar is well stocked, with more than 300 different labels.

PRECI Al Porcello Felice

€€

Frazione Castelvecchio, 06047 **Tel** *0743 93 90 05*   **Road map** *E5*

This restaurant is part of an *agriturismo* that grows much of its own produce according to organic principles. The location, in the middle of the Umbrian hills, is fabulous. Come here for good home-cooked fare, prepared using the freshest ingredients and following traditional local recipes. In the evening, pizzas are made in the wood-burning oven.

SAN GEMINI Gattaluna

 €€

Viale Garibaldi 6, 05029 **Tel** *0744 33 40 46*   **Road map** *D6*

Set in a fantastic position high on a hill above medieval San Gemini, Gattaluna offers some fabulous views from its terrace tables. The restaurant – often used for weddings and other functions, including poolside parties – serves fragrant pizzas, as well as some excellent dishes from the local tradition and tempting home-made desserts.

SCHEGGINO Del Ponte

 €€€

Via di Borgo 15, 06040 **Tel** *074 36 12 53*   **Road map** *E5*

This pleasant restaurant in the middle of the village of Scheggino serves an excellent range of specialities from the Valnerina valley – in particular, good freshwater fish such as trout. Other local options to try include the black truffle, and there are some excellent cheeses and cold meats. It is also possible to stay in the small hotel.

SPELLO Il Molino

 €€€

Piazza Giacomo Matteotti 6, 06038 **Tel** *0742 65 13 05*   **Road map** *D4*

Set in a converted 14th-century olive mill in central Spello, this restaurant in Hotel Palazzo Bocci *(see p150)* is simple but refined in style. The menu features good typical recipes of the region, as well as some innovative combinations. Specialities include game, truffles, porcini and charcoal-grilled meats that you can watch being prepared.

SPELLO La Bastiglia

€€€€€

Via Salnitraria 1, 06049 **Tel** *0742 65 18 23*   **Road map** *D4*

Furnished with antiques, this elegant hotel restaurant *(see p150)* is set within an 18th-century mill. The menu changes according to the season and is mainly based on local recipes, with a choice of fish and vegetarian dishes too. The pasta, bread and desserts are all home-made. Try the delicious wood pigeon in Sagrantino wine sauce.

SPOLETO Le Casaline

 €

Località Poreta di Spoleto, Frazione Casaline, 06142 **Tel** *0743 52 11 13*   **Road map** *D5*

An oasis of calm in a restored 18th-century mill. Try the gnocchi stuffed with mushrooms, the *rigatoni alla norcina* (pasta tubes with mushrooms, peas, truffles and sausage) or the *cinghiale alla cacciatora* (wild boar in a wine-and-tomato sauce). The menu also offers many peasant-inspired goose dishes.

SPOLETO Il Panciolle

 €€

Vicolo degli Eroli 1/Via Duomo, 06049 **Tel** *0743 22 12 41*   **Road map** *D5*

The main highlights of this restaurant are the large terrace shaded by a spreading pine tree for summer dining, and the stone-walled room where the meat for the main courses is grilled over a large open fire. Try the *strangozzi alla montanara* (hand-rolled pasta strands with minced vegetables and chilli peppers).

SPOLETO Il Tartufo

 €€

Piazza Garibaldi 24, 06049 **Tel** *0743 402 36*   **Road map** *D5*

The floor of the basement dining room of this restaurant specializing in truffles dates back to ancient Rome. The well-tried regional specialities include such delights as *zuppa di farro* (spelt soup); courgette flowers stuffed with cheese, aubergine and truffles and duck in Sagrantino wine sauce.

SPOLETO Il Tempio del Gusto

Via Arco di Druso 9, 06049 **Tel** *074 34 71 21*

Road map *D5*

This restaurant is located in a fascinating building, with architectural remains dating from the 1st century BC and a wine cellar that is even more ancient. The food served is excellent, with many dishes based on old recipes. Imaginative use is made of fresh herbs, as well as other locally produced ingredients. There is a very good wine list.

SPOLETO Agghielli

Località Pompagnano, 06049 **Tel** *0743 22 50 10*

Road map *D5*

The atmosphere at this restaurant set in its own gardens, about 5 km (3 miles) outside Spoleto, is romantic and intimate. Many of the ingredients used in the dishes are produced at the owner's farm, which works according to strict organic principles. There is also an interesting choice of dishes from the Renaissance period.

SPOLETO Al Palazzaccio da Piero

Località Palazzaccio 33, Poreta, 06049 **Tel** *0743 52 01 68*

Road map *D5*

This is a well-established, family-run restaurant on the Via Flaminia – a road dating from Roman times – not far from the centre of Spoleto, and a frequent haunt of lovers of good food. A warm welcome awaits you, not to mention a menu featuring good traditional Umbrian delights, the main speciality being the fragrant local truffles.

SPOLETO Il Capanno

Località Torrecola 6, 06049 **Tel** *074 35 41 19*

Road map *D5*

You can dine among the trees in the garden of this restaurant, set in the fabulous hills just outside Spoleto. The menu is based on local flavours and changes according to the season. The pasta with mushroom and wood pigeon is particularly good, and there is a wide range of charcoal-grilled meats. Two bedrooms are also available.

SPOLETO Sabatini

Corso Mazzini 54, 06049 **Tel** *0743 22 18 31*

Road map *D5*

This smart restaurant in the centre of Spoleto has its own extensive garden, ideal for dinner on a summer's evening. The house specialities include *strangozzi allo spoletino*, the local pasta with a tasty sauce of tomato, garlic and chilli pepper. The lamb cooked with fresh porcini mushrooms is another great option.

SPOLETO San Lorenzo

Piazza Sordini 6, 06049 **Tel** *0743 22 18 47*

Road map *D5*

Some great food is served at this restaurant in central Spoleto. The menu offers plenty of traditional Umbrian dishes with some interesting variations. The *vellutata di ceci* (cream-of-chickpea soup) with prawns is delicious, as is the pork filet cooked in a red-wine sauce with juniper berries. Speciality food-and-wine events are often held here.

SPOLETO Trattoria del Festival

Via Brignone 8, 06049 **Tel** *0743 22 09 93*

Road map *D5*

This elegant but rustic restaurant set in a 16th-century building in Spoleto's town centre serves dishes that are mostly based on traditional recipes, and the local truffles are very much in evidence. All the pasta is made by hand on the premises. Pizzas are also available, and there is also a good wine list.

SPOLETO Tric Trac

Via dell'Arringo 10, 06049 **Tel** *074 34 45 92*

Road map *D5*

This restaurant has a fantastic setting, looking out over Spoleto's beautiful Piazza Duomo. The food served is rooted in local traditions, but there is a wide choice of dishes that will appeal to all. Also operating as an *enoteca*, or wine bar, Tric Trac features a particularly well-thought-out wine list, which includes the best labels from various Italian regions.

SPOLETO Apollinare

Via Santa Agata 14, 06049 **Tel** *0743 22 32 56*

Road map *D5*

This refined restaurant has a fascinating location, set among walls that are of Roman origin and were later part of a former Franciscan monastery. The choice of food is a combination of the traditional and the creative. You can also choose from various set menus, including a surprise menu, as well as vegetarian, fish and traditional dishes.

STRONCONE Taverna di Portanova

Via di Porta Nuova 1 **Tel** *074 46 04 96*

Road map *D6*

The setting for this restaurant is a converted convent with a gorgeous open fire, in the hills south of Terni. Great care is taken over the recipes, and a variety of fresh local herbs and other ingredients is used. The *zuppa di Suor Anita* is a good one to try – made with beans, chickpeas and mushrooms, and served in a hollowed-out bread roll.

TERNI Da Carlino

Via Piemonte 1, 05100 **Tel** *0744 42 01 63*

Road map *D6*

Robust, rustic food is served in this historic building in town. Start off with the *crostini* (toasts) served alongside local salami, followed perhaps by tagliatelle with truffles, lamb or a fish dish. The house speciality is *stracci* (home-made pasta) tossed in a sauce of veal and fresh mozzarella.

TERNI Lu Somaru

Viale Cesare Battisti 106, 05100 **Tel** *0744 30 47 87*

Road map *D6*

This is a warm and friendly place to eat near the centre of Terni. The theme is Tyrolean, so there are plenty of alternatives to the traditional Umbrian flavours on offer everywhere else. Fragrant pizzas are also served. Sit out in the garden – a great place to spend a warm summer's evening – or in the welcoming interior.

Key to Price Guide *see p156* **Key to Symbols** *see back cover flap*

TERNI Oste della Mal'ora

Via Tre Archi 5, 05100 **Tel** *0744 40 66 83* **Road map** *D6*

This is a lovely, atmospheric little place, with decor reminiscent of an old-style hostelry. There is a variety of different foods on the menu, including Umbrian specialities from the hills and lake areas, and the choice of cheeses is particularly good. It is also possible to come just for a drink or an afternoon snack.

TERNI La Piazzetta

Via Cavour 9, 05100 **Tel** *074 45 81 88* **Road map** *D6*

The menu changes daily at this stylish and chic little restaurant in the centre of Terni. The food on offer includes traditional regional specialities, but these are often made with an original and creative twist. There are also some delicious fish dishes. The wine list is carefully thought out, with recommendations made to match the food.

TERNI Villa Graziani

Vocabolo Valle 10, Papigno, 05037 **Tel** *074 46 71 38* **Road map** *D6*

A charming 16th-century villa, not far from the Cascate delle Marmore waterfall, houses this lovely restaurant. There's a children's play area here, and the atmosphere is friendly and welcoming. The food served includes some very good examples of local Umbrian cuisine, the grilled meats and traditional pastas being the house specialities.

TODI La Mulinella

Località Pontenaia 29, 06059 **Tel** *075 894 47 79* **Road map** *C5*

In the countryside about 2 km (1 mile) from Todi, this restaurant serves simple, reliable dishes. The wood-fired breads and home-made pastas and desserts are excellent. Also recommended are the *carni alle brace* (grilled meats) with seasonal vegetables and the *pasta in ragù di anatra* (duck) or *oca* (goose).

TODI Antica Osteria della Valle

Via Ciuffelli 19, 06059 **Tel** *0758 94 48 48* **Road map** *C5*

This cosy restaurant sticks closely to Umbrian culinary traditions. The hearty dishes, prepared using locally produced ingredients, are always tasty and the portions generous. The *crostini* are great starters, and the desserts, such as the *semifreddo alle mandorle tostate* (chilled pudding with toasted almonds), are memorable.

TODI Jacopone

Piazza Iacopone 3, 06059 **Tel** *0758 94 23 66* **Road map** *C5*

Located in Todi's town centre, this simple restaurant serves a variety of tasty dishes, including wild boar and mixed charcoal-grilled meats. The pastas are not to be overlooked either: try the *strangozzi agli asparagi piccanti* (the local pasta with spicy asparagus) or the house speciality, *pasticcio di Jacopone* (a kind of cannelloni with truffle).

TODI Lucaroni

Via Cortesi 57, 06059 **Tel** *075 894 26 94* **Road map** *C5*

In the picture-perfect hilltown of Todi, this restaurant serves up regional specialities based on fish, meat and game (including hare, duck and lamb), often lacing dishes with truffles in season. The puddings, such as a *crema* (cream) topped with warm chocolate, are delicate and exquisite.

TODI Pane e Vino

Via Augusto Ciuffelli 33, 06059 **Tel** *0758 94 54 48* **Road map** *C5*

Located in a lovely part of central Todi, near the church of San Fortunato, this welcoming restaurant exudes calm and tranquillity. The excellent food is based on traditional recipes. There is a fantastic range of antipasti, some delicious pasta dishes, such as the chickpea and porcini mushroom dish, and hearty meat dishes.

TODI Ristorante Umbria

Via San Bonaventura 13, 06059 **Tel** *0758 94 27 37* **Road map** *C5*

In the 15th century, a group of local gourmets used to meet on the premises of this atmospheric restaurant in Todi's lovely old town centre. There's an attractive open fire in winter, while in summer a table on the panoramic terrace is a great idea. The menu covers a wide range of regional and local specialities, and there is a good wine list.

TREVI La Taverna del Pescatore

Via Flaminia Vecchia 50, 06039 **Tel** *0742 78 09 20* **Road map** *D5*

At this relaxed restaurant, the freshest of local produce is combined with freshwater fish and cooked in simple yet exquisite recipes based on old Umbrian recipes. Try the *gamberi di fiume alle brace* or *all'arrabbiata* (crayfish grilled or served spicy hot). The service is gracious and attentive.

TREVI La Vecchia Posta

Piazza Mazzini 14, 06039 **Tel** *0742 38 16 90* **Road map** *D5*

This simple, informal trattoria is located right on the main square of the stunning hilltop town of Trevi. The decor is attractively rustic, and the dishes on offer are always tasty and carefully prepared. The local olive oil is fantastic, and there's also a good wine list. Come here for an authentic taste of genuine Umbrian fare.

TREVI Maggiolini

Via San Francesco 20, 06039 **Tel** *0742 38 15 34* **Road map** *D5*

This attractive, well-established restaurant has brick-vaulted ceilings and outside tables for summer dining. The food served includes plenty of local specialities cooked according to tradition – charcoal-grilled meats and so on – as well as more creative fare. There is an interesting selection of omelettes, and the pasta is all home-made.

SHOPPING IN UMBRIA

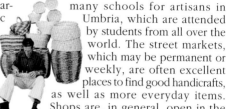

The small shops lining the narrow streets of the historic centres of Umbria's towns and the craft workshops seen in small Umbrian villages make the region a wonderful place for shopping. It is not simply a question of buying traditional furniture, ceramics or textiles; it is also possible to track down workshops producing new and modern interpretations of ancient crafts, created by real masters of their art. Their fame is such that there are

A basket-maker at work

many schools for artisans in Umbria, which are attended by students from all over the world. The street markets, which may be permanent or weekly, are often excellent places to find good handicrafts, as well as more everyday items. Shops are, in general, open in the morning from 9am to 1pm and in the afternoon from 3 to 8pm. In the major tourist centres, such as Perugia and Assisi, shops are often open on Sunday as well.

Pottery shop in Deruta, a town famous for its ceramics

CERAMICS

The ancient art of making pottery is one of the most traditional of Umbrian crafts. It was practised by the Etruscans and then resumed in the Middle Ages.

The ceramics of Deruta are among the most famous in Umbria, for their sheer quality and their bright colours. Today, the introduction of new styles and designs has breathed fresh life into a series of workshops run by artist-potters, whose work can be seen in Perugia, Orvieto, Deruta, Gubbio and Umbertide.

WOOD

The woodworkers of Umbria are not simply carpenters or restorers. Umbrian artisans working in wood, though famous for their solid and traditional furniture, have also introduced some individual

lines, such as wooden models (Perugia), sculpture (Orvieto) and modern furniture (Assisi). Most carpentry workshops are keen to produce furniture and other items for individual customers. However, these custom-made pieces can be very costly.

TEXTILES AND EMBROIDERY

For some years now in Umbria the tradition of hand-weaving fabric, using methods and designs dating back as far as the Middle Ages, has been

Worker with a hand loom used in the production of typical Umbrian textiles

making a comeback. Rugs, bedspreads, and household linens, all with an antique feel, are regaining popularity in the shops of many Umbrian towns.

Another well-known tradition is that of "punto Assisi", or Assisi embroidery. Less widespread but equally fine is embroidery on tulle, originating from Panicale, south of Lake Trasimeno.

ANTIQUES

Traditional Umbrian taste, a sense of the past, and increasing numbers of visitors have helped antiques shops and galleries to prosper. Items on sale range from antique books and other printed material to statues, furniture, jewellery, carpets and even icons. There are, in addition, regular antiques markets, such as those held in Assisi, Todi and Perugia.

WINE AND OLIVE OIL

Umbrian wine companies vary considerably in size, from the small vineyard owner to large modern industrial units. Wine is a serious matter in Umbria and the quality of its red and white wines now rivals the world's best.

Vineyards can often be visited, and wines tasted and purchased on site. In some cases the wine tasting, with sampling of cheeses and salami included, commands a fee and must be booked in advance. Apart from the traditional wine cooperatives, the most famous places to go to are the Lungarotti company in Torgiano; Antinori, not far from Orvieto; and Decugnano dei Barbi, near Corbara.

In Umbria, the production of olive oil is an ancient and much-respected tradition. A good proportion of the oil made in Umbria is bottled with the quality mark DOP (Denominazione di Origine Protetta – or protected denomination of origin), which guarantees the origin of the olives used and the method of pressing. The best places to buy oil are at the olive presses *(frantoi)*, which can be visited in November and December; here you can see how the olives are made into olive oil in a matter of hours. The price of a good-quality oil bought on site will be at least twice that of any everyday extra-virgin oil bought in an ordinary shop.

Delicatessen in Norcia, a typical shop selling local produce

GASTRONOMY

Another popular buy is the traditional produce of the region. The cured meats – especially those from Norcia, although they can be found almost everywhere – are one of the top delicacies. The variety is impressive: salami, hams and sausages, cured or fresh. Bottled vegetables in oil or brine are widely available, as are locally made jams.

Focaccia with cheese (which is traditional at Easter) is particularly good in southern Umbria, and Umbrian sheep's milk cheeses, both mature and fresh, are also excellent.

Cereals and vegetables are another important and popular Umbrian staple, and are often grown organically. In addition to the lentils of Castelluccio, look for spelt *(farro)* and chickling *(cicerchia)*, a type of pea.

DIRECTORY

CRAFTS

**L'Antica Deruta
(ceramics)**
SS E45, Deruta.
www.anticaderuta.com

**Artigianato
Ferro Artistico
(ironwork)**
Via Baldassini 22, Gubbio.

**Bottega del legno
di Gualverio
Michelangeli
(woodwork)**
Via Michelangeli 3,
Orvieto.

**Ceramiche
artigianali
(ceramics)**
Via Storelli 42,
Gualdo Tadino.

**Ceramiche Rometti
(ceramics)**
Traversa Garibaldi 73,
Umbertide.

**Duca di Montefeltro
(ceramics)**
Via dei Consoli 33, Gubbio.

**La Fucina
(metalwork)**
Via dei Muratori, Orvieto.

**Laboratorio
Tela Umbra
(textiles)**
Via Sant'Antonio 3,
Città di Castello.

**Mastri Cartai
Editori (paper)**
Via Alessi 4, Perugia.

**Officina Libris
(leather-bound
goods)**
Via dei Consoli 39,
Gubbio.

**La Spola
(general crafts)**
Via Garibaldi 66, Torgiano.

**Tele Umbre
(tapestry)**
Via Piccotti 1, Gubbio.

**Tessuto Artistico
Umbro
(textiles)**
Piazza del Comune 1,
Montefalco.

ANTIQUES FAIRS

**Assisi Antiquariato
(end Apr–May)**
Centro Umbriafiere
Bastia Umbria.
www.assisiantiquariato.it

**Rassegna Antiquaria
(end Oct–early Nov)**
Rocca Paolina, Perugia.

**Rassegna
Antiquaria d'Italia
(mid-end Apr)**
Palazzo Vignola, Todi.

GASTRONOMY

L'Agricola Goretti
Strada Pino 4, Pila
(nr Perugia).

**Bartolini
(porcini, truffles,
oils etc.)**
33 Via XX Settembre,
Gubbio.

Bottega Barbanera
Piazza della Repubblica
34, Foligno.

**Cantina Terre
de' Trinci**
Via Fiamenga 57, Foligno.

**Fratelli Ansuini
(cured meats)**
Viale della Stazione, Norcia.

**Giò Arte e Vini
(wine)**
Via Ruggero d'Andreotto
19, Perugia.

**Macelleria Giulietti
(meat products)**
Corso Cavour 13,
Città di Castello.

**Pasticceria Muzzi
(cakes and biscuits)**
Via Roma 38, Foligno.

**Pasticceria Sandri
(cakes, biscuits
and chocolates)**
Corso Vannucci 32,
Perugia.

**La Spezieria
Bavicchi (spices)**
Piazza Matteotti 37,
Perugia.

**Urbani Tartufi
(truffles)**
SS Valnerina, 31.3 km,
Santa Anatolia di Narco.

What to Buy in Umbria

The varied crafts of Umbria, derived from tradition but still open to new ideas, can be found either in shops or actually at the artists' own workshops. Old-fashioned ceramics sit side by side with works by great contemporary artists such as Cagli and Leonardi. Antique linen, lovingly produced by hand on a loom, is piled up next to more up-to-date and fashionable knitwear produced by Umbrian factories. It would also be impossible to ignore the delicious food of the region. Salami, of course, but also preserves, lentils, black truffles and chocolate, enabling visitors to take home something of the flavour of Umbria.

Potter at work in his studio

CERAMICS

Ceramics production – of which Deruta is the capital – is inspired by techniques and designs from a centuries-old tradition. An interesting new and flourishing trend is for new artists to make modern pieces, which have been inspired by their own imagination and by the study of new production methods.

Whistle from Ficulle

Vases and jars in painted majolica

Basket and lid

Basket for fruit

BASKETS

The reeds that grow around Lake Trasimeno are gathered for use today, as they were in centuries past. A sturdy but flexible plant material, the reed is used to make all kinds of objects. Baskets, mats and traps for fishing on the lake are on sale in the towns of Passignano, Castiglione del Lago and Tuoro.

TEXTILES AND EMBROIDERY

In several studios in Perugia, and in a few other towns, it is possible to buy household linen, fabrics and carpets, woven on a loom according to ancient methods. Umbrian embroidery and lace (made in Assisi, Panicale and Orvieto) are still widely available.

Detail from antique fabric

Cashmere wool *is used to make high-quality garments. The most famous company name is that of Brunello Cucinelli.*

Ars panicalensis *is the name given to the technique of embroidering on tulle, originating in Panicale and now done throughout Umbria. The pieces have the delicacy of lace.*

KNITWEAR

Umbria is a region with a series of small but dedicated knitwear companies producing garments using different types of wool. Clothes made from cashmere wool are particularly desirable.

BOOKBINDING

The old traditions of bookselling, bookbinding and book restoration are by no means dead in Umbria. Bookplates, diaries, notebooks, and albums are made with paper that reproduces the designs and colours of the Renaissance, a tradition that began with the followers of St Francis.

Book plate

WOOD

A man called Michelangeli launched the trend for good-quality woodwork in Orvieto. There is now a small but flourishing trade in wooden statues and animals, as well as garden sculptures. Items made from olive wood are now a tourist attraction in Assisi.

Hand-made wooden aeroplane

PORK SAUSAGES AND SALAMI

The meat and salami of Norcia are superb. You can choose from hams (made from pig or wild boar), fresh sausages, cured pork sausage, *capocollo* (made with neck of pig), and wild boar salami among many other delicacies. Good salami from small producers is found all over the region.

Shop selling a selection of fine hams, sausages and salamis

The prized black truffle

White truffle

TRUFFLES

The world's most prized type of black truffle (*tartufo nero*) grows in the Valnerina, especially around Norcia, and is gathered from November to March. The white truffle, gathered from October to December, is rare but less prized.

CHOCOLATE AND SWEETS

The manufacture of chocolate in the city of Perugia dates back to the early 1900s. Traditional sweets can be found all over the region, and a chocolate festival is held in Perugia every October.

PERUGINA

Baci Perugina, individually wrapped hazelnut chocolates, are the bestselling line of a business established in 1907. Their introduction led to a fresh appreciation of Italian confectionery. "Baci" means kisses and each sweet wrapper contains a little quotation about love, in four languages. Historic Perugina adverts are on display in Perugia's Museo Storico.

SURVIVAL
GUIDE

PRACTICAL INFORMATION

Along with an exceptional variety of landscapes, museums and places of historical and artistic interest, Umbria can offer a good range of services. The distances between the main centres are not great, making this, therefore, an ideal place for visitors eager to explore. The museums and galleries are, in general,

Regione dell' Umbria logo

modern, well run, welcoming and accessible to all (an increasing number have access for people with disabilities). The regional authority, Regione dell'Umbria, can offer a wide range of maps and lists of events through the various tourist offices. Banks and medical services are widely available throughout the region.

Mountain biking in the hills around Gubbio

WHEN TO VISIT

Umbria is one of the richest regions in Italy in terms of its attractions (natural and man-made) and its calendar of traditional, cultural and religious events. As a result, Umbria attracts large numbers of visitors between May and September. If you have the option, it is certainly best to arrange to visit either in May and June or September and October, thereby avoiding the crowded peak summer months. In summer, Umbria can also be exceedingly hot. In winter, when snow falls in the mountains, temperatures are low and the winds cold.

TOURIST INFORMATION

The two provinces that form Umbria – Perugia and Terni – each have their own Azienda di Promozione Turistica (APT), responsible for the promotion of tourism in that particular province.
There is a tourist office in every town of a decent size. In smaller centres, offices

called Pro Loco are able to supply historical or cultural information, in addition to information about restaurants and lodgings. Specialist tour guides providing individual attention are available in some towns, too. In addition,

Tourist office (APT) sign

there are numerous organizations which deal with all kinds of sporting events and activities *(see pp22–3)*. For those planning a cycling holiday, and for lovers of mountain biking, the APT provides a booklet called *Umbria in bicicletta* ("Umbria by bicycle").

Informa Giovani, set up by the Comune di Perugia (the Perugia town council), is aimed at young people, and can provide suggestions as well as addresses relating to culture, sport, music, wildlife, holidays, work opportunities, and youth associations.

SIGHTSEEING

Museums in Umbria are run either by the local town council or by the Italian government. In general, state

museums are open from 9am to 7pm, and often close on Monday, and on Sunday afternoon. Winter hours tend to be shorter. Museums run by the local authority have more varied timetables, and may even close over lunch. The use of a flash or a tripod is forbidden in most museums.

Church opening hours are unpredictable, but many close between noon and 3 or 4pm. When visiting churches, you should dress suitably. Tourists are discouraged from touring churches during services, and may be excluded from special religious festivals.

COMMUNICATIONS

Post offices can be found in all towns and there is often more than one branch. Main post offices are usually open from 8:30am to 7:30pm Monday to Saturday. Smaller offices, however, are often open in the morning only, from 8:30am to 1:30pm; on Saturday and the last day of the month, these post offices close at noon.

If all you want is stamps *(francobolli)* for postcards and normal letters, you can buy these at any tobacconist's *(tabacchi)* with the black and white T sign.

The number of public telephones has fallen in tandem with the rise of the mobile phone. Those that remain use telephone cards, available from tobacconists and some newspaper kiosks.

Telephone company logo

◁ **The picturesque Piazza del Popolo in Todi**

DIALLING CODES

- To phone another number in Italy you must include the full area code.
- For international calls, country codes are: UK & Ireland 00 39; USA & Canada 0 11 39; Australia 00 11 39.
- For reverse charge calls, dial 170.
- For directory enquiries dial 1240 (for Italy) or 176 (international).
- For the British Operator, dial 17200 44.
- US Operators: 172 10 11 (AT&T); 172 10 22 (MG Worldphone); 172 18 77 (Sprint).
- Australian Operators: 1225 (Telstra); 172 11 61 (Opus).

TAX EXEMPTION

Value added tax (IVA in Italy) ranges from 12 to 35 per cent. Non-EU citizens can claim an IVA rebate, provided the total expenditure is over €155. It is easiest to get a refund if you shop where you see the "Euro Free Tax" sign. Show your passport, complete a form, and the IVA will be deducted from your bill. Or show your purchases and their receipts at customs upon departure; they will stamp the receipts. Send these to the vendor and a refund should then be sent to you.

STUDENT INFORMATION

An International Student Identity Card (ISIC) can be used to get a reduction on admission charges to many museums and other tourist attractions. The ISIC card also gives access to a 24-hour phone helpline. For discount travel and information, visit any branch of the Centro Turistico Studentesco (CTS).

ELECTRICAL ADAPTORS

The voltage in Italy is 220 volts, with two-pin round-pronged plugs. It is worth buying adaptor plugs before you leave as they are difficult to find in Italy. Most hotels with three or more stars have hairdryers and shaving points in all bedrooms, but check the voltage first, to be safe.

ITALIAN TIME

Italy is one hour ahead of Greenwich Mean Time (GMT). The time difference is: London: –1 hour; New York: –6 hours; Perth: +7 hours; Auckland: +11 hours. These figures may vary briefly in summer with local time changes. Italy uses the 24-hour clock (eg 10pm = 22:00).

CONVERSION CHART

Imperial to Metric
1 inch = 2.54 centimetres
1 foot = 30 centimetres
1 mile = 1.6 kilometres
1 ounce = 28 grams
1 pound = 454 grams
1 pint = 0.57 litre
1 gallon = 4.6 litres

Metric to Imperial
1 centimetre = 0.4 inch
1 metre = 3 feet 3 inches
1 kilometre = 0.6 mile
1 gram = 0.04 ounce
1 kilogram = 2.2 pounds
1 litre = 1.8 pints

DIRECTORY

ITALIAN STATE TOURIST OFFICES ABROAD

Canada
175 Bloor Street East, Suite 907, South Tower, Toronto M4W 3R8.
Tel 416-925-4882.

Ireland & United Kingdom
1 Princes St, London W1B 2AY.
Tel 020 7408 1254.

United States
630 Fifth Avenue, Suite 1565, New York, NY 10111.
Tel 212-245-4822.

STATE TOURIST OFFICES IN UMBRIA

Regional Tourist Office (APT)
Via Mazzini 21, Perugia.
Tel 075 575 951.

Assisi
Tel 075 812 450.
info@iat.assisi.pg.it

Orvieto
Tel 0763 341 772.
info@iat.orvieto.tr.it

Perugia
Tel 075 573 6458.
info@iat.perugia.it

Spoleto
Tel 0743 238 920.
info@iat.spoleto.pg.it

Trasimeno
Tel 075 965 2738.
info@iat.castiglione dellago.pg.it

OTHER TOURIST INFORMATION

Associazione Guide Turistiche (tour guides)
Via Dono Doni 18, Assisi.
Tel 075 815 228.
www.assoguide.it

Centro Turistico Studentesco (CTS)
Viale Sempione 6, Città di Castello.
Tel 075 855 3353.
www.cts.it

Informa Giovani
Via Idalia 1, Perugia.
Tel 075 572 06 46.
www.comune.perugia.it/ informagiovani

EMBASSIES AND CONSULATES

Canada
Via Salaria 243, Rome.
Tel 06 854 441.

Ireland
Piazza Campitelli 3, Rome.
Tel 06 697 9121.

United Kingdom
Via XX Settembre 80a, Rome.
Tel 06 4220 0001.

United States
Via Vittorio Veneto 121a, Rome. *Tel* 06 46 741.

WEBSITES

Regione Umbria
www.regioneumbria.eu
www.italian touristboard.co.uk
www.italiantourism.com

EMERGENCIES

General emergencies
Tel 113.

Carabinieri (police)
Tel 112.

Fire service
Tel 115.

Car breakdown
Tel 116.

Ambulance
Tel 118.

Hospital
Via Bonacci Brunamonti 51, Perugia.
Tel 800 118 020 or 075 57 81.

Health and Safety

Umbria is a safe region. However, if you are in diffculties, each town has a police headquarters, open 24 hours a day. Medical care in Umbria can be excellent, but be sure to take out medical insurance.

Police vehicle, equipped for off-road use

Vehicle used by the Vigili del Fuoco for smaller fires

HOSPITALS AND PHARMACIES

Pharmacy sign

Pharmacies are open 9am–1pm and 4–8pm, Monday to Friday, and mornings only on Saturdays.

Every Umbrian city has its own hospital. In emergencies, go to the *Pronto Soccorso* (Casualty) or telephone for help. EU citizens are entitled to free treatment if they have a European Health Insurance Card (EHIC), but making a claim is a bureaucratic process. Always ensure that your travel insurance includes medical cover.

POLICE

In Italy the forces of law and order are organized into two divisions: the *Carabinieri* and the police *(Polizia)*, to which can be added, at urban level, the municipal police, including traffic police *(Vigili Urbani)*. Traffic police can also deal with minor matters and can provide information and deal with emergency situations. They wear a dark uniform in winter and a light one in summer, with the city coat of arms usually on the pocket. *Carabinieri* are responsible for public order. They wear black trousers with a red stripe down the side, and a white band across the body. Patrols are often seen on the streets.

A team of *carabinieri* in traffic police uniform

The duties of the *Polizia* are more wide-ranging and are, in general, concerned with criminal investigations. The uniform is blue, with a white belt and hat. To report a theft or other serious problem, go to the nearest police station or dial 113.

FIREFIGHTERS

In such a green and wooded region as Umbria, problems with fires are perhaps inevitable, even if the fairly damp climate and the scarcity of winds do not favour the spread of fire. Even so, particularly if you are planning an outdoor holiday, be sure to observe all the standard countryside code practices, especially with regard to not lighting a fire outside the designated areas and making sure cigarettes are completely extinguished.

Municipal policeman

The region has many fire stations, and fire engines respond rapidly to alarm calls. Firefighters also attend to other kinds of emergencies.

PERSONAL SAFETY

Use common sense to keep safe. Do not carry large sums in cash and, if you have valuables, leave them in the safe at your hotel if possible. Pickpockets frequent main railway stations and crowded tourist sights. If travelling by car, lock the vehicle and don't leave any items in view.

It is essential to arrange full insurance cover before you travel, and you may wish to keep a separate photocopy of personal documents so that you can request duplicates in the event of theft.

In Umbria, there are no areas that need to be avoided. It is safe to walk around town streets in the evenings, and even late at night; of course, make sure you are always aware of your surroundings and use your common sense if you feel any unease.

Banking and Local Currency

Foreigners arriving in Umbria may change currency in a number of ways, but it is still wise to arrive with euros in your pocket. Credit cards are widely accepted for purchases and can be used to withdraw money.

Sign at a cash machine, useful for withdrawing cash with a debit card

BANKS AND CURRENCY EXCHANGE

In the larger towns there are bureaux de change as well as currency-converting machines. It is also possible to change money in hotels and in travel agencies, but you'll get a better exchange rate in the banks. Commission charges can be hefty, so it's worth shopping around.

Italian banks are normally open from 8:30am to 1:30pm, and then from 3pm to 4pm,

from Monday to Friday, but these hours may vary from place to place; banks often close early the day before a public holiday. Your hotel reception or the tourist office should be able to help with information. Opening hours of bureaux de change and other places are much more variable. Some form of identification will be needed for all kinds of money transactions.

All towns have cashpoint (ATM) machines *(bancomat)*, which allow you to take money out with a debit card or a credit card and a PIN number.

VISA, American Express, MasterCard and Diners Club are the most commonly seen credit cards and there should be no problems getting them accepted.

Logo of the Banca dell'Umbria

THE EURO

The Euro (€) is the common currency of the European Union. It went into general circulation on 1 January 2002, initially for 12 participating countries. Italy was one of those 12 countries, and the lira was phased out in February 2002. EU members using the Euro as their sole official currency are known as the Eurozone. Several EU members have opted out of joining this common currency.

Euro notes are identical throughout the Eurozone, each one including designs of fictional architectural structures and monuments. The coins, however, have one side identical (the value side), and one side with an image unique to each country. Both notes and coins are exchangeable in each participating country.

When travelling, it is best not to carry euro notes of large denominations, since not all businesses have large amounts of change.

Banknotes and Coins

Banknotes come in seven denominations. The €5 note is grey, €10 is pink, €20 is blue, €50 is orange, €100 is green, €200 is yellow and €500 is purple. There are eight different coins. The €1 and €2 coins are silver and gold; those worth 50, 20 and 10 cents are gold, while the 5-, 2- and 1-cent coins are bronze.

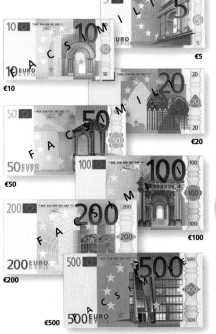

€5
€10
€20
€50
€100
€200
€500

€2 coin   **€1 coin**

50 cents   **20 cents**   **10 cents**

5 cents   **2 cents**   **1 cent**

TRAVEL INFORMATION

Umbria lies at the geographical heart of Italy. Despite the hills and the mountains of the Apennines, road and rail infrastructures are well maintained and well organized; this, combined with the relatively small size of the region, makes it easy and straightforward to travel from one place to another by car. Road and tourist signs are helpful and up-to-date. Driving and parking can be

Logo of state railway
Ferrovie dello Sato

difficult in towns, but buses and taxis are plentiful, and most towns are small enough to be explored easily on foot. The railway network has few branch lines but there are frequent and reliable connections by coach where there are no trains. Umbria itself is easily reached by air or coach. Ferries link the villages on the shores of Lake Trasimeno as well as the lake islands.

Hiring a car, a practical and convenient way of getting around Umbria

ARRIVING BY AIR

The Umbrian Regional Airport of Sant'Egidio is 12 km (7 miles) from both Perugia and Assisi. Scheduled Alitalia flights arrive here from Milan Malpensa and the main Italian international airports; in high season there are also some charter flights. Ryanair flies to Perugia daily from London Stansted. Buses between the airport and the centre of Perugia are timed to coincide with the arrival of scheduled flights. Taxis are also available at the airport, as is car hire: the major companies (Avis, Europcar and Hertz) offer pre-booked fly-drive arrangements.

One option is to fly to Rome or another nearby airport, such as Ancona, Pisa or Florence, and take the train or drive from there. Rome to Perugia by car, for example, takes two hours.

TRAVELLING BY CAR

The Autostrada del Sole (A1) from Milan, via Florence, skirts Umbria along the Tuscan

border before continuing on to Rome. At the Val di Chiana exit a road runs east to Perugia. Other useful exit points are Chiusi Chianciano, Orvieto and Orte, from where a fast road runs to Terni and links up with the Via Flaminia. The latter is the most important state road in Umbria, running from north to south. The condition of the roads is good; only within the Apennines does driving become more challenging.

A car is by far the best way to explore Umbria, enabling you to reach the most remote villages and making it easier to enjoy the scenery.

Car hire is expensive and should be booked ahead. You must be over 21 and have held a licence for at least a year. Visitors from outside the EU may need to show an international licence.

A toll is payable for use of the motorways *(autostrade)*. Tolls are high, but you can usually pay by credit card.

Note that petrol stations may close at lunch time and rarely stay open late.

TRAVELLING BY TRAIN

Umbria has two railway lines: Ferrovie dello Stato (FS) and the private Ferrovia Centrale Umbra (FCU). FS operates the main routes, and its stations do not sell FCU tickets.

The FS Milan–Rome line stops at Orte, Orvieto and the rail junction at Terentola. From here there is another FS line running to Perugia and Foligno, stopping at a few places on Lake Trasimeno and passing close to Assisi. Two Eurostar (ES) and four regional trains provide a daily direct link between Perugia and Rome. Other useful FS lines are the one linking Florence to Perugia and the Rome–Ancona (stopping at Terni, Foligno, Spoleto and Orte).

The FCU Terni–Perugia line serves Todi and then goes on to Città di Castello and Sansepolcro, in Tuscany. Perugia has two stations: Sant'Anna and San Giovanni. The former is used only by FCU trains; the latter by both the FCU and FS.

Train stations may be some distance from the hill town after which they are named. Give yourself enough time to make your way back to the station to catch the return train.

A train run by the state company Ferrovie dello Stato

You must buy tickets before departure. Be sure to validate both outward and return tickets in the machines provided on the platform, before boarding the train, or you will be fined. Always check before doing so that the train you plan to board stops at the station you want: InterCity and Eurostar trains stop only at major stations. Most InterCity and all Eurostar trains have a compulsory seat-reservation policy included in the fare.

Fares are still among the cheapest in Europe, but check in advance with Rail Europe (*see box*) for details of money-saving passes.

TRAVELLING BY COACH

Intercity coach travel can be faster than travelling by train. Perugia is the main hub for coach services. It has direct links to several Italian cities, with stops in various Umbrian towns en route. A daily service from Roma Tiburtina, Rome's main coach station, stops in Todi, Assisi and Deruta en route to Perugia. There are daily coaches between Rome and Gubbio and Città di Castello, as well as Norcia. Perugia is accessible by coach from Florence; many coaches also stop at Città di Castello (via Arezzo).

Coaches from Perugia to Assisi run six or seven times a day, while Todi has around five services a day and Gubbio ten. Coach services are often reduced at weekends, particularly on Sundays, and also vary between summer and winter.

TOWN BUSES

In Perugia the Azienda Perugina di Mobilità operates services within the city and out to the suburbs, among them buses linking the train terminal with the coach station. Tickets are valid for different lengths of time and prices vary accordingly. Bus tickets can be purchased from newspaper kiosks and *tabacchi*. Season tickets are also available, including tourist tickets that are valid for 24 or 48 hours.

In Assisi, regular buses link the railway station, 5 km (3 miles) away at Santa Maria degli Angeli, to the centre. In Todi, too, the railway station is linked to the town by bus.

At Terni, buses run by the Azienda Trasporti Pubblici (ATC) serve the town and also travel as far as the Cascata delle Marmore.

Ferry logo

TAXIS

Hire a cab only from an official taxi stand or else reserve it by phone. If you telephone, the meter will run from the time of your call. Extra is charged for each piece of luggage put in the boot, for rides at night, on Sundays and public holidays, and for airport trips (fix a price before you set off).

FERRIES

On Lake Trasimeno ferries link Castiglione del Lago, the islands of Isola Polvese, Isola Maggiore and Isola Minore, as well as Tuoro sul Trasimeno and Passignano sul Trasimeno.

DIRECTORY

AIRPORTS

Perugia
Aeroporto Regionale Umbro di Sant'Egidio. *Tel* 075 592 141.
www.airport.umbria.it

RAIL INFORMATION

Ferrovia Centrale Umbra (FCU)
Tel 075 575 401.
www.fcu.it

Ferrovie dello Stato (FS)
Tel 892021.
www.trenitalia.it

Rail Europe
Tel 08448 484 064 (UK).
www.raileurope.co.uk
Tel 1-877-257-2887, 1-800-622-8600 (US). www.raileurope.com

COACH INFORMATION

Società Umbro Laziale Gestione Autolinee
Tel 075 500 9641 or 800 099 661 (free from landlines).
www.sulga.it

BUS INFORMATION

ATC Terni
Tel 0744 492 711.
www.atcterni.it

Azienda Perugina di Mobilità (APM)
Tel 075 506 781 or 800 512 141 (free from landlines).
www.apmperugia.it

CAR HIRE

Avis (Perugia)
Tel 075 500 0395.
www.avis.com

Europcar (Perugia)
Tel 075 692 0615.
www.europcar.it

Hertz (Perugia)
Tel 075 500 2439.
www.hertz.com

TAXIS

Assisi	*Tel* 075 804 0275.
Foligno	*Tel* 0742 344 280.
Orvieto	*Tel* 0763 301 903.
Perugia	*Tel* 075 500 4888.
Spoleto	*Tel* 0743 220 489.
Terni	*Tel* 0744 425 768.
Todi	*Tel* 075 894 2525.

One of the ferries linking the islands and towns on Lake Trasimeno

General Index

Page numbers in **bold** type
refer to main entries

Acknowledgments

Dorling Kindersley would like to thank all those whose contribution and assistance have made the preparation of this book possible.

Special Thanks

Archivio Electa-Milano, Assessorato del Turismo Regione Umbria, APT di Perugia, APT di Assisi, APT di Foligno, APT di Spoleto, Consorzio del Parco del Lago Trasimeno, Consorzio del Parco del Monte Cucco, Ente Parco dei Monti Sibillini, Guido Stecchi for consultation and help with pages 154–5, and all the companies who have assisted with their products.

Photography

Ghigo Roli (Modena)

Translator

Fiona Wild

Editor

Emily Hatchwell

Design and Editorial Assistance

PICTURE RESEARCH Ellen Root
REVISIONS EDITOR Anna Freiberger
REVISIONS DESIGNER Collette Sadler
Beverley Ager, Marta Bescos Sanchez, Uma Bhattacharya, Gadi Farfour, Vinod Harish, Mohammad Hassan, Jasneet Kaur, Vincent Kurien, Sarah Lane, Leonie Loudon, Sam Merrell, Rebecca Milner, Helen Partington, Sangita Patel, Gillian Price, Rada Radojicic, Sands Publishing Solutions, Azeem Siddiqui, Ellie Smith, Susana Smith, Conrad Van Dyk

Additional Photography

John Heseltine, Ian O'Leary, Christine Webb

Photography Permissions

The publisher would like to thank all the churches, museums, hotels, restaurants, art galleries, parks and all those who supplied material and contributed to the publication of this guide, too numerous to be named individually. While every effort has been made to contact the copyright holders, we apologize for any omissions and will be happy to include them in subsequent editions of this publication.

Picture Credits

t = top; tl = top left; tlc = top left centre; tc = top centre; tr = top right; cla = centre left above; ca = centre above; cra = centre right above; cl = centre left; c = centre; cr = centre right; clb = centre left below; cb = centre below; crb = centre right below; bl = bottom left; b = below; bc = bottom centre; bcl = bottom centre left; br = bottom right; (d) = detail.

4CORNERS IMAGES: Gaudenzio Luciano 11br; Ripani Massimo 10br

AGRITURISMO CIGLIANO: 143bl; ALAMY IMAGES: David Ball 10cla; Cubo Images srl/Enrico Caracciolo 155cc; Norma Joseph 154cla, 155tl; Torchy 10tc; Christine Webb 11cl; FABRIZIO ARDITO (Rome): 2–3, 16tl, 33bl, 61tl, 61cr, 69tc, 71tr, 86br, 89c, 92tr, 92bl, 131cr, 134cl, 135tc, 137cr; THE ART ARCHIVE: Galleria Nazionale dell'Umbria Perugia/Dagli Orti 88tr; Palazzo Trinci Foligno/Dagli Orti 102c.

ADRIANO BACCHELLA (Milan): 16c; THE BRIDGEMAN ART LIBRARY: Galleria Nazionale dell'Umbria, Perugia, Italy Altarpiece: Annunciation; Madonna and Child with Saints; Miracles of St. Anthony, St. Francis and St. Elizabeth Piero della Francesca 88bl.

DAVID CAPASSO (Modena): 42bl, 103cl, 104tl, 105cr; CORBIS: Elio Ciol 17b.

IL DAGHERROTIPO: Stefania Servili 11tr.

FERROVIE DELLO STATO: 178br; FONDAZIONE FESTIVAL DEI DUE MONDI: 45bc; GIOVANNI FRANCESIO (Mantua): 54tl, 54cr, 56 all photos, 57 all photos, 63t, 63b, 64 all photos, 65 all photos, 66tr, 66bl, 67tl, 67cr, 67b, 82c, 82br, 83cl, 83cr, 94 all photos.

GETTY IMAGES: Photodisc/Buena Vista Images 45cb.

ROBERT HARDING PICTURE LIBRARY: T. Gervis 16b.

TIM JEPSON: 15b.

MARCO MANDIBOLA (Milan): 51b, 61bc, 78c, 100bl, 102tl, 105bl, 130bc; GUIDO MANNUCCI (Florence): 33cr, 91cl; MARKA (Milan): D. Donadoni 96, 153bc, 172–3; R. Gropozzo 153t; Sechi 140–1

PETER NOBLE: 176b

RISTORANTE LE MURA: 152c.

ANNA SERRANO (Rome): 16cb, 18tr, 18crb, 19bl, 32tc, 32cr; GUIDO STECCHI (Milan): 154cla, 154cra, 154bl.

JACKET
Front – PHOTOLIBRARY: Tips Italia/Francesco Tomasinelli. Back – ALAMY IMAGES: E. J. Baumeister Jr. tl; Tom Bean cla; Andre Jenny clb; David Noton bl. Spine – PHOTOLIBRARY: Tips Italia/Francesco Tomasinelli t.

All other images © Dorling Kindersley. For further information see: **www.dkimages.com**

Phrase Book

In An Emergency

Help!	Aiuto!	eye-**yoo**-toh
Stop!	Fermate!	fair-**mah**-teh
Call a doctor.	Chiama un medico	kee-**ah**-mah oon **meh**-dee-koh
Call an ambulance.	Chiama un' ambulanza	kee-**ah**-mah oon am-boo-**lan**-tsa
Call the police.	Chiama la polizia	kee-**ah**-mah lah pol-ee-**tsee**-ah
Call the fire brigade.	Chiama i pompieri	kee-**ah**-mah ee pom-pee-**air**-ee
Where is the telephone?	Dov'è il telefono?	dov-**eh** eel teh-**leh**-foh-noh?
The nearest hospital?	L'ospedale più vicino?	loss-peh-**dah**-leh pee-**oo**-vee-**chee**-noh?

Communication Essentials

Yes/No	Sì/No	**see**/noh
Please	Per favore	pair fah-**vor**-eh
Thank you	Grazie	**grah**-tsee-eh
Excuse me	Mi scusi	mee **skoo**-zee
Hello	Buon giorno	bwon **jor**-noh
Good bye	Arrivederci	ah-ree-veh-**dair**-chee
Good evening	Buona sera	**bwon**-ah **sair**-ah
morning	la mattina	lah mah-**tee**-nah
afternoon	il pomeriggio	eel poh-meh-**ree**-joh
evening	la sera	lah **sair**-ah
yesterday	ieri	ee-**air**-ee
today	oggi	**oh**-jee
tomorrow	domani	doh-**mah**-nee
here	qui	**kwee**
there	la	**lah**
What?	Quale?	**kwah**-leh?
When?	Quando?	**kwan**-doh?
Why?	Perchè?	pair-**keh**?
Where?	Dove?	**doh**-veh

Useful Phrases

How are you?	Come sta?	**koh**-meh stah?
Very well, thank you.	Molto bene, grazie.	**moll**-toh **beh**-neh, **grah**-tsee-eh
Pleased to meet you.	Piacere di conoscerla.	pee-ah-**chair**-eh dee cob-**noh**-shair-lah
See you soon.	A più tardi.	ah pee-**oo** tar-dee
That's fine.	Va bene.	va **beh**-neh
Where is/are ...?	Dov'è/Dove sono ...?	dov-eh/**doveh** soh-noh?
How long does it take to get to ...?	Quanto tempo ci vuole per andare a ...?	kwan-toh **tem**-poh chee voo-**oh**-leh pair an-**dar**-eh ab...?
How do I get to ...?	Come faccio per arrivare a ...?	koh-meh **fah**-choh pair arri-**var**-eh ab...?
Do you speak English?	Parla inglese?	par-lah en-**gleh**-zeh?
I don't understand.	Non capisco.	non ka-**pee**-skoh
Could you speak more slowly, please?	Può parlare più lentamente, per favore?	pwoh par-**lah**-reh pee-oo len-ta-**men**-teh pair fah-**vor**-eh
I'm sorry.	Mi dispiace.	mee dee-spee-**ah**-cheh

Useful Words

big	grande	**gran**-deh
small	piccolo	**pee**-koh-loh
hot	caldo	**kal**-doh
cold	freddo	**fred**-doh
good	buono	**bwoh**-noh
bad	cattivo	kat-**tee**-voh
enough	basta	**bas**-tah
well	bene	**beh**-neh
open	aperto	ah-**pair**-toh
closed	chiuso	kee-**oo**-zoh
left	a sinistra	ah see-**nee**-strah
right	a destra	ah **dess**-trah
straight on	sempre dritto	**sem**-preh **dree**-toh
near	vicino	vee-**chee**-noh
far	lontano	lon-**tah**-noh
up	su	**soo**
down	giù	**joo**
early	presto	**press**-toh
late	tardi	**tar**-dee
entrance	entrata	en-**trah**-tah
exit	uscita	oo-**shee**-ta
toilet	il gabinetto	eel gab-bee-**net**-toh
free, unoccupied	libero	**lee**-bair-oh
free, no charge	gratuito	grah-**too**-ee-toh
out of order	guasto	**gwass**-to
strike (train etc.)	sciopero	**sho**-pay-ro

Making a Telephone Call

I'd like to place a long-distance call.	Vorrei fare una interurbana.	vor-**ray** far-eh oona in-tair-oor-**bah**-nah
I'd like to make a reverse-charge call.	Vorrei fare una telefonata a carico del destinatario.	vor-**ray** far-eh oona teh-leh-fon-ah-tab ah **kar**-ee-koh dell dess-tee-nah-**tar**-ree-oh
I'll try again later.	Ritelefono più tardi.	ree-teh-**leh**-foh-noh pee-oo tar-dee
Can I leave a message?	Posso lasciare un messaggio?	**poss**-oh lash-**ah**-reh oon mess-**sah**-joh?
Hold on.	Un attimo, per favore	oon ah-tee-moh, pair fah-**vor**-eh
Could you speak up a little please?	Può parlare più forte, per favore?	pwoh par-**lah**-reh pee-oo for-teh, pair fah-**vor**-eh?
local call	la telefonata locale	lah teh-leh-fon-**ah**-ta loh-**kah**-leh

Shopping

How much does this cost?	Quant'è, per favore?	kwan-**teh** pair fah-**vor**-eh?
I would like ...	Vorrei...	vor-**ray**
Do you have ...?	Avete ...?	ah-**veh**-teh...?
I'm just looking.	Sto soltanto guardando.	stoh sol-**tan**-toh gwar-**dan**-doh
Do you take credit cards?	Accettate carte di credito?	ah-chet-tah-teh kar-teh dee creh-dee-toh?
What time do you open/close?	A che ora apre/chiude?	ah keh or-ah ah-preh/kee-oo-deh?
this one	questo	**kweh**-stoh
that one	quello	**kwell**-oh
expensive	caro	**kar**-oh .
cheap	a buon prezzo	ah bwon **pret**-soh
size, clothes	la taglia	lah **tah**-lee-ah
size, shoes	il numero	eel **noo**-mair-oh
white	bianco	bee-**ang**-koh
black	nero	**neh**-roh
red	rosso	**ross**-oh
yellow	giallo	**jal**-loh
green	verde	**vair**-deh
blue	blu/azzurro	bloo/at-**zoo**-row
brown	marrone	mar-**roh**-neh

Types of Shop

antique dealer	l'antiquario	lan-tee-**kwah**-ree-oh
bakery	la panetteria	lah pah-net-tair-**ree**-ah
bank	la banca	lah **bang**-kah
bookshop	la libreria	lah lee-breh-**ree**-ah
butcher's	la macelleria	lah mah-chell-eh-**ree**-ah
cake shop	la pasticceria	lah pas-tee-chair-**ee**-ah
chemist's	la farmacia	lah far-mah-**chee**-ah
delicatessen	la salumeria	lah sah-loo-meh-**ree**-ah
department store	il grande magazzino	eel **gran**-deh mag-gad-**zee**-noh
fishmonger's	la pescheria	lah pess-keh-**ree**-ah
florist	il fioraio	eel fee-or-**eye**-oh
greengrocer	il fruttivendolo	eel froo-tee-**ven**-doh-loh
grocery	alimentari	ah-lee-men-**tah**-ree
hairdresser	il parrucchiere	eel par-oo-kee-**air**-eh
ice-cream parlour	la gelateria	lah jel-lah-tair-**ree**-ah
market	il mercato	eel mair-**kah**-toh
news-stand	l'edicola	leh-**dee**-koh-lah
post office	l'ufficio postale	loo-**fee**-choh pos-**tah**-leh
shoe shop	il negozio di scarpe	eel neh-goh-tsioh dee **skar**-peh
supermarket	il supermercato	su-pair-mair-**kah**-toh
tobacconist	il tabaccaio	eel tab-bak-**eye**-oh
travel agency	l'agenzia di viaggi	lah-jen-**tsee**-ah dee vee-**ad**-jee

Sightseeing

art gallery	la pinacoteca	lah peena-koh-**teh**-kah
bus stop	la fermata dell'autobus	lah fair-**mah**-tah dell ow-toh-booss
church	la chiesa	lah kee-**eh**-zah
	la basilica	lah bah-**seel**-i-kah
closed for the public holiday	chiuso per la festa	kee-oo-zoh pair lah **fess**-tah
garden	il giardino	eel jar-**dee**-no
library	la biblioteca	lah beeb-lee-oh-**teh**-kah
museum	il museo	eel moo-**zeh**-oh
railway station	la stazione	lah stah-tsee-**oh**-neh
tourist information	l'ufficio turistico	loo-**fee**-choh too-**ree**-stee-koh

Staying in a Hotel

Do you have any vacant rooms?	Avete camere libere?	ah-veh-teh kah-mair-eh lee-bair-eh?
double room	una camera doppia	oona kah-mair-ah doh-pee-ah
with double bed	con letto matrimoniale	kon let-toh mah-tree-moh-nee-ah-leh
twin room	una camera con due letti	oona kah-mair-ah kon doo-eh let-tee
single room	una camera singola	oona kah-mair-ah sing-goh-lah
room with a bath, shower	una camera con bagno, con doccia	oona kah-mair-ah kon ban-yoh, kon dot-chah
porter	il facchino	eel fah-kee-noh
key	la chiave	lah kee-ah-veh
I have a reservation.	Ho fatto una prenotazione.	oh fat-toh oona preh-noh-tah-tsee-oh-neh

Eating Out

Have you got a table for ...?	Avete una tavola per ... ?	ah-veh-teh oona tah-voh-lah pair ...?
I'd like to reserve a table.	Vorrei riservare una tavola.	vor-ray ree-sair-vah-reh oona tah-voh-lah
breakfast	colazione	koh-lah-tsee-oh-neh
lunch	pranzo	pran-tsoh
dinner	cena	cheh-nah
Enjoy your meal.	Buon appetito.	bwon ah-peh-tee-toh
The bill, please.	Il conto, per favore.	eel kon-toh pair fah-vor-eh
I am a vegetarian.	Sono vegetariano/a.	soh-noh veh-jeh-tar-ee-ah-noh/nah
waitress	cameriera	kah-mair-ee-air-ah
waiter	cameriere	kah-mair-ee-air-eh
fixed price menu	il menù a prezzo fisso	eel meh-noo ah pret-soh fee-soh
dish of the day	piatto del giorno	pee-ah-toh dell jor-no
starter	antipasto	an-tee-pass-toh
first course	il primo	eel pree-moh
main course	il secondo	eel seh-kon-doh
vegetables	il contorno	eel kon-tor-noh
dessert	il dolce	eel doll-cheh
cover charge	il coperto	eel koh-pair-toh
wine list	la lista dei vini	lah lee-stah day vee-nee
rare	al sangue	al sang-gweh
medium	al puntino	al poon-tee-noh
well done	ben cotto	ben kot-toh
glass	il bicchiere	eel bee-kee-air-eh
bottle	la bottiglia	lah bot-teel-yah
knife	il coltello	eel kol-tell-oh
fork	la forchetta	lah for-ket-tah
spoon	il cucchiaio	eel koo-kee-eye-oh

Menu Decoder

l'abbacchio	lab-back-kee-oh	lamb
l'aceto	lah-cheh-toh	vinegar
l'acqua	lah-kwah	water
l'acqua minerale gasata/naturale	lah-kwah mee-nair-ah-leh gah-zah-tah/ nah-too-rah-leh	mineral water fizzy/still
l'aglio	lahl-yoh	garlic
al forno	al for-noh	baked
alla griglia	ah-lah greel-yah	grilled
l'anatra	lah-nah-trah	duck
l'aragosta	lah-rah-goss-tah	lobster
l'arancia	lah-ran-chah	orange
arrosto	ar-ross-toh	roast
la birra	lah beer-rah	beer
la bistecca	lah bee-stek-kah	steak
il brodo	eel broh-doh	broth
il burro	eel boor-oh	butter
il caffè	eel kah-feh	coffee
il carciofo	eel kar-choff-oh	artichoke
la carne	la kar-neh	meat
carne di maiale	kar-neh dee mah-yah-leh	pork
la cipolla	lah chee-poll-ah	onion
i fagioli	ee fah-joh-lee	beans
il formaggio	eel for-mad-joh	cheese
le fragole	leh frah-goh-leh	strawberries
frutta fresca	froo-tah fress-kah	fresh fruit
frutti di mare	froo-tee dee mah-reh	seafood
i funghi	ee foon-gee	mushrooms
i gamberi	ee gam-bair-ee	prawns
il gelato	eel jel-lah-toh	ice cream
l'insalata	leen-sah-lah-tah	salad
il latte	eel laht-teh	milk
i legumi	ee leh-goo-mee	vegetables
lesso	less-oh	boiled
il manzo	eel man-tsoh	beef
la mela	lah meh-lah	apple
la melanzana	lah meh-lan-tsah-nah	aubergine
la minestra	lah mee-ness-trah	soup
l'olio	loll-yoh	oil
l'oliva	loh-lee-vah	olive
il pane	eel pah-neh	bread
il panino	eel pah-nee-noh	roll
le patate	leh pah-tah-teh	potatoes
patatine fritte	pah-tah-teen-eh free-teh	chips
il pepe	eel peh-peh	pepper
la pesca	lah pess-kah	peach
il pesce	eel pesh-eh	fish
il pollo	eel poll-oh	chicken
il pomodoro	eel poh-moh-dor-oh	tomato
il prosciutto	eel pro-shoo-toh	ham
cotto/crudo	kot-toh/kroo-doh	cooked/cured
il riso	eel ree-zoh	rice
il sale	eel sah-leh	salt
la salsiccia	lah sal-see-chah	sausage
secco	sek-koh	dry
succo d'arancia/ di limone	soo-koh dah-ran-chah/ dee lee-moh-neh	orange/lemon juice
il tè	eel teh	tea
la tisana	lah tee-zah-nah	herb tea
il tonno	ton-noh	tuna
la torta	lah tor-tah	cake
l'uovo	loo-oh-voh	egg
l'uva	loo-vah	grapes
vino bianco	vee-noh bee-ang-koh	white wine
vino rosso	vee-noh ross-oh	red wine
il vitello	eel vee-tell-oh	veal
le vongole	leh von-goh-leh	baby clams
lo zucchero	loh zoo-kair-oh	sugar
gli zucchini	lyee dzo-kee-nee	courgettes
la zuppa	lah tsoo-pah	soup

Numbers

1	uno	oo-noh
2	due	doo-eh
3	tre	treh
4	quattro	kwat-roh
5	cinque	ching-kweh
6	sei	say-ee
7	sette	set-teh
8	otto	ot-toh
9	nove	noh-veh
10	dieci	dee-eh-chee
11	undici	oon-dee-chee
12	dodici	doh-dee-chee
13	tredici	tray-dee-chee
14	quattordici	kwat-tor-dee-chee
15	quindici	kwin-dee-chee
16	sedici	say-dee-chee
17	diciassette	dee-chah-set-teh
18	diciotto	dee-chot-toh
19	diciannove	dee-chah-noh-veh
20	venti	ven-tee
30	trenta	tren-tah
40	quaranta	kwah-ran-tah
50	cinquanta	ching-kwan-tah
60	sessanta	sess-an-tah
70	settanta	set-tan-tah
80	ottanta	ot-tan-tah
90	novanta	noh-van-tah
100	cento	chen-toh
1,000	mille	mee-leh
2,000	duemila	doo-eh mee-lah
5,000	cinquemila	ching-kweh mee-lah
1,000,000	un milione	oon meel-yoh-neh

Time

one minute	un minuto	oon mee-noo-toh
one hour	un'ora	oon or-ah
half an hour	mezz'ora	medz-or-ah
a day	un giorno	oon jor-noh
a week	una settimana	oona set-tee-mah-nah
Monday	lunedì	loo-neh-dee
Tuesday	martedì	mar-teh-dee
Wednesday	mercoledì	mair-koh-leh-dee
Thursday	giovedì	joh-veh-dee
Friday	venerdì	ven-air-dee
Saturday	sabato	sah-bah-toh
Sunday	domenica	doh-meh-nee-kah

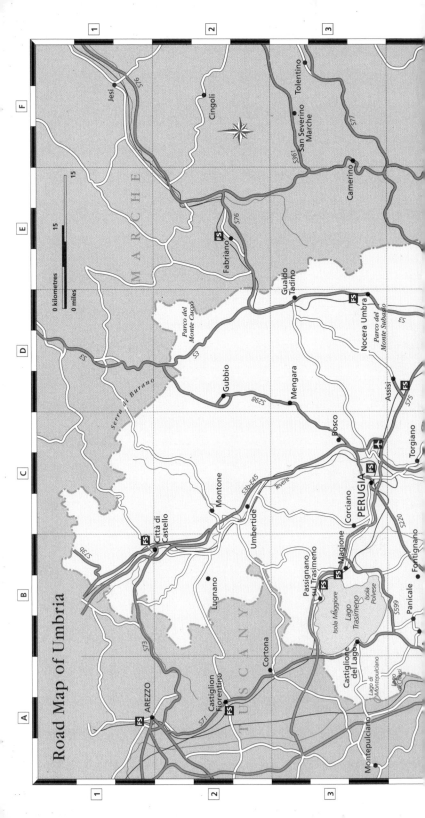

Road Map of Umbria